CBT and Existential Psychology

CBT and Existential Psychology

Philosophy, Psychology and Therapy

Michael Worrell
Consultant Clinical Psychologist
Central and North West London Mental Health NHS Trust
United Kingdom

Including dialogues with Thomas Heidenreich, Alexander Noyon and Ernesto Spinelli

WILEY Blackwell

This edition first published 2023

Registered Offices
John Wiley & Sons, Inc., 111 River Street, Hoboken, NJ 07030, USA
John Wiley & Sons, Ltd, The Atrium, Southern Gate, Chichester, West Sussex, PO19 8SQ, UK

Editorial Office
The Atrium, Southern Gate, Chichester, West Sussex, PO19 8SQ, UK

For details of our global editorial offices, customer services, and more information about Wiley products visit us at www.wiley.com.

Wiley also publishes its books in a variety of electronic formats and by print-on-demand. Some content that appears in standard print versions of this book may not be available in other formats.

For general information on our other products and services or for technical support, please contact our Customer Care Department within the United States at (800) 762-2974, outside the United States at (317) 572-3993 or fax (317) 572-4002.

Library of Congress Cataloguing-in-Publication Data applied for
Paperback ISBN 9781119310969

Cover Design: Wiley
Cover Image: © BlueOrange Studio/Adobe Stock Photos

Set in 9.5/12.5pt STIXTwoText by Straive, Pondicherry, India
Printed and bound by CPI Group (UK) Ltd, Croydon, CR0 4YY

C069884_210922

This book is dedicated to my sons, Tomas and Daniel
and to Anna

Contents

About the Author

Michael Worrell, PhD, is a Consultant Clinical Psychologist and leads the Central London CBT Training Centre, within Central and North West London Foundation NHS Trust. He is accredited as a CBT Therapist, Supervisor and Trainer with the British Association for Behavioural and Cognitive Psychotherapies and is registered as an Existential Psychotherapist with the United Kingdom Council for Psychotherapy. He is a visiting professor at Regents University London.

Contributors

Professor Thomas Heidenreich, PhD, is a psychologist and a psychotherapist. He has worked as a scientific assistant at the Departments of Psychology and Psychiatry of the Frankfurt Goethe University. Since 2006, he has been a professor of Psychology for Social Work and Nursing at Esslingen University. He is an experienced CBT therapist and has numerous publications on existential issues over the past 15 years. He has worked as a lecturer and supervisor in several institutes for psychotherapy training. In 2019, Thomas was co-chair of the scientific committee for the 9th World Congress of Behavioural and Cognitive Therapies in Berlin.

Professor Alexander Noyon, PhD, is a psychologist and a psychotherapist. He has worked in hospitals and, as a scientific assistant, at the Frankfurt Goethe University. Since 2000, he has worked as a therapist in private practice. Since 2007, he has been Professor for Psychology in Social Work at Mannheim University of Applied Sciences. He is an experienced CBT therapist who has also trained in existential psychotherapy (Logotherapy). He is also a lecturer and clinical supervisor.

Professor Ernesto Spinelli, PhD, is an existential phenomenological psychotherapist in private practice. He has published many papers and books on various aspects of existential therapy and has provided training workshop in the approach around the world. He was the Chair of the Society for Existential Analysis between 1993 and 1999. He is a Fellow of the British Psychological Society (BPS) and the British Association for Counselling and Psychotherapy (BACP). In 2000, he was the recipient of the BPS Division of Counselling Psychology Award for Outstanding Contribution to the Profession.

Acknowledgements

I am grateful to Wiley and, in particular, to Monica Rogers, for her patience, support and enthusiasm for this project. I would like to thank Professor Ernesto Spinelli, Professor Thomas Heidenreich and Professor Alexander Noyon, for their willingness to engage with me in dialogue on this topic. I have also benefitted from many extensive and challenging discussions with Ernesto regarding the relationship between CBT and existential therapy and he has provided feedback and suggestions on many chapters. I would also like to thank the fantastic group of trainers and supervisors with whom I had the good fortune of learning existential phenomenological therapy in the 1990s including Professor Ernesto Spinelli, Professor Emmy van Deurzen, Lucia Moja-Strasser (who continues to both support and challenge my therapeutic practice), The late Dr Hans Cohn (who would have raised an eyebrow and asked some very difficult questions about this whole project), and the late Dr Freddie Strasser, by far the coolest existential therapist I have ever met.

I would also like to thank the team of clinical psychologists and CBT therapists who I have the great pleasure of working with at the London CBT training Centre particularly Dr Rita Woo, Dr Rita Santos, Tamara Cilliers, Dr. Alexander Margetts and Dr Louise Payne. I would also like to thank Philip Tata for supporting me in my career in the NHS despite his concern, now possibly realised, that I was in fact 'a rogue priest'. I would also like to thank Dr Carlton Coulter for the challenging, philosophically, and clinically rich discussions, attempting to clarify what we think we mean by the many terms we are using, as well as for constructive feedback on several chapters. Thanks also to Dr Anna Streeruwitz and Dr Stephen Adams-Langley for their willingness to read and share their reflections and suggestions on the book. Additionally, I would like to thank the many trainees in CBT who have responded warmly and with considerable patience during my overly enthusiastic lectures on why they immediately need to read as much existential therapy literature as possible to become better CBT therapists. I think I might even have convinced one or two.

Michael Worrell
London, 2022

Preface

This book is perhaps an unusual one for a text with 'CBT' in the title. In most cases, CBT texts are of the form of 'CBT for X', where 'X' stands for a wide range of specific and diagnosable forms of psychological suffering. The content of such texts normally would cover interventions that are based upon research evidence, and which are promoted as 'evidence based' strategies for 'overcoming' the particular condition. As I have been involved in the training and supervision of CBT therapists, as well as clinical psychologists, counsellors, psychotherapists, psychiatric nurses, and others interested in CBT for over 25 years, I am well acquainted with literature of this type. While I was trained in, and have practiced, applied behavioural analysis and CBT, I have had a long-standing interest in Existential approaches and have trained in existential phenomenological therapy at what has become known as the 'British School' of Existential Analysis in the early 1990s. During my training in existential therapy, I was often struck by the points of contact and agreement with various perspectives within behaviour therapy and CBT. And yet very little was written of this, as existential therapy was mostly developed in dialogue, and at times conflict, with psychoanalysis. As will be seen, there is an existing literature that attempts to create such a dialogue between CBT and existential therapy, however it is scattered and incomplete. This book is an attempt to take this dialogue forward. In my view, the insights and methods of existential therapy are of immeasurable value in this current climate of evidence-based practice, disorder-specific interventions and manualised therapies.

Almost a half of this book was written during the COVID-19 pandemic, an event that the existentialists would regard as an 'ultimate situation' or 'boundary situation'. Such situations, bring us into direct, disturbing and anxiety provoking awareness of the 'givens of existence'. The pandemic is most certainly an expression of, as Heidegger (1962) would have it, our 'thrownness'. Our vulnerability to the virus arises from our fundamental relatedness to each other and the natural world. Our way of coping, the enforced, or embraced, strategies of 'distancing' and 'isolation' also bring us into contact with our ultimate separateness and existential isolation. The multiple, and extreme forms, of conspiracy theory that have arisen, are also a disturbing reminder of the 'drive to meaning' that is fundamental to human experience. This book focuses upon the relevance of existential thought for our practice as therapists and I invite you to reflect upon your own experience of the givens of existence as a reference point. Existential thinking and methods ultimately need to be embodied and 'lived' for their full meaning and implications to be revealed.

1

Introduction

The quest for certainty blocks the search for meaning.

—Erich Fromm.

Cognitive behavioural therapy (CBT) has established itself as the dominant force in western psychotherapy. It has been identified as the treatment of choice by a range of health agencies, such as the UK National Institute of Clinical Excellence (NICE), for many of the most commonly encountered forms of psychological distress. In the United Kingdom and elsewhere, training in CBT has greatly expanded in an effort to increase public access to this form of evidence-based therapy. This has caused considerable alarm to proponents of non-CBT models, some of whom have taken a highly critical and challenging stance to what they perceive to be 'the CBT tsunami' (Dalal, 2018). Others have become so alarmed that they fear the advance of CBT will lead to the prospect of '100 years of psychotherapy wisdom' being lost (Lees, 2016). During the 1990s, there appeared to be the possibility of further developments towards more integrative ways of practising. Indeed, one view of CBT has always been that it was intended to be a form of integrative therapy (Alford & Beck, 1997). In the current situation of the rapid expansion of CBT, there appears to be a hardening of views, with critical discussions around CBT appearing to have a limited impact due to their tendency to adopt and then attack 'straw man' versions of CBT that the CBT practitioner is unable to recognise (see the collection of papers in House & Loewenthal, 2008, for a range of both straw man and reasoned critiques).

CBT and Existential Psychology: Philosophy, Psychology and Therapy, First Edition. Michael Worrell.

From the outside, it can appear as if CBT is sitting proudly, if unjustifiably, on its laurels and is immune to any form of challenge. At the same time, *within* CBT there remains a range of unresolved clinical, empirical, theoretical and philosophical dilemmas and controversies. It is widely accepted that, rather than being a unified school of therapy, CBT is in fact a diverse range of therapies and theories that display both a family resemblance and significant points of disagreement. In a controversial paper, Hayes (2004) argued that there exists three generations, or 'waves', of CBT. The first wave, originating in the 1950s, focused on the identification and application of basic principles of learning. The second wave, originating in the work of Beck and Ellis, as well as the social learning theory of Bandura, shifted the focus to cognitive mediation of behavioural and emotional change. Hayes (2004) argues that the second wave also involved the loss of a strong link between the applied techniques of CBT and basic laboratory-based science on fundamental principles; instead, the second wave favoured a more clinical approach to the evaluation of efficacy of treatment packages for specified diagnoses, formalised as treatment manuals. The third wave, according to Hayes (2004), came to fruition in the late 1990s and has involved an emphasis on assisting clients to change their *relationship* with cognitions and other distressing psychological experiences—instead of direct cognitive change efforts, mindful awareness and acceptance of distressing experience is promoted along with the identification of forms of value consistent behaviour.

Given the diversity and controversy described earlier, what is the basis of the family resemblance? At a fundamental level, despite differences in technique and concept, diverse forms of CBT agree that the overall project is one of developing a form of psychotherapy based upon scientific principles and validated via the scientific method of experimentation. The basic notion is embodied to such an extent in classical Beckian CBT that the metaphor offered to the client is one of 'learning to become one's own therapist by adopting the scientific-experimental method to one's beliefs' (Westbrook et al., 2017). However, some of the controversies that exist in the field are expressive of basic philosophical differences in how the activity of 'science' should be understood, carried out and evaluated.

Consider the still unresolved question of the relationship between thoughts, emotions and behaviours highlighted above. While classical Beckian CBT maintains that the mediating factor in achieving beneficial outcomes is cognitive change, and that it makes sense to differentiate cognition from emotion and behaviour, acceptance and commitment therapy (ACT) asserts that beneficial outcomes are more likely when both the therapist and client step away from direct attempts at achieving cognitive change and instead focus on the possibility of acceptance. Furthermore, ACT disputes that cognitions can be separable from behaviour in any meaningful sense. They also cannot be regarded as being causal. More recently, additional controversy has arisen from the fact that both groups of researchers and practitioners claim empirical support for their positions, in contrast to those of other CBT perspectives, from the very same experimental research findings. This dilemma has led some to propose that different versions of CBT do not simply represent a range of opposing techniques and concepts but are in fact expressions of entirely different philosophical worldviews (Herbert et al., 2016).

Contemporary practitioners of CBT, and new practitioners in particular, are thus faced with a bewildering range of theories and strategies and, at times, competing propositions of how best to be of service to their clients. The forms of CBT favoured in government-funded services, however, have tended to strongly emphasise the delivery of the so-called second wave 'disorder specific' and manualised interventions. This has led to criticism from outside CBT (House & Lowenthal, 2008) that CBT is in essence a quasi-medical approach, reliant upon diagnostic classification, that attempts to 'remove symptoms' and 'adjust' clients to the prevailing socio-political ideology of neo-liberalism. The apparent success of the *CBT for x* approach covers over the fact that, in the history of cognitive and behavioural therapies, there has always been a strong tradition of challenging the necessity, usefulness, reliability and validity of psychiatric classification as a basis for providing therapy. This challenge has arisen again as erstwhile opponents in the behaviour-versus-cognition wars have called a truce and proposed that further developments in CBT may be dependent on moving away from any reliance or endorsement of psychiatric classification of mental disease entities, and moving towards an approach that emphasises the identification of key *processes*, such as attentional fixation, cognitive fusion, rumination, avoidance and negative affect that are common across different forms of psychological suffering. These researchers suggest (Hayes & Hoffmann, 2018, p. 15): 'This approach might counter the drawback of training clinicians in disorder-specific CBT protocols, which often leads to an oversimplification of human suffering, inflexibility on the part of the clinician and low adherence to evidence-based practices'. Furthermore, these authors suggest that an approach based upon the identification of key psychological processes and upon the development of evidence-based ways of working with these processes that rely upon the intensive exploration of the experience and context of the unique client—an approach that abandons the psychiatric-medical system of diagnosis—may lead to the eventual 'death' of CBT as a distinct approach; Hayes and Hoffmann (2018, p. 436) state:

> This will not occur because all evidence-based methods will be shown to emerge from CBT. Rather, as CBT reorients towards issues that were previously the focus of other therapy traditions, there will be fewer and fewer reasons to distinguish CBT from analytic, existential, humanistic, or systemic work.

These authors, who identify themselves as leaders of both the cognitive and contextual behavioural science wings of contemporary CBT, thus appear to re-open the possibility of dialogue with alternative perspectives, including that of existential therapy.

Existential Therapy and CBT: An Interrupted and Incomplete Dialogue

At first glance, existential therapy seems the most unlikely of partners in any dialogue that has even the faintest hope of identifying areas of convergence and agreement with CBT. Nevertheless, the suggestion that various forms of CBT and existential phenomenology may have points in common, and may potentially enrich and challenge each other, is by no means a new one. As early as 1963, a symposium considering the relative strengths and limitations of behaviourism and phenomenology was held at Rice University (Day, 1969). In addition, the possibility that phenomenology and radical behaviourism, particularly the psychology of B.F. Skinner, share points of contact has been noted numerous times in the literature (e.g. Butcher, 1984; Fallon, 1992). Clark et al. (1999), writing from a more cognitive perspective, suggested that the philosophical perspective most consistent with the practice of CBT was existential phenomenology. In fact, as will be discussed further, Beck et al. (1979), in their seminal text on cognitive therapy for depression, acknowledge Ludwig Binswanger, an early proponent of existential therapy, as an inspiration for the development of cognitive therapy. More recently, Corrie and Milton (2000) have called for greater dialogue between the approaches. Additionally, Fewtrell and O'Conner (1995) and O'Conner (2015) have explored the possibility of incorporating phenomenologically derived perspectives into CBT. The possibility of finding ways to integrate forms of CBT with existential perspectives has also been advanced by Edwards (1990), Ottens and Hannah (1998) and Sotskova et al. (2016).

Existential therapy tends to distinguish itself from other models by virtue of it being an explicitly philosophical approach to therapy, as opposed to a scientific or medical one (van Deurzen-Smith, 1997). Existential therapy gains its distinctive flavour through its concern with issues of *being* and *existence*, that is, the meanings we construct, or find, regarding our lives and how these meanings relate to various forms of psychological, behavioural and relational distress. As Cohn (1997) explains, the term 'existence' can be understood as the human being's quality of *standing out*. In existential philosophy, this sense of standing out also connotes a special way in which human beings are said to, alone in existence, have an awareness of and openness towards Being. Also, according to this philosophy, human beings are best understood in terms of a fundamental inter-relational grounding expressed in the notion of 'Being-in-the-world'. Existential psychology and therapy, drawing upon insights from a range of existential and phenomenological philosophers, propose that many of the dilemmas and concerns that clients bring to therapy are expressive of basic and universal aspects of existence itself. Such fundamental aspects of existence include the finite nature of human life, the ubiquity and inevitability of anxiety and uncertainty and that human existence is always embodied and temporal. In this approach, the problems that clients bring to therapy are often conceptualised as *problems in living* rather than necessarily being expressive of forms of psychopathology. The question follows: How can such an approach offer anything to therapists interested in developing a form of psychotherapy based on scientific principles?

In answering this question, much may depend on one's understanding of the nature of science and the scientific worldview that is embraced.

O'Donohue and Ferguson (2016) have noted that while the project of developing a scientifically based form of psychotherapy is defining for CBT therapists, the understanding of what is meant by science and what versions of scientific activity are appropriate to CBT remains an unanswered question. Existential therapists are by no means hostile towards scientific understandings and approaches to therapy; however, they trace their stance towards questions of science to a distinction made by the psychologist and philosopher Wilhelm Dilthey (1833–1911). Dilthey contrasted what he referred to as the explanatory natural sciences, *naturwissenschaften,* and the descriptive or interpretative sciences, *geisteswissenschaften*, also referred to as the human sciences. In brief, Dilthey advocated for a form of psychology based upon a human science which was understood as being inherently historical and contextual and concerned with issues of meaning and understanding rather than causality and prediction (Burston & Frie, 2006). The human science perspective, a form of 'descriptive contextualism', can be seen as a philosophical worldview as Hughes (2018, p. 26) defines it: 'A philosophical worldview can be defined as the coherent set of interrelated assumptions that provides the preanalytic framework that sets the stage for scientific or therapeutic activity'.

From a human science perspective, it is as possible to be methodologically rigorous, structured and focused, and as concerned with empirical phenomena, as it is in natural science. However, from a human science perspective, concerns regarding causality, explanation and prediction are seen as extraneous and likely to significantly bias the conduct of any effort at research and understanding. Efforts at descriptive and contextualised *understanding* constitute the goal of human science projects. As Cohn (2005, p. 222) has stated, this concerns: 'the slow process of exploring and clarifying the many-stranded tangle of a life situation that can never be complete and does not lead to final answers'. For Cohn (2005), understanding involves a 'broadening out of contexts' rather than a targeted and reductive 'narrowing down':

> The perceived phenomenon gains clarity, richness and meaningfulness whenever a new aspect of its totality is discovered. The concern is always with amplification and exploration rather than explanation (2005, p. 224).

Existential therapy embraces this perspective and, as such, can also be understood as allied to a human science approach as much as it can be understood as a particular expression or application of existential philosophy. As applied to therapy, a human science perspective suggests that the goals of therapeutic conversations are more directed to the possibilities of dialogue and understanding rather than psychoeducation, cure or the technical overcoming of difficulties or, indeed, the prediction and control of behaviour.

Hughes (2018) argues that it is an invalid and pointless exercise to evaluate the results of work from one philosophical worldview against the criteria embraced by another philosophical worldview. Instead, what can be embraced is an attempt at entering into that alternative worldview in order that its possibilities and limitations can be considered. This has relevance for the discussion presented in this book as I will often be drawing the reader's attention to the implications of an existential perspective that may be very challenging or alien for a CBT therapist to consider. In short, I will be drawing on a distinction made by existential therapist Ernesto Spinelli (2015) that I feel to be both valid and useful. Spinelli suggests that the insights and arguments of existential philosophy and therapy can be considered at two levels. The first level considers the various themes identified by existential philosophers, psychologists and therapists, such as death, isolation, meaning, freedom and choice. As argued by Yalom (1980)—possibly the most well-known and widely read existential therapist—any therapeutic approach that is able to thoughtfully consider such universal themes can be considered an existential approach. As will be shown throughout this text, many versions of CBT do indeed consider such themes, or have the potential to do so, in meaningful and productive ways, and, as such, CBT can be considered, as Spinelli has it, to be a form of existentially attuned therapy. The second level, however, is by far more challenging as it involves a more thoroughgoing encounter with the underlying philosophical worldview of existential phenomenology; this encounter is likely to challenge and bring into question the more typical philosophical worldview implicitly or explicitly embraced by different forms of CBT.

In my view, Clark et al.'s (1999) suggestion that existential phenomenology is consistent with CBT is highly instructive and one that this book intends to elaborate upon. Contemporary standard CBT (the most commonly practised form of essentially cognitively based CBT), at the level of scientific investigation and validation of its methods, expresses a worldview best understood as either positivist or post-positivist (Hughes, 2018). This worldview is essentially a reductionist and mechanistic one that asserts that there is an external reality governed by natural laws that can be systematically studied. Scientific models (as well as an individual's beliefs/their personal worldview) are valid to the extent that they are in correspondence with the actual nature of the external world. At the level of practice, however, CBT therapists find themselves drawing upon significantly more constructivist notions (which are themselves derivations and developments of existential phenomenological views). It appears that in many respects, contemporary CBT mixes aspects of positivist and constructivist worldviews and that it would be of some benefit to explore the implications, challenges and dilemmas that this produces. The same is not the case for other versions of CBT, most notably ACT, which expresses and maintains a pragmatic-contextualist worldview in both theory, research and practice. This contextualist perspective, as will be shown, also has substantial points of contact with, as well as difference from, existential phenomenological views.

Aims of This Book

This book aims to take the dialogue between existential phenomenology and CBT forward. In doing so, I am also aiming to include as much of the current breadth of CBT thinking and practice as is possible and practicable in a text of this type. My principal aim is to convince adherents of CBT that there is much within existential thinking to enrich, challenge and support their therapeutic practice. Because CBT was developed in a way that acknowledges the significance of existential therapy, well trained and critically informed CBT therapists should be aware of this and be able to draw upon this rich and varied literature. My second aim is to convince those therapists aligned with existential therapy to take a second and even a third look (or wave) at CBT. In my experience, the ability of existential therapists to take a constructively critical view of CBT has been severely hampered by a limited understanding of, and contact with, diverse forms of CBT. There is much within contemporary versions of CBT that existential therapists could potentially find of value, as well as much with which they will undoubtedly disagree. Much of the discussion to date has focused on the adequacy, reliability and validity of the empirical research held to support a view of CBT as the treatment of choice to the exclusion of other modalities. This book is less concerned with the issue of the adequacy and appropriateness of empirical research methodologies, as it is with the underlying worldviews characteristic of CBT and existential therapy.

As my principal aim is to promote a constructive, if challenging, dialogue, it is important to clarify from the outset what this book is *not* attempting to achieve. I am not proposing a new form of therapy called 'existential CBT'. Rather, I will attempt to show how various forms of current CBT are already, in at least some respects, existentially attuned. I am also not suggesting that the contributions of existential thought can simply be integrated easily and fully within existing forms of CBT. So, there is no manual being presented here. The attempt is to provide the basis for a constructive and challenging dialogue—as challenging of existential therapists as of CBT therapists—one that avoids the pitfall of straw man versions of either approach. As I have trained, practised and provided teaching and supervision from the perspective of both approaches, I am hopeful that I am able to do this task some justice. It is of course for the reader to decide to what extent I am successful in this as undoubtedly there will be aspects of what I present that both CBT therapists and existential therapists disagree with and dispute. This is, of course, what true dialogue will allow and promote.

Structure of This Book

This book is presented in four parts. In Part 1, I introduce the reader to existential thinking in the form of existential philosophy, existential psychology and existential therapy. At times, I use the term 'existential psychology' to cover both philosophy, psychology and therapy, an obviously academically unacceptable practice that I adopt simply for convenience. There are many excellent texts available that provide a comprehensive introduction to the key existential philosophers and the fundamental arguments of existential thought. What is needed for my purpose here is a brief overview that identifies the key themes and figures in a way that sets the scene for what comes later. Chapter 2 therefore is a brief and incomplete overview of existential philosophy *as* philosophy. Many writers within the existential field have assumed that the key themes and ideas of existential thinking are unsuitable for the methods of experimental science—such an attitude would immediately create a barrier for those coming to the field with an interest in experimental science, as this book would then only be concerned with questions of philosophical worldview and therapeutic practice. However, a number of researchers have in fact made important contributions to a natural science focused approach to existential themes and issues, and this field of work is discussed in Chapter 3 on existential psychology. Additionally, Chapter 3 reviews some of the research that has been conducted within CBT but from a standpoint more in tune with the concerns of a human science approach. This will also allow for the presentation of the phenomenological method, a fundamental aspect of the human science approach of existential therapy. Chapters 4 (theory) and 5 (practice) are focused on the theoretical ideas, assumptions and ways of working within the many different versions of existential therapy. It will be clarified that just as there is no single unified school of CBT, the same is true of existential therapy.

In Part 2, I review what would be considered to be the major versions of contemporary CBT. The starting point in Chapter 6 is standard Beckian CBT, the most commonly practised form of CBT worldwide. It will be seen how this form of CBT converges with existential thinking by virtue of its focus on meaning, while at the same time significantly diverging via its adoption of a more Cartesian notion of an information processing system. Chapter 7 will consider the development of schema-focused approaches that significantly deepen questions of meaning, while also widening the view of the role and significance of emotion and the therapeutic relationship in a way that opens up lines of possible convergence with existential therapy. Chapter 8 considers the wide range of constructivist and postmodern versions of CBT that in some ways constitute an unofficial and incomplete fourth wave of CBT. In many respects, these versions of CBT draw upon ideas and arguments that are direct developments and elaborations of existential phenomenological thinking. Chapter 9 considers the development of third wave CBT approaches that focus on issues of acceptance, mindfulness and inter-relation that again substantially converge with existential therapy. This is especially the case with ACT where there is a substantial convergence in underlying philosophical worldviews, but where the difference in these worldviews also provides considerable scope for debate and disagreement. In Chapter 10, I attempt to draw together the various strands and points of contact, disagreement and potential dialogue between these different versions of CBT and existential perspectives.

Part 3 of this book considers a range of phenomena and issues where an existential perspective may be of value. Chapter 11 discusses the role of the therapeutic relationship and how an existential view provides a number of significant challenges to CBT. Chapter 12 considers the issue of existential anxiety, a theme that will be addressed at various points, and the extent to which the so-called clinical expressions of anxiety have their basis in a more fundamental and shared existential anxiety. Chapter 13 considers the phenomena of dreams and how these may be worked within CBT, enriched by both existential perspectives on the nature and significance of dreams, as well as structured phenomenological ways of working. Chapter 14 is an inconclusive conclusion that attempts to clarify the various levels at which CBT and existential therapy can both enrich and challenge each other.

At various points in the book, I will discuss a range of clinical examples that seek to illustrate the various existential themes being discussed. Existential therapists are likely to have an immediate conditioned negative emotional response to the term 'clinical', so I invite these readers to substitute the term 'therapy story' to help reduce their subjective units of discomfort to a tolerable degree. These examples are drawn from my own experience working as a therapist—to protect the confidentiality of former clients, I have changed identifying information to the extent that these examples are more constructions than 'reports', and as such they implicate and express my own concerns and thinking more than they do the issues of any particular individual.

The essence of therapy from an existential perspective is dialogue or conversation. In keeping with this, the Part 4 of this book is a series of dialogues on the issue of the inter-relation of CBT and existential thinking and therapy. The first dialogue is a three-way conversation between me and two highly experienced CBT therapists, Thomas Heidenreich and Alexander Noyon, who also have a long-standing interest in existential thinking and who incorporate existential views into their practice as CBT therapists, researchers, trainers and supervisors. The second dialogue is with Ernesto Spinelli, an internationally recognised authority in existential therapy. I hope these dialogues will inspire the readers' engagement, conversation and wrestling with the issues and ideas raised in this book.

Part 1

Existential Philosophy, Psychology and Therapy

2

Existential Philosophy

Over his friend, Enkidu, Gilgamesh cried bitterly, roaming the wilderness.
'I am going to die! —am I not like Enkidu?!
Deep sadness penetrates my core,
I fear death, and now roam the wilderness—'

—The Epic of Gilgamesh Tablet IV (somewhere between 2750 and 2500 BCE).

CBT practitioners, by nature pragmatic and empirically inclined, when presented with the possibility of an existentially attuned form of CBT, are likely to ask: 'What have the existentialists ever done for us?' In this book, it is argued that existential philosophy, psychology and therapy can offer much to CBT therapists. To explore this, it is necessary to have some grounding in the various perspectives and ideas of the existential philosophers. Rather than review in depth, the thinking of specific existential philosophers, which would require a single text of considerable length to even approach adequacy, an overview is presented of the field as a whole and, following this, key concerns and themes of existential philosophy are discussed.

CBT and Existential Psychology: Philosophy, Psychology and Therapy,
First Edition. Michael Worrell.

A Lightning Tour of Existential Philosophy

The boundaries around the field of existential and existential phenomenological philosophy are nothing if not blurry. If the central issue is to explore philosophical perspectives that address what it means to live as a human being, then it is possible to claim that the views of western philosophers from antiquity, beginning with the Greek stoics and sceptics, and a diverse range of non-western philosophies should all be considered (van Deurzen-Smith, 1997). It is clearly true that such contributions are worthy of serious consideration; however, the more specific form of philosophy that is of interest here concerns not only various themes or dimensions relevant to an understanding of human existence but also the manner in which these themes were and are addressed. The discussion is therefore restricted to philosophers identifiable in some fashion with existential phenomenology. The philosophical perspectives identifiable within this grouping attempted to address key aspects of the nature of human existence, as clarified by phenomenological description and analysis. To place these in context, it will be useful to identify several important precursors, as well as a range of related voices and contributions that were/are in some form of dialogue with the existential phenomenological thinkers.

Precursors

The two most influential thinkers that are precursors to contemporary existential phenomenological perspectives are the contributions of **Soren Kierkegaard** and **Friedrich Nietzsche**. Kierkegaard (1813–1855) was a Danish Christian philosopher who is now regarded as the father of existentialism. Reacting to what he saw as the dry, abstract and totalising philosophy of Hegel, he forcefully argued that philosophy must remain focused on the existing individual. He is most appreciated for his contributions to understanding the nature of anxiety as an inherent and unavoidable aspect of human existence. Nietzsche (1844–1900) was a German philosopher (in) famous for his pronouncement that 'God is dead'. Highly provocative in his style, he criticised what he regarded as the *slave mentality* of conventional society and urged people to become *supermen*, meaning autonomous individuals living embodied lives of passion and power. Nietzsche's work is as relevant to the development of psychoanalysis and postmodernism as it is to existential philosophy (see Bazzano, 2019, for an in-depth discussion of the impact of Nietzsche's thought on psychotherapy).

Both philosophers were highly influential for a range of existential phenomenological philosophers. Concerns around issues of authenticity and anxiety are traceable to their ideas. At the same time, their philosophies appear to emphasise the centrality of an isolated individual as the source point for experience and value. Existential phenomenological philosophers, by contrast, have emphasised an irreducible relational foundation of human existence that is substantially at variance with the notion of the primacy of the existing individual (Spinelli, 2016).

Phenomenological Foundations

Although the term 'phenomenology' predates his work, **Edmund Husserl** is nevertheless credited as being the founder of phenomenology. Husserl (1859–1938) developed phenomenology as a radical new approach to philosophy that was also intended to provide solid foundations for the empirical sciences. Husserl's phenomenology focused on the question of consciousness and emphasised the notion of 'intentionality', that is, that consciousness has a quality of directedness, that it is always consciousness *of* something. Husserl's work was of prime importance to the existential phenomenological thinkers that followed him, even in their serious disagreements with him on central aspects of the phenomenological project. Key insights as well as aspects of phenomenology as a method are discussed further.

Existential Phenomenological Philosophers

Karl Jaspers (1883–1969) was a German philosopher and psychiatrist who developed descriptive studies of psychopathological states in his *General Psychopathology* (1963) and suggested that symptoms of mental illness should be diagnosable via their form rather than their content. His philosophical work, drawing on Kierkegaard and Nietzsche, emphasised the issue of individual freedom as well as the inevitable 'boundary situations' that human beings face, such as death and loss.

Martin Heidegger (1889–1976), a German philosopher, is widely considered as the most significant and influential existential thinker, let alone one of the most important philosophers of the twentieth century. Heidegger's focus was on the issue of Being itself, asking 'What does it mean that there is something rather than nothing at all?' In his magnum opus *Being and Time* (1962), Heidegger argued that human beings have a fundamental pre-understanding of the nature of Being and that the nature of their own being remained an issue for them. His descriptions of the fundamental dimensions of human existence—including the existential nature of anxiety and guilt, the notion of the human being as 'thrown', and being-towards-death—have been greatly influential for most existential therapists. At the same time, he remains a controversial figure due to the fact that he was in the 1930s a member of the Nazi party and did not subsequently publicly account for this. This raised the issue of the extent to which his political actions are consistent with or a betrayal of his philosophy as well as the question of to what extent a form of psychotherapy can be developed based upon his philosophy (see Cohn, 2002 for a discussion of this issue).

Jean-Paul Sartre (1905–1980), a French philosopher, writer and playwright, is possibly the philosopher most clearly identifiable as being an existentialist. Sartre remains a highly influential philosopher and social critic who emphasised the centrality of human freedom and responsibility. His descriptions of forms of 'bad faith' are highly psychologically acute and revealing of the various ways in which human beings tend to avoid an awareness of, and responsibility for, choice. Sartre proposed a form of 'existential psychoanalysis' and also provided an analysis of the nature of emotions as being forms of meaning (emotions clarify for us in what way 'things matter') and are a 'magical' means by which people 'transform their world'. Betty Cannon (1991) has developed a form of existential psychotherapy based principally on the work of Sartre and how his philosophy can be read as providing alternative understandings of the psychoanalytic notions of the unconscious and transference.

Maurice Merleau-Ponty (1907–1961), a French philosopher, made particularly valuable contributions to an existential phenomenological understanding of embodied relational experience. While a number of existential phenomenological philosophers are notable for their hostility to psychology as a discipline, Merleau-Ponty made use of the findings of contemporary psychologists, such as the findings of the Gestalt school.

Other Contributors

There is a wide range of other philosophers whose work has not been mentioned above, including, for example, Simone de Beauvoir (1908–1986), Paul Tillich (1996–1965) and Gabriel Marcel (1889–1973). Their absence is not due to their lower status, but due to the need for brevity. Three additional philosophers are, however, important to briefly describe due to the significant challenges and correctives they offered that served to emphasise the relational nature of human existence.

Martin Buber (1887–1965) was an Austrian Jewish and Israeli philosopher and theologian whose work has been highly influential among many existential and humanistic psychotherapists; he is known in the world of psychotherapy for having engaged in a dialogue with Carl Rogers (Anderson & Cissna, 1997). Buber's work emphasises the fundamentally relational nature of human existence, and he challenged what he saw as an emphasis on 'individuals' in other perspectives. He is best known for his descriptions of I-Thou versus I-It forms of relating, both of which are essential aspects, or forms, of human dialogue.

Emmanuel Levinas (1906–1995), from Lithuania, is known as a French philosopher who prioritised ethics and the status of 'the other'. For Levinas, the other is not knowable and cannot be made into an object of the self. Levinas provides a highly demanding philosophy in which the other holds primacy in a face-to-face encounter and in which 'responsibility for the other' is foundational for our existence (see Heaton, 2014).

Hans-Georg Gadamer (1900–2002) was a German philosopher whose work on hermeneutics dealt with the nature of human understanding. Hermeneutics is concerned with the issue and methodology of interpreting texts. He was critical of the work of empirically minded researchers who sought an *objective* understanding of human action. In his major text, *Truth and Method* (2004), he described the process of interpreting the meanings of a text in terms of a 'fusion of horizons' in which both the text and the interpreter of the text always find themselves within a particular historical tradition and language. For Gadamer, the hermeneutic process is one of dialogue and conversation, and the meanings to be found in a text will change depending upon the questions asked of it.

Contemporary Developments

The existential philosophical movement was itself overtaken by developments in post-structuralism and postmodernism. Many contemporary existential therapists are thus as influenced by the works of philosophers such as Foucault (1980) and Derrida (2001) as they are by the philosophers mentioned above. Nevertheless, there continue to be developments within philosophy that are, in important respects, continuations of central existential phenomenological themes, or that are important reinterpretations and elaborations of these. In this respect, the work of **Hubert Dreyfus** (1929–2017) is of particular relevance. Dreyfus, an American philosopher, used the central insights of Martin Heidegger to critique dominant models of cognitive psychology, as well as research into artificial intelligence (AI) (Dreyfus, 1972). Opposing current models of human information processing as being 'computer like' and based on processing of internal cognitive representations via 'if-then' rules, Dreyfus argues that human consciousness is always an embodied consciousness-in-the-world. In order to approach the form of intelligence most characteristic of human intelligence, argued Dreyfus, AI devices would need to be based on the key aspect of what it is to be human, namely, they would need to be embodied in such a way that 'things matter'. Of interest too is the work of **Dan Zahavi** (1967–), a Danish philosopher whose work has focused on a phenomenological analysis of pre-reflective consciousness and which has addressed the topics of shame, shared emotions and experiences of 'we' (Zahavi, 2015).

Key Propositions of Existential Phenomenology

If one were expecting that the field of existential philosophy would present itself as a coherent and consistent view of human existence—a view that could find easy or, indeed, manualisable application to the field of psychotherapy—then disappointment, dread and despair are the most likely consequences. Most of the existential philosophers discussed above would have refused the title *existential philosopher* and had the possibility of a symposium been presented, one in which they could compare and contrast their views, the most likely point of agreement would be that each philosopher had misunderstood or misrepresented what the other had intended. Cooper (2003) acknowledges that existential philosophy is, as a field 'difficult, contradictory and ill-defined'. For CBT therapists, the language used by existential philosophers, as well as existential therapists, can be alienating. Some philosophers, such as Kierkegaard, often make their arguments indirectly, using pseudonyms to express points of view and arguments that are not actually those of the writer. Others, such as Heidegger, either invent new terms or use ordinary (German) language in a manner that is substantially different from ordinary usage and that relies on an understanding of etymology. Cohn (2002) describes how in Heidegger's classic and unavoidable work *Being and Time* (1962) there is no sustained clear argument that leads to a conclusion, and he suggests that Heidegger's thinking can be compared to a musical score in which Being is the recurring theme.

Macquarrie (1973) asserts that existentialism is more a style of philosophising than a set of agreed philosophical doctrines, a style that is concerned with concrete realities of human existence, such as death, freedom, guilt, responsibility and the like. Similarly, Friedman (1991, p. 3) suggests that existentialism is best characterised as a *mood* that he understands as consisting of 'a reaction against the static, the abstract, the purely rational, the merely irrational, in favour of the dynamic and the concrete, personal involvement and engagement, action, choice and commitment'.

In contrast, Cooper (1999) has argued that the main existential thinkers are identifiable as belonging to the same family, not on the basis of a style or mood but rather because they would all have at some point, as philosophers, subscribed to what he identifies as an 'existentialist manifesto'. This manifesto is centrally concerned with an understanding of how human beings and the world are related to each other. Cooper argues that existentialism is often misunderstood as presenting a view of human beings as always isolated and alienated from the world. This view, while often an accurate portrayal of how some individuals may experience their existence, is based upon a misunderstanding. Existentialism, argues Cooper, asserts that human beings and the world are fundamentally a single unitary phenomenon. This notion of human existence as always Being-in-the-world can be difficult to grasp—but before attempting to discuss what this might mean, it is important to clarify the manner in which this question is asked and explored by existential philosophy. This then brings us to the significance of phenomenology.

Phenomenology

Phenomenology aims at gaining a descriptive understanding of the nature of phenomena rather than a causal or explanatory analysis. Cerbone (2015) has provided a useful orientating experiential exercise that allows an approach to the key concerns and methods of phenomenological analysis. Consider the experience of holding a cup of coffee in one's hands. We will take responsibility for this example and imagine that it is a regular 'flat white' (a form of coffee claimed to have been invented in Australia, but whose origins remain contested) that we are holding while sitting in an Italian café in Hammersmith underground station in London. The café advertises itself as serving 'the best' Italian coffee in London. The waiting staff come from various nationalities and the décor, intended to evoke the unique, relaxed but sophisticated vibe of an Italian city, has existed for less than 12 months and is but one of a, for the most part identical, chain of cafes. As Cerbone (2015) notes, a wide variety of questions could be asked regarding this experience. For example, a behavioural psychologist might enquire into our reinforcement history so as to address the question of the likely probability of future purchases of similar flat whites. Such an enquiry might be productive in that it may emerge that in fact the claims of perfect coffee are somewhat inconsistent with past experience such that a variable schedule of reinforcement has been set up. The sufficiently high ratio of excellent flat whites may have led to a high probability of future purchases (further reinforced by the application of the notorious behavioural strategy known as 'the loyalty card'—a strategy that I consistently resist in an act of absurd existential defiance).

Alternatively, a postmodern or narratively informed psychologist might be most interested in the wide range of referential signs intended to evoke authenticity, sophistication and the like, and might inquire into the possibility that purchasing and consuming regular flat whites is a performance of identity, a caffeinated punctuation of existence that asserts a shallow and unstable individuality in a manner authorised and approved by a late (latte?) capitalist neo-liberal ideology. A physiologically or biologically oriented researcher may be interested in the effects of caffeine on the brain or in the neural pathways activated by the touch of the cup and its emanating heat, as well as the visual pathways that provide the possibility for the cup to be registered in the brain as an internal representation of a flat white. All of these questions, and more, may be of interest. However, none of them are central to the project of phenomenology. Phenomenology, understood as an effort to study phenomena as 'that which appears', would seek to enquire into the question of how the flat white presents itself as what it is. That is, phenomenology seeks a descriptive clarification of how the phenomena presents itself and is experienced. This might include the observation, for example, that when slowly turning the cup in my hand, I am only ever presented with one side of the cup and yet, at the same time, I apprehend the cup as a whole cup of coffee. Furthermore, it presents itself as 'about to be enjoyed'—the experience of 'bitter-smoothness' already present within the anticipation.

Is Your Coffee the 'Real Thing'?

Historically within philosophy, one of the most difficult and possibly irresolvable questions concerns the relationship between 'the appearance of things' (phenomena) and things as they 'really are'. Is it the case that our conscious awareness provides us with direct and accurate information about how the world actually is, or is the world as we experience it solely a product of our own species-based and culturally conditioned limited faculties? As noted earlier, phenomenology is principally the philosophical perspective developed and elaborated by Husserl and his collaborators. Husserl's project was to develop a science of phenomena that would seek to clarify how phenomena present themselves to our consciousness. As Spinelli (2005) has described, for Husserl, the basis for any meaning-based construct (such as a flat white) lies in the fundamental relationship between consciousness and reality that is termed 'intentionality'. This should not be confused with the more specifically psychological concept of 'an intention'. Rather, intentionality refers to an irreducible relationship and 'direction' between consciousness and the world. Any act of consciousness is seen to be 'about' something. For example, being angry is always directed in some fashion—there is no anger, as such, but only *anger about something* (my flat white being less than perfect, for example). A consequence of this notion is that we can never say we have a truly objective or God's-eye view of what reality is in itself, separate from our conscious awareness of it. The world as we experience it always remains an interpreted reality (Spinelli, 2005). We cannot know, for example, what the cup of flat white is in itself, separate from the way we apprehend it in consciousness or in the act of drinking it. Even if we were to take the cup of coffee to a lab and examine its chemical composition or examine the porcelain under an electron microscope, we could not say we were any closer to what the cup of coffee 'really is'. Such scientific analyses of what the cup of coffee is in itself are also the results of human interpretation—interpretation, furthermore, that is always carried out within a particular context and in the service of chosen purposes.

Intentionality, as a foundational idea, describes an irreducible relationship between consciousness and the world. In this perspective, the cup of coffee is not seen as simply the product of, or in some sense contained within, a separate conscious mind. Consciousness does not itself produce the coffee cup. Instead, each fundamentally co-constitute the other; both the coffee and the drinker bring meaning to each other (Ihde, 1986, Spinelli, 2005).

In addition to the fundamental idea of intentionality, phenomenology claims it is possible to gain a more adequate or richer understanding of the way phenomena present themselves to consciousness, thereby offering greater clarity on the nature of consciousness and its acts of interpretation. In other words, the phenomenological method is in essence a research project designed to help the investigator gain an ever more adequate, but never complete or final, description of the phenomena of consciousness. The specifics of the phenomenological method are discussed in further detail in Chapter 3.

In summary, phenomenology and the phenomenological method are concerned with the rigorous and structured exploration of experience. As will be discussed in later chapters, there is a great deal within phenomenology that is congruent with the emphasis on guided discovery, as the principal method within CBT to clarify a client's experience. For now, however, we turn to an exploration of how phenomenology has been used by philosophers interested in turning the focus of exploration away from the nature of consciousness to the nature of Being itself. It is in this turn towards existence that phenomenology becomes existential phenomenology.

The Phenomenology of Existence

While for Husserl, and others, the phenomenological project concerned principally the attempt to understand consciousness, for Heidegger, and the existential phenomenologists that followed him, the central issue concerns the attempt to describe the nature of Being itself. Questions about how to describe the nature of Being are regarded as belonging to the field of ontology. The question of Being is said by Heidegger (1962) to be commonly forgotten and, indeed, it can be a challenge to even grasp what the question of Being might mean. At a basic level, the question of Being refers to the issue of: 'Why, or what does it mean, that there is something at all rather than nothing?' It refers to the attempt to understand the nature of is-ness and existence. The term 'existential' can be expressed also as to 'ex-ist' meaning 'to stand out from' (Cohn, 2002). This indicates a special sense in which human beings standout in their existence in a manner that is radically different from that which characterises the existence of objects. An object, such as a chair, may be understood principally in terms of its essence or, indeed, essences. Thus, a chair can be said to be understood to the degree that we can identify its various essences, such as having height appropriate for human posture, being capable of securely supporting weight or indeed being 'available to be sat upon'. From this the essence of chair may be clarified in terms of human projects and embodied action. A human being, by contrast, cannot be completely understood in terms of essences. The essence of a human being, following Sartre (1991), lies in its existence and the sense in which its 'existence precedes its essence'; that is, human beings are seen as, in an important sense, 'incomplete' and 'open'. Thus, even if one were able to complete some form of total functional analysis such that an individual's full reinforcement history could be revealed, allowing for the possibility of prediction and influence of their behaviour, it could not be claimed that the totality of that human being was understood. Thus, existential philosophers can be read as making various attempts at understanding and describing the fundamental aspects of what it means to exist in the specific ways that human beings exist.

Relatedness and Being-in-the-World

One way of understanding the most central concerns of existential thinking is that it is founded upon a particular way of understanding the nature of 'relatedness'. That is, what is the nature of the relationship between human beings and the world, the relationship between human beings and each other and also the relationship between human beings as minds-and-bodies. This perspective is in many respects a response or reaction to the types of understanding that most characterise the field of psychology, and indeed Western culture, which can be traced to the philosophy of Rene Descartes (1596–1650). Descartes was particularly concerned with a quest for certainty in order to build up a philosophy from first principles. In a project of radical doubt, Descartes arrived at the now famous statement 'I think therefore I am'. Descartes postulated that his existence as a 'thinking thing' was the one thing of which he could be certain. However, this then introduced a series of splits or separations in which, for example, the nature of mind needed to be seen as fundamentally different to the nature of matter. Similarly, mind was seen as fundamentally separate although somehow related to body. Additionally, the relationship between one mind and the mind of another individual then becomes an issue. Such Cartesian dualisms have gone on to become the subject of intense debate. CBT has often been characterised as expressing a Cartesian point of view, particularly through its insistence that cognition can be meaningfully separated from emotion.

In essence, the existential perspective, particularly within the philosophy of Heidegger (1962), challenged all such Cartesian separations, along with any notion that individual subjects can be considered as fundamentally separate from the world. Heidegger describes human existence as Being-in-the-world (the hyphens here serve to express the degree to which the human being and the world are fundamentally aspects of a single process). Heidegger's concept of Being-in-the-world is also represented by the term ‘Dasein’. Dasein is used in the sense of ‘being there’, as well as ‘the “there” of being’ or ‘the place where being reveals itself’ (Cohn, 2002). Human beings, in Heidegger’s philosophy, are best characterised in terms of an ‘openness towards being’, rather than as being like solid objects. Additionally, Heidegger characterises our inevitable involvement with the world and various projects in terms of ‘care’ or ‘concern’—the world as experienced by human beings is always already meaningful. Things, such as chairs and coffee cups, ‘matter’ in terms of embodied human projects (Cohn, 2002).

Being and Being-with-Others

Cooper’s (1999) ‘existential manifesto’ asserts that existential philosophy is concerned with the ways in which human beings experience themselves as being estranged or set apart from the world. This emphasis also finds expression in those versions of existential psychotherapy, such as that presented by Yalom (1980), that highlight the ways in which each human being is in a fundamental sense isolated and unique. This emphasis on individual isolation and alienation is in many respects, however, a misrepresentation of the most central insight of existential phenomenology. As Cooper notes, the main thrust of existential thinking demonstrates how any sense of estrangement is secondary to a more fundamental and irreducible relatedness between human beings and the world. For Heidegger, Being-in-the-world is also always a Being-with-others. Our relationships with others are primary and foundational for any sense of an individual self to emerge. Even where an individual chooses to live a life of isolation from others this can itself only be understood in terms of a primary relatedness.

Meaning and Meaninglessness

Psychotherapists, of varying orientations, who have looked to existential philosophy for inspiration have frequently highlighted the way in which meaning is prioritised as a central dimension of what it is to be human. Heidegger’s project (1962) was the attempt to understand and elucidate the *meaning* of Being. Heidegger, in his descriptions of facticity and thrownness, describes the ways in which we find ourselves 'always already' situated in a context of meaningful relationships given to us by culture and language. Sartre, too, describes the ways in which human beings confront the central task of actualising meaning in the form of a 'life project'. Certainly, one direct way in which existential philosophy and therapy may be of relevance to CBT is in highlighting forms of meaning, particularly more global forms of *meaning in and of life* that are not addressed by a focus on specific cognitions associated with forms of psychological distress. However, it would be an error to emphasise meaning at the expense of what may exist at its opposite pole, namely, meaninglessness.

Existential philosophy, in as much as it emphasises the primacy of meaning, also asserts that meaninglessness (or the absurd) is inherent to human existence. That is, any meanings that human beings either construct or find, including broader forms of value and 'meaning of life', however enriching, motivating and life-affirming, can only ever be partial, incomplete and uncertain attempts at capturing or solidifying meaning. Spinelli (2015) has argued that the existential emphasis on the openness and incompleteness of human existence can also be understood in terms of the primary principle of uncertainty. That is, uncertainty is an inherent aspect of any being's attempts at finding and fixing some form of certainty. Existential philosophy proposes that our direct and pre-reflective experience of relational being, which is characterised by flux and change, is never fully capturable in a reflective construction of meaning (Spinelli, 2015). As will be discussed in greater depth later in this book, considering meaning from the perspective of an inherent and ultimately irresolvable tension between meaning and meaninglessness has substantial implications for how the process of beneficial change is understood in therapy.

Freedom and Limitations

Existential philosophy and existential therapy are perhaps best known for their emphasis on freedom—that human beings have the possibility of making free choices and cannot be reduced to a deterministic understanding—but that, at the same time, individuals often avoid and cover up the possibility of freedom and choice. Sartre is perhaps the existential philosopher who most emphasises this aspect of human existence, at least in his early work *Being and Nothingness* (1991). In this important book, Sartre states (1991, p. 34) 'man is condemned to be free; because once thrown into the world, he is responsible for everything he does', indicating that the only choice that is not available is that of not choosing, because to ignore freedom and the possibility of choice is itself seen as a choice or a response to this existential given. At the same time, it is possible to misunderstand this emphasis on freedom because, in many ways, the philosophy of Sartre and other existential philosophers have just as much to say about the limitations on freedom and choice and on how freedom is always context-bound, that is, freedom and choice are only possible within a set of limitations and structural conditions. Heidegger uses the expression 'thrownness' to describe the limits to our freedom and control. We are, in this sense, thrown into a particular context—a family, culture and language. In addition, it cannot be maintained that we are free to choose many of the events that befall us. Rather, our freedom consists more in the possibility—which can be evaded or denied—of taking up a particular attitude or response to what has befallen us. Heidegger emphasises our facticity, meaning the givens of our history and context that cannot in themselves be changed. The most fundamental limitation and given of human existence is that of mortality. Heidegger describes human beings as being-towards-death. In this sense, death is not simply an unavoidable event that will occur at some point in the future but is rather an intrinsic background aspect of every lived moment in time. In summary, then, while freedom and choice are themselves unavoidable and intrinsic to our existence, they also present themselves within a context in which we, through no choice of our own, are thrown into existence and, at some point, thrown out of existence. Our freedom then consists in the possibilities for how we face these aspects of human existence.

Embodiment and Emotion

In contrast to the Cartesian view, which seems to prioritise a disembodied consciousness separate from the world, the existential perspective emphasises that human existence is always fundamentally an embodied existence. Merleau-Ponty (1962) in particular has emphasised this dimension of existence. For Merleau-Ponty, it is only through our lived embodiment that we are able to encounter and respond to the world. As well as having implications for an understanding of bodily experience, this emphasis on embodiment also has consequences for understanding seemingly more cognitive aspects of existence. For Heidegger, the way in which we understand and know the world is based upon this embodied dimension. To use a very Heideggerian example, the way in which we know the meaning of a tool such as a hammer is not fundamentally in terms of a cognitive category or representation of hammers or a theory of hammers, but rather we only know the truth of the meaning of a hammer through the embodied act of using it. The hammer itself will most often only emerge as an object of reflection and categorisation at the moment in which it ceases to function as it should (substituting photocopier or printer for hammer might make clearer what Heidegger is getting at).

Another key aspect of our embodiment, according to existential philosophers, is that our experience is always emotional. In place of emotions, however, Heidegger used the terms 'mood' and 'attunement' to describe the emotional dimension of existence. Attunement is used here in the sense of how a musical instrument may be tuned. In contrast to the CBT perspective that often considers emotions to arise as a result of various cognitive processes, moods are seen as more primary and as themselves meaningful and revealing of the way human beings exist. There is also an important sense in which moods are not regarded as either *arising from* or residing internally. To get a sense of this, it is helpful to consider the term 'attunement' also in terms of the way in which a radio may be tuned to different stations. When a radio is tuned to a particular frequency, it may pick up and play some music; however, it is not quite correct to say that the radio is itself making the music or that the music exists inside the radio. It is possible, however, to consider the CBT emphasis on 'selective attention'—referring to how a depressed individual may be directed towards features in his life that resonate with his depressed state—as touching upon this perspective.

Existential Anxiety

For many existential philosophers, the mood or attunement that is most characteristic of human beings, and that in an important sense defines them as human beings, is that of anxiety. Kierkegaard (1980, p. 61) described anxiety as 'the dizziness of freedom'. Thus, existential anxiety is seen as arising from the awareness of the given dimensions of existence, of our thrownness, facticity and mortality, and the need to make a project out of our limited time in existence via choices that present no guarantee of success or ultimate meaning. Anxiety thus arises from our responsibility to make choices and for the results that follow in a situation in which existence presents us with no excuses. For Heidegger (1962), anxiety also arises from our awareness that many of the culturally based assumptions and practices about 'the way one does things' are themselves without solid foundations.

When we are in a state of inauthenticity or bad faith, we may deceive ourselves into thinking that we have solid, defined and durable identities—in so doing, we attempt to flee from and avoid contact with the insubstantial and groundless nature of our existence. It is important to recognise that, from an existential perspective, anxiety, or 'angst' as it is sometimes labelled, is not to be thought of as simply a form of anxiety that can be considered alongside other forms, such as generalised anxiety or panic anxiety, rather, existential anxiety is fundamental and implicit in all our experience. Thus, while in an important sense, panic anxiety (often expressing a direct fear of imminent death) can be seen as being an expression of existential anxiety, equally it can be seen that existential anxiety may be expressed in an individual's artistic work or in successful attempts to project oneself forward in a valued form of life. Existential anxiety is not something that can be eliminated: habituation will not eliminate it, nor is there a rational belief or behavioural experiment that will enable an individual to overcome it. Rather, existential anxiety is ontological: it is an inherent and fundamental aspect of what it is to be human.

Existential Guilt

In addition to anxiety as an inherent aspect of human existence, Heidegger and others argue that human beings are always fundamentally guilty. This should not be interpreted in any moralistic sense because this guilt, like anxiety, is ontological in nature and is unavoidable. Guilt in this context refers to the fact that, arising from our thrownness and facticity, and our need to make choices, we are always in the position of having said 'no' to a range of other possibilities. In our choice to train and work as CBT therapists, for example, we will have necessarily said no to a range of other possibilities, such as being a carpenter or a politician. Even if such alternate possibilities were not considered, it remains the case that we always lag behind our possibilities for being. In choosing one or a series of directions for our life, we will inevitably close down other possibilities that may weigh upon us as the road not travelled. Thus, the existential perspective presents us with a view of existence in which there is a range of inevitable tensions, for example between possibility and actuality and between freedom and limitation. These tensions are not themselves ever fully resolvable, nor do they constitute problems for which there is a correct solution, rather they are tensions that must be lived. Additionally, such tensions must be lived within time—we do not have the possibility of stopping and starting again.

Time

CBT often presents itself as being concerned with the present rather than the past, and in this appears to draw close to other humanistic therapies that also emphasise the importance of the present moment. The existential view of time is somewhat more complex. Time, as an ontological dimension of Being, is fundamental. There is a sense in which, in the same way that *we are anxious*, human beings *are* temporal. Cohn (2002, p. 67) states: 'Human beings can thus be seen not so much to live *in* time as to be living it. At every moment, the past is the soil from which we are already stretching out towards a future'. The present moment contains both the past and is also already directed towards the future. Similarly, Hersch (2015, p. 117) states that human experience is part of 'an ongoing, necessarily incomplete process of becoming, one which is situated in time, in the full multi-dimensional sense of time where past, present and future co-imply each other as a totality'.

The existential understanding of time has implications for the manner in which the past is dealt with in therapy, as well as how we deal with such future-directed activities such as goal setting and value clarification. The past as *currently presenting* and *already future-directed* becomes a focus for descriptive clarification as much as any attempt to help a client stay in contact with the present moment. Both existential anxiety and existential guilt express this dimension of temporality. We experience existential anxiety as an aspect of our projecting ourselves forward into a finite future and encounter our existential guilt as we reflect back on the possibilities for being that have already, inevitably, been lost. There is no present moment as such apart from this unfolding and enfolding recollecting-presenting-directing.

The Ontic and the Ontological

The preceding section has discussed a range of the so-called existential givens, such as being-with-others, thrownness, facticity, existential anxiety and guilt and existence as embodied and temporal. These dimensions of existence are understood as being ontological in that they pertain to the fundamental aspects of human existence. This ontological dimension can be considered as being the ground from which the figure of experience emerges. There is also an important sense in which the experience of any particular human being (who is regarded as being specific and ontic) always includes ontological aspects that may remain implicit. The difference and relationship between the ontological and the ontic are important for therapy. It is important that ontological aspects of the human being are not somehow equalised with a range of ontic features so that, for example, a therapist attempts to treat existential anxiety alongside, for example, rumination or selective attention as just one more trans-diagnostic variable to be identified and treated—this would be to misunderstand their ontological status. Therapy, as Cohn (2002) asserts, remains focused on the ontic phenomena presented by a particular client; however, the possibility of clarifying the ontological dimensions of these ontic phenomena may present itself and be of value.

Summary

Existential philosophers have proposed a range of fundamental aspects of human existence, or existential givens, including:

- existence means always being-in-the-world and with-others,
- meaning and meaninglessness is a fundamental existential tension,
- freedom and limitation,
- anxiety and guilt are existential and inevitable,
- existence is embodied,
- existence as attunement or mood is fundamental and
- existence as temporal and being-towards-death.

Existential philosophers have attempted to address such concerns from a specifically phenomenological viewpoint, i.e. via a structured method of investigation that prioritises the descriptive clarification of directly encountered phenomena rather than prioritising efforts at gaining a causal analysis.

Existential Reflections

In a small group (three to four people) of peers, consider the following questions:

- Existential philosophy has proposed a range of givens of existence that are proposed as universal. These givens are said to characterise human existence across culture, class and gender. To what extent do you agree with the givens that have been identified? Are there aspects of existence you believe to be more fundamental or to be missing from this list?
- Many CBT interventions, although not all, focus on a specific clinical problem and seek improvement in that problem. What difference does it make to the field of therapy, and CBT in particular, to suggest that we need to contextualise such problems in relation to the nature of human existence as a whole?
- To what extent and in what ways could the activity of conducting therapy be said to be itself philosophical?

3

Existential Psychology

When you are a Bear of Very Little Brain, and you Think of Things, you find sometimes that a Thing which seemed very Thingish inside you is quite different when it gets out into the open and has other people looking at it.

—A.A. Milne, *The House at Pooh Corner* (1928).

Can there really be such a thing as an existential psychology, where the discipline of psychology is defined as an empirical-quantitative science? Of all, the points of possible disagreement and conflict between cognitive behavioural therapy (CBT) practitioners and existential therapists, the issue of the appropriateness of experimental and quantitative methods must surely be the most difficult. After all, how is it possible to measure authentic being-towards-death? For CBT therapists, as I argued in Chapter 1, the use of experimental and quantitative methods is fundamental. While a range of tensions and disagreements appear to be successfully held within the family of CBT therapies, general agreement appears to exist that the basic project is to advance a scientifically grounded and experimentally verified form of psychological therapy (Salkovskis, 2002). Existential and other critically minded therapists, on the other hand, are more likely to assert that the scientific method—viewed as being an overextension of methods and assumptions suitable for the study of natural phenomena, but unsuitable for the study of human beings—is incapable of throwing light on fundamental human concerns, including the practice of therapy, without distorting its subject

CBT and Existential Psychology: Philosophy, Psychology and Therapy,
First Edition. Michael Worrell.

matter (Bohart & House, 2008). The natural scientific method is seen as inevitably based on 'essentialism', i.e., the attempt to divide up phenomena into parts and to enquire regarding their causal relationships. The insistence that 'existence precedes essence' appears to rule out any approach to phenomena that seeks to delineate and measure the relationship between separate elements. Echoing this apparent incommensurability, Pyszczynski et al. (2004, p. 4) state: 'For the most part, experimentalists and existentialists acknowledged the existence of each other only when pointing to the fundamental absurdity of what the other was trying to accomplish.'

Despite this, a new field of enquiry has arisen that has been labelled experimental existential psychology. Recently, a number of writers within CBT have drawn attention to this research and argued for the incorporation of its insights into CBT practice. In so doing, it has been suggested that an integration between CBT and existential psychotherapy may be viable due to the strong empirical findings in this still developing field (Iverach et al., 2014).

As well as exploring the field of experimental existential psychology, this chapter will examine the extent to which qualitative methods of research consistent with a human science perspective have been used within CBT. The field of qualitative research is vast and beyond the scope of this chapter to cover comprehensively; however, the extent to which existential phenomenological research methods have been used within CBT research is of obvious relevance to the aims of this book. I hope to show that incorporating existential phenomenological research perspectives into CBT is not only of interest from a methodological point of view but has also led to a number of provocative results that may have relevance to the project of developing an existentially attuned CBT.

Experimental Existential Psychology

This relatively new field can be considered a reconfiguration of some of the central concerns and research methods of social psychology. The objective is to reorient the work of social psychologists away from a focus on micro level social interactions towards larger themes and existential concerns. This work began in the 1980s, largely inspired by the work of cultural anthropologist Ernest Becker (1973) on the pervasiveness of anxiety about death across cultures, as well as by the work of Irving Yalom (1980). Pyszczynski et al. (2015) reviewed how hundreds of social psychological experiments, mostly focusing on non-clinical populations, have looked at questions relating to what they call 'the big five' existential concerns, namely death, isolation, identity, freedom and meaning. By far, the greatest amount of research has been conducted upon the issue of death awareness and death anxiety, under the appropriate but alarming title of 'terror management theory' (TMT).

Terror Management Theory (TMT)

According to TMT, cultural worldviews and self-esteem (defined as a sense of occupying a socially recognised role that establishes and stabilises relationships with others) serve an 'anxiety buffering' function to assist us in managing the fear of death (Pyszczynski et al., 2015). In his book *Existential Psychotherapy*, Yalom (1980) made a similar argument when he identified two commonly occurring defences against death anxiety: the illusion of 'the ultimate rescuer' and the illusion of 'specialness'. Yalom identifies the illusion of specialness as the irrational belief that I, unlike all others, will somehow escape death. This belief is not thought by Yalom to be consciously held or endorsed but may be encountered during a range of unwelcome and unpredictable events that are reminders of mortality. Yalom gives the personal example of a visit to an optometrist where the attending professional stated that his worsening eyesight was 'on schedule' leading Yalom to experience significant indignation. (It is possible that optometrists have a finely honed existential sensibility, as my own consultant recently remarked, 'Well yes, I think we can expect that as time goes on this will of course just get worse and worse until, well, until it, um, stops, really'.) According to TMT, such interactions serve as unwelcome instances of 'mortality salience' and have been found to be associated with a range of effects (other than changing optometrist).

The other illusion as a defence against death anxiety, according to Yalom, is that of the ultimate rescuer, which does not necessarily involve belief in a deity but may include efforts to remain closely identified with a charismatic individual or cultural group that serves to maintain a sense of permanence and invulnerability. In TMT, the maintenance of cultural worldviews and attachment relationships can be seen to serve the same function as that of the ultimate rescuer. Similarly, the belief in personal specialness is understood in terms of the drive to maintain self-esteem. Both illusions, or defences, can be seen as expressions of the fundamental existential tension between individual separation/uniqueness versus communion/merging with others. It must be emphasised that while Yalom studied and provided vivid descriptions of how death anxiety is encountered in clinical practice and how various problems in living express attempts to avoid awareness of mortality, in TMT, the maintenance of worldviews and self-esteem may have both negative and positive consequences.

On first reading, both the experimental paradigms used and the populations studied in TMT research appear somewhat remote from the concerns of practising therapists. However, on closer reading, results of many of these experimental studies are consistent with the proposition of existential philosophy that anxiety regarding death (an expression of existential anxiety) is pervasive and often implicit in daily life. Additionally, the results are consistent with the propositions of a range of existential therapies that, in situations in which they confront reminders of their own mortality, people will frequently resort to a range of avoidance strategies or strategies to bolster their self-esteem and worldview, sometimes with negative individual and societal consequences. At times, anxiety regarding mortality may be encountered through forms of change that are not, on the surface, of obvious resonance with death itself. This could include, for example, the anxiety experienced when a significant aspect of one's self-concept or worldview is opened up to reconsideration, even if this change is also desired.

In an ingenious series of studies by McGregor et al. (1998), participants' aggressive responses were studied in situations where others challenged their worldviews. In one study, participants with moderate conservative or liberal worldviews were asked to write a paragraph explaining their perspective on United States politics, which they were led to believe would be supported and affirmed by another participant. Participants were then exposed to a mortality salience procedure in which they were asked to describe their emotions around the thought of their death, as well as their thoughts and emotions regarding what might happen after they died. Participants in a control condition were asked to describe their thoughts and feelings regarding an upcoming exam (existentially minded therapists might comment that such a control condition is not without its existential resonance either). Participants were then presented with fake paragraphs allegedly written by another participant which either challenged or confirmed their political views. Subsequently, the participants were engaged in a food tasting experiment in which the fake participant was required to eat all the food provided—the participant was also informed that the fake participant did not like spicy food and that it was up to the participant to decide how much hot sauce to serve the fake participant. The amount of hot sauce served to the fake participant was then taken as a measure of the participant's aggression (the experimenters pointed out that there had been real cases of individuals using hot sauce as a weapon to harm others). In the mortality salience condition, participants were found to allocate more than double the amount of hot sauce to the writer of the fake paragraph that challenged their worldview in comparison to those participants who received a worldview consistent paragraph.

These results were interpreted as being consistent with a central idea of TMT that under conditions of increased mortality salience, people will act aggressively towards, or potentially harm, those who threaten their worldview. Results such as these illustrate the degree to which mortality salience may influence human behaviour, even when these behaviours have no clear or obvious connection to death. A wide range of TMT studies have provided evidence that mortality salience may influence behaviour and perception across a range of different domains, including religion, politics, racism, scapegoating, driving, violence and terrorism (Iverach et al., 2014).

Death Anxiety as a Transdiagnostic Phenomena

Several authors have suggested that CBT perspectives on the nature of anxiety may be enhanced by incorporating the results of terror management research and the insights and methods of existential psychotherapy (Menzies et al., 2018). As noted earlier, TMT proposes that worldviews and self-esteem may function to buffer against the experience of death anxiety. The theory also suggests that a range of factors may act to weaken the effectiveness of this buffering, including genetic predisposition, traumatic events, insecure attachment relationships, stressful life contexts and other difficulties (Maxfield et al., 2014). In addition, a range of threats to meaning, self-esteem and relatedness may act to increase vulnerability to experiencing emotional distress. TMT, consistent with a range of existential views, suggests that various forms of psychopathology may be understood as efforts to cope with death anxiety and existential terror (Iverach et al., 2014). Both Yalom (1980) and Cohn (2002) have presented basic diagrammatic representations of the fundamental proposition of existential philosophy and therapy that various problems in living may be expressive of an individual's attempts to avoid awareness of the givens of existence, such as mortality. Using the additional insights regarding the nature of anxiety buffering provided by TMT, Figure 3.1 is a diagrammatic representation of how fundamental existential concerns may be related to both problems in living and the more successful methods for managing existential anxiety, such as efforts at valued living and enacting meaningful life projects.

Figure 3.1, consistent with TMT, suggests that a wide range of situations in daily life may function as mortality salience triggers, which act as reminders of the fundamental aspects of existence, such as our inevitable deaths. Existential philosophy and therapy might prefer to express this in terms of a potential background awareness rather than 'salience' or 'triggers' which seem more mechanistic terms. The diagram also asserts the existence of feedback loops linked to both the pathway leading to problems in living and the pathway leading to creative coping. There is no final resolution or solution to the issue of existential anxiety: whatever position we adopt will involve some degree of existential downside.

As will be discussed in Chapter 6, a significant focus of standard CBT has been the attempt to identify and intervene in the specific cognitive and behavioural processes at work within a wide range of anxiety disorders. More recently, this work has further advanced to consider the possibility that there exists a range of transdiagnostic processes that may better account for the high degree of overlap between supposedly separate disorders. A number of authors have also suggested that, fundamentally, what is revealed in the cognitive-behavioural study and treatment

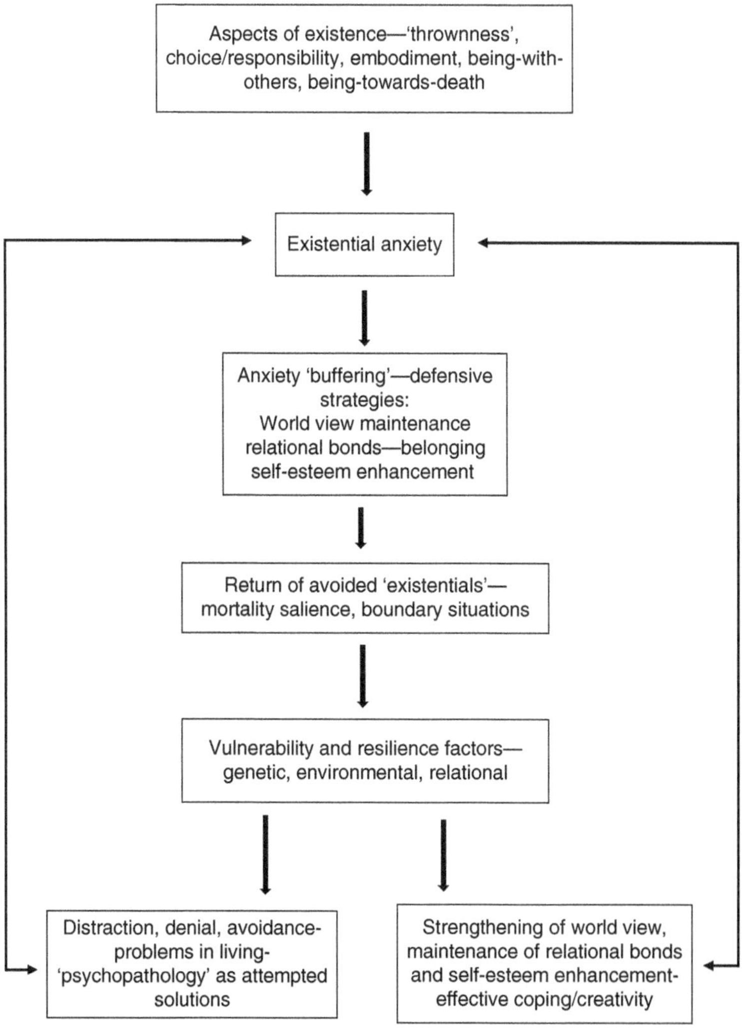

Figure 3.1 A model of existential anxiety.

of severe anxiety is the presence of a range of existential givens that the afflicted individual struggles to accept and respond to (Wolfe, 2008). Iverach (2018), in a review of the research, concludes that there is substantial evidence to support the argument that death anxiety is an important transdiagnostic factor implicated in the vulnerability to and the maintenance of anxiety disorders. Iverach (2018) describes supportive evidence for this in studies on obsessions and compulsions, panic attacks, phobias, social anxiety, agoraphobia, separation anxiety, health anxiety, traumatic stress reactions and eating disorders.

Research conducted into obsessions and compulsions provides a particularly impactful illustration of the extent to which existential concerns may lie at the heart of various forms of psychological distress. Menzies and Dar-Nimrod (2017) explored the relationship between the degree of death anxiety and various indicators of OCD in 171 diagnosed OCD sufferers. Moderate to large correlations were reported between the level of death anxiety and the level of OCD severity, as well as with the number of hospitalisations, medication use and diagnoses of comorbid anxiety disorders. Following the TMT paradigm, Menzies and Dar-Nimrod (2017) also conducted an experiment in which 66 OCD washers and 66 OCD non-washers were allocated to either a mortality salience or a dental pain priming condition. Following each of the priming conditions, participants were engaged in a range of distraction tasks and were then able to wash conductive gel (which had been applied during the distracting skin conductance recording procedure) off their hands. As expected, the OCD washers washed their hands for longer and used more soap than the OCD non-washers. In addition, participants engaged in the mortality salience condition demonstrated greater intensity of cleaning than participants exposed to the dental pain condition. The authors of this study concluded that this provided some evidence consistent with the hypothesis that death anxiety may drive OCD washing behaviour.

The literature review by Iverach (2018) found that, alongside death anxiety, existential anxiety and a sense of meaninglessness were also present in individuals experiencing depression. Iverach concluded that depression could be considered, from a TMT perspective, to be an ineffective attempt to buffer existential anxiety. Similarly, experimental research has provided evidence of greater worldview defence in response to mortality salience for mildly depressed individuals compared to non-depressed individuals (Iverach, 2018). Iverach et al. (2014) argued that the strength of such findings supports the notion that CBT treatments for anxiety and depression could be supplemented by drawing from a range of existential psychotherapies.

In summary, there appears to be a substantial body of research, arising primarily from the experimental paradigm of TMT, that supports a central proposition of existential philosophy and therapy, namely that problems in living, such as anxiety and depression, may at least in part be expressions of efforts to cope with the experience of existential anxiety. Furthermore, the strength of these finding has led some authors, primarily those within the CBT tradition, to argue for the incorporation into CBT of insights and strategies from existential therapy.

Existential Uncertainty and Intolerance of Uncertainty

Existential philosophy and psychology assert that uncertainty is an inherent and unavoidable aspect of existence. According to Spinelli (2015, p. 22), existential uncertainty refers to the 'inevitable and inescapable openness of possibility in any and all of our reflections upon our existence'.

Recently, CBT therapists have argued that intolerance of uncertainty could be one of the most significant factors implicated in a range of different forms of psychological distress. McEvoy and Erceg-Hurn (2016) argued that intolerance of uncertainty may constitute both an important transdiagnostic factor as well as a 'trans-therapy' factor. That is, intolerance for uncertainty may be a key factor that is altered by a range of differing therapies even when this is not an explicit target of those therapies. As such, they consider intolerance of uncertainty could be a 'universal process'.

Intolerance of uncertainty has been defined in various ways, such as a 'dispositional fear of the unknown' (Carleton, 2012). Echoing existential psychologists such as Rollo May (1983), Carleton (2012) suggested that uncertainty is fundamental to anxiety, whereby future negative events are anticipated but remain uncertain, in contrast to fear, wherein negative events are more certain and imminent. Within a CBT perspective, the Intolerance of Uncertainty Model (Dugas & Robichaud, 2007) was originally developed in order to explain the development of severe and uncontrollable worry (i.e. generalised anxiety disorder). Dugas and Robichaud note that people who experience excessive worry appear to be caught between an intolerance of uncertainty and various forms of certainty that worry is both necessary and helpful despite contrasting experiences and beliefs that their worry feels out of control. McEvoy and Erceg-Hurn (2016) found evidence that intolerance of uncertainty is implicated across a wide range of anxiety difficulties, as well as depression. In their review of research literature, the authors concluded that positive changes in the level of intolerance for uncertainty were associated with positive symptom change in generalised anxiety and social anxiety. McEvoy and Erceg-Hurn conclude that further research is required to determine the extent to which intolerance of uncertainty is a universal process implicated in vulnerability to psychological distress and its successful remediation. As of yet, no direct link has been made between the literature looking at intolerance of uncertainty and the literature of existential philosophy and psychology that asserts that uncertainty is an inherent aspect of existence.

Menzies et al. (2018) argued that many of the fears and anxieties described in the CBT literature highlight the inherent irrationality of the beliefs that are disclosed. In contrast, anxiety regarding death needs to be acknowledged as essentially rational as it is an outcome that will eventually occur. Similarly, in as much as intolerance of uncertainty may be associated with forms of distorted cognition such as repetitive negative thinking, nevertheless certain uncertainties and uncertain certainties remain an unavoidable aspect of existence.

The discussion so far has sought to demonstrate that while existential therapists have tended to show a strong aversion to experimental psychological science, nevertheless there are trends in the experimental literature that can be interpreted as supporting several of the key propositions of existential philosophy. However, such findings are unlikely to motivate existential therapists to take up the cause of experimental science. Instead, existential therapists, along with a range of humanistic therapists and others, assert that a range of qualitative methodologies are more suitable to the task of exploring the unique and specific aspects of their chosen models. As noted earlier, the range of qualitative research literature is vast and beyond the scope of this chapter. While there may be much in this broad field of qualitative research that may be of considerable interest and importance, a no less interesting issue is the surprising extent to which existential phenomenological research methods (as well as methods that represent derivations of this) have found their way into the field of CBT—and a consideration of what such studies may reveal is explored next.

Existential Phenomenological Research Within CBT

Existentially oriented psychologists have developed a wide range of qualitative research methods consistent with the aim of understanding human phenomena (Valle & Halling, 1989). The specific forms of these methodologies do not concern us here. In essence, all of these methods represent attempts to provide descriptive clarifications of lived experience rather than causal analyses. An understanding of the basics of this is, however, essential because existential psychologists and therapists have argued that the practice of existential therapy can be understood as a type of phenomenological research rather than a quasi-medical intervention. In this, there is a direct parallel to those CBT authors who have suggested that CBT involves an invitation to the client to become something of a scientific investigator with respect to their own experiences and beliefs (Westbrook et al., 2017).

Spinelli (2005) has provided a description of the phenomenological method that is highly useful. Other authors have also described various steps for a phenomenological method, however, there is neither an agreed or final version of what such a method should look like, nor the extent to which it might be possible to fully adhere to one—so this topic remains an area of debate (Moran, 2000). Let us look at this in more detail. Spinelli (2005) suggested that the phenomenological method can be understood in terms of three steps or rules. These rules overlap rather than being clearly distinct, and it is probably better to think of them as interacting phases of an ongoing analysis rather than a linear programme that arrives at a final answer. The steps are defined as follows:

The Rule of Reduction

This is possibly the most challenging of the three rules to follow. Phenomenologists urge that in any attempt to gain a more adequate understanding of a phenomenon it is essential that any preconceptions or theories regarding that phenomenon be identified and set aside (placed in brackets). For example, in encountering the flat white in Chapter 2 it would be important to set aside theories that attempt to explain why I am ordering a flat white, such as notions of a reinforcement history or the drinker's beliefs around self-identity. This is analogous to the situation of encountering a client in therapy who has been diagnosed as suffering from depression. This diagnosis, and any theories or assumptions regarding what depression is, are (at least temporarily) set aside in order that a richer and more open view is possible. This is quite different then from a hypothesis testing model in which an initial hypothesis is set out (this client is depressed, and this is in part maintained by self-critical thinking) and then tested against experience as to its adequacy (is there evidence of self-critical thinking? For example). Phenomenologists, such as Merleau-Ponty (1962), have demonstrated that this first step of setting aside assumptions and theories can never be final or complete—no stance can be taken that is free of all interpretative bias or assumption. Nevertheless, it is asserted that the effort of identifying and reducing interpretative bias is of significant benefit—hence this step is referred to as one of reduction.

The Rule of Description

Having attained a greater level of experiential openness to direct experience, the second step urges the investigator to 'describe, but don't explain'. Like the first step of reduction, there is an acknowledgment that the rule of description is also limited in that all aspects of description may themselves include unacknowledged explanatory assumptions. Nevertheless, it is maintained that remaining at the level of description allows for the possibility of clarifying aspects of experience that are often missed in the rush to find causal explanation. Thus, in encountering the flat white, we are urged not to immediately compare and contrast this flat white to our memories of previous experiences—something we might do in an effort to understand why on this occasion the barista has used too much milk or too little coffee. Instead, the challenge of the phenomenological method is to remain in contact with the details of experience itself and to describe that which emerges from this contact—in this example, this may include the taste of the coffee, the feel of the cup in the hand, the smell of the coffee emerging from a background of other smells, such as the various pastries on offer that were not ordered. As Spinelli (2005) notes, the various Cognitive Behavioural analyses of states of anxiety serve to reveal the extent to which people in the grip of anxiety may fail to adhere to the rule of description—for example, people experiencing a panic attack may be aware of their beating heart and a wobbliness in their legs and jump to the explanatory causal theory that they are having a heart attack or are losing their mind. It can be seen that an important aspect of CBT approaches to working with anxiety involves assisting clients to be in touch with the details of their experience of anxiety while aiming to set aside their initial theories that such experiences are an indication of an imminent threat to life, in order that alternative less threatening descriptions become possible.

The Rule of Equalization

According to Spinelli (2005), the third step of the phenomenological method requires that practitioners refrain from placing a 'hierarchy of significance' on any aspects of direct experience that have been revealed through descriptive clarification. Again, it is acknowledged that full equalization is impossible, however, the attempt to avoid imposing value judgements on levels of significance is seen as an essential step in maintaining a more adequate degree of openness to the phenomenon under investigation. So, to continue with our flat white, the phenomenological investigator is urged to refrain from concluding that the essence of the flat white lies primarily in the frothiness of the milk over either the strength of the coffee, the size of the cup, or the presence or absence of the small Italian chocolate treat that the barista normally (but not always) provides. Similarly, the failure to follow this rule can be seen in the case of a CBT therapist who is working with our client experiencing panic attacks. Our CBT therapist may be anxious to ensure that they are on model and focused on quickly identifying the client's catastrophic beliefs which have been hypothesised as being at the root of the maintenance of the difficulty. The client's statement 'I will die of a heart attack' may be seized upon as the key variable to be worked with. However, had our therapist adhered to the rule of equalization, it may have been clarified that, for this client, the catastrophe is less about the heart attack and death, and more about the client's fears of what will happen to her children in such an event. This is, of course, still consistent with the cognitive model of panic, however, in this case, adherence to a more phenomenologically informed method may allow the CBT therapist to use their model with a greater respect for the way the phenomenon reveals itself.

In existential phenomenological research investigations, the intended output of the research is a rich description of the phenomena of interest, intended to give the researcher, participants and reader a sense of access to the phenomena. For example, Fischer (1989, p. 134) reported on a phenomenological study of anxiety, including the following rich description of becoming and being anxious:

> being anxious . . . means that one experiences a sense of being blocked, an inability to move forward undividedly. Confronted with multiple, problematic, and often contradictory meanings of the situation, one is captured, at least temporarily, by its ambiguity, its lack of a univocal meaning. Expressing this sense of being blocked and captured is a burgeoning uncertainty as to what to do, for that matter, as to one's ability to do anything effectively.

This segment, part of a much longer description, can be seen in no way to contradict the more explanatory models of anxiety provided by CBT. On the other hand, it can be seen to provide a richer description of the experience of anxiety as it is lived.

Existential Phenomenological Research Methods in CBT

While certainly limited when compared to the amount of quantitative research conducted within CBT, a number of CBT researchers have started to use a range of qualitative methodologies in order to understand in more depth clients' experiences of undergoing CBT. In part, this broadening out of research methods is in response to the need to include the client's voice more often. In addition, it has been suggested that gaining a broader understanding of the client's experience of CBT may assist in the larger task of accounting for the factors that are involved in producing beneficial change. Most often, CBT researchers have made use of Interpretative Phenomenological Analysis (Smith et al., 2009) and have acknowledged the extent to which this methodology is based on insights from existential phenomenology.

My purpose in the following is not to provide a substantial review of the published qualitative research into CBT, but to highlight some key areas that, taken as a whole, appear to both support some propositions of CBT as well as challenge and critique other aspects in a manner that has resonance with the perspective of existential phenomenology.

The Client's Experience of Change

Most standard CBT models conceptualise the nature of specific forms of psychological distress in terms of tightly delineated cognitive and behavioural processes. For example, in the area of social anxiety, CBT interventions focus a great deal on the hypothesised role of an 'internal focus of attention' and safety behaviours (Clark & Wells, 1995). In an intriguing study to investigate the experiences of clients undergoing such interventions for social anxiety, McManus et al. (2010) conducted an interpretative phenomenological analysis of interviews with eight participants and found that the findings were largely consistent with the CBT emphasis on identifying specific cognitive and behavioural factors. However, the strongest finding from the analysis of transcripts was that clients experience their social anxiety as 'a way of being' rather than suffering from a specific 'condition'. Social anxiety was experienced as affecting all aspects of their lives and as isolating them from other people in their world. In addition, the positive changes experienced through CBT were experienced as a 'transformation of being' rather than simply a reduction of symptoms.

A very similar finding was reported by Shearing et al. (2011) who used interpretative phenomenological analysis to explore clients' lived experience of undergoing a 'reliving' process during CBT for post-traumatic stress disorder (PTSD). This study found that the clients experienced the process of reliving to be an ultimately beneficial one resulting in a reduction in the frequency and intensity of flashbacks. While a change of symptoms was often described, at the same time, clients described their lived experience of change as regaining a sense of agency in the world, with the authors reporting (Shearing et al., 2011, p. 466): 'Participants spoke about experiencing a changing sense of themselves, their interactions with their worlds, and their future. It appeared that participants were speaking about regaining a sense of agency in the world, replacing a previous sense of being stuck and powerless.' The authors go on to suggest that their results indicate that therapy for PTSD involves a process of regaining a valued sense of self, suggesting that Lee (2006) is correct when she states that therapy involves the task of creating a meaningful life 'when faced with living in a meaningless world'.

In addition to experiencing the process of change in terms of identity rather than simply symptom reduction, the participants in the McManus et al. (2010, p. 584) study highlighted the extent to which the relationship with their therapist was key for them in being able to effect this change, stating:

> Trust and belief in the therapist, and in the therapists' skills, were central to many of the positive experiences which participants reported. The importance of liking the therapist as a person resonated throughout the transcripts; understanding, validation and support were perceived to be paramount.

The centrality of the client's experience of the therapeutic relationship has also been highlighted in other qualitative studies of CBT. For example, Messari and Hallam (2003) explored clients' experiences of CBT for psychosis and found that clients valued open, honest therapeutic relationships as well as some more explicitly educational components. Similarly, in an interpretative phenomenological analysis of participants' experience of undergoing CBT for bulimia, Onslow et al. (2015) highlighted the centrality of the client's experience of a positive therapeutic relationship. These general findings regarding the relational context in standard CBT have also been found with clients reporting on the centrality of relationship factors in their experiences of Schema Therapy for personality disorder (Napel-Schutz et al., 2011), as well as Acceptance and Commitment Therapy for psychosis (Bacon et al., 2014).

Challenging Findings

The qualitative results described earlier can be interpreted as largely supportive of some key propositions within CBT. At the same time, the results appear to suggest that clients experience change primarily in terms of a general reorientation of their way of being in the world, a change that has ramification across domains and is not restricted to a reduction of specific symptoms. These results also suggest that such changes are experienced within the context of a safe and supportive therapeutic relationship and that clients attribute a good proportion of positive change to aspects of this relational context. A number of qualitative studies have also emerged that can be read as providing a challenge to certain assumptions made by CBT therapists regarding what works in therapy.

The best example of this is offered by studies that focused on the client's experience of the process of formulation in therapy. Clinical formulations are promoted within standard CBT as an essential intervention that will allow the therapist to individualise CBT treatment and assist in shifting the client's understanding of the nature of their difficulties in a manner that will facilitate their engagement in therapy (Kuyken et al., 2009). To a large extent, this emphasis on formulation in CBT has become accepted wisdom, and competence in constructing formulations is focused upon specifically in CBT training and supervision.

A series of qualitative studies have emerged, however, that seem to provide a more complicated picture. Chadwick et al. (2003) interviewed 13 clients about their experience of CBT for psychosis; Pain et al. (2008) undertook a qualitative study into therapists' and clients' experiences of case formulation in CBT for psychosis; Kahlon et al. (2014) looked at clients' experience of formulation during CBT for depression; and Redhead et al. (2015) describe a similar study focusing on formulation with clients' who received CBT for depression and anxiety. While it was reported across these studies that therapists experience a range of benefits from creating formulations, the experience of clients towards the process and content of formulations was consistently more complex. Pain et al. (2008) also found clients' responses to formulations to be 'cognitively, behaviourally and emotionally complex, and subject to change over time'. Consistent with standard CBT theory, formulations appear to help clients to make sense of their difficulties and to normalise these rather than seeing them as reflections of a defective or incompetent self.

However, negative responses were also described, with often a third of the clients included in these studies reporting a range of negative emotional reactions, such as sadness, confusion and distress in response to the process of formulation. At times, this appeared, across studies, to be related to therapeutic processes whereby the CBT therapist was experienced by the client as having taken over or to be handing down a formulation to the client rather than the formulation emerging through a process of dialogue. Client distress also appeared at times to be related to the felt implications of the formulation. That is, the client experienced the formulation as having negative implications for their sense of self. At other times, these negative responses appeared to be more related to the therapist having got it wrong, such that the formulation was experienced as inaccurate and unhelpful. The possibility of negative emotional responses from clients has also been explored in a qualitative paper by Nilsson et al. (2007), who looked at descriptive findings from studies of both satisfied and dissatisfied recipients of CBT or psychodynamic therapy. In regard to the CBT findings, the negative responses appeared to be related to the client's experience that the therapist had behaved in an intrusive or oppressive manner 'applying a rigid predetermined therapy design' (Nilsson et al., 2007, p. 563).

The finding that helpful therapeutic strategies may at times be associated with unpredicted and difficult negative client reactions has been found with a range of forms of CBT, such as Schema Therapy (ST). Napel-Schutz et al. (2011) reported on a qualitative study of clients' experiences of imagery strategies in ST. While the use of imagery was found to be helpful, clients indicated a desire for the potential negative emotional impact of these interventions to be more greatly appreciated by therapists. Imagery interventions were at times experienced by clients as being unpredictable and as provoking unwelcome experiences of uncertainty and fear.

On the other end of the scale, some qualitative studies pointed to helpful aspects of treatment, as judged by clients, where these aspects are regarded in standard CBT as things to be avoided. In the earlier study of bulimia by Onslow et al. (2015), clients rated positively a range of therapist behaviours that were 'off model'. The authors quote from Fairburn (2008) who states: 'Experience can be a dangerous thing; the wise therapist adheres to the manual.' However, in this study, the most experienced therapists were also the most likely to deviate from the model, and their behaviour in doing so was highlighted by clients as being highly beneficial. As the authors state (Fairburn, 2008, p. 175): 'Despite Fairburn's warning, most individuals experienced these "deviations" as extremely helpful, with others feeling inexperienced therapists were "just following the book"'.

The earlier discussion is by no means an exhaustive review of the literature on qualitative investigations of CBT. In addition, some of the studies reviewed above could be critiqued from a more rigorous existential phenomenological perspective due to methodological weaknesses. For example, in the study by McManus et al. (2010) it is very difficult to determine the extent to which, if at all, the investigators attempted to bracket their theoretical preconceptions regarding the nature of social anxiety. However, taken as a whole, the findings are suggestive of a number of conclusions. Firstly, there is qualitative evidence that clients value many of the specific interventions used by a range of differing CBT models. These strategies are experienced by clients in a relational context with the therapist, with the quality of this context experienced by clients as highly important and impactful. Secondly, the research indicates that, as much as their interventions may be of value, CBT therapists are wise to attend to the possibility of unpredictable negative client responses. Finally, clients' experiences of change appear to be global, pointing to issues of self and self-in-relation-to-others, rather occurring primarily in terms of isolated and decontextualized symptom reduction.

Summary

- While existential phenomenological philosophy has been described as 'the science of Being' (Craig, 2015), the question of the extent to which there can be an existential psychology is an open one.
- Experimentally minded researchers have conducted productive and revealing research into a range of existential themes.
- CBT researchers have increasingly drawn upon methods of research aligned more usually to a human science and existential phenomenological framework.
- In so doing, they have produced a range of findings that may challenge views of CBT that emphasise its supposed quasi-medical nature as a treatment for specific symptoms.

Existential Reflections

In a small group of peers, consider the following experiments into mortality salience:

- Each take a blank sheet of paper and write the words 'birth' and 'death' at opposite ends. Start drawing a line from birth to death. Stop the line where you feel you currently are in your life. Be aware of any emotions and thoughts that arise as you do this.
- Imagine that each of you have been given an envelope inside of which is the exact date and time of your death as well as the manner of your death. Would you choose to open this envelope? Consider the thoughts and emotions that arise as you consider the question.
- Consider the extent to which the statement 'I am a CBT therapist' or 'I am an existential therapist' is central to your identity and worldview. Imagine a situation in which undisputable scientific evidence is revealed that all forms of CBT or existential therapy, are ineffective and that their theoretical concepts are incorrect. What would 'the death of CBT' or 'death of existential therapy' mean to you?
- If you are not a CBT or existential therapist, repeat the above exercise with your own preferred modality.

4

Existential Therapies—Theory

> *The existential analyst . . . not only is in possession of existential-analytic and psychotherapeutic competence, but . . . he must dare to risk committing his own existence in the struggle for the freedom of his partner's.*
>
> —Ludwig Binswanger (1963).

Existential phenomenological philosophy does not constitute a unified body of work that can be applied to psychotherapy in any straightforward fashion. Instead, each existential therapist and school of existential therapy can be seen to interpret and draw on different aspects of a range of philosophical thinking in an effort to delineate a form of practice that is true to the principles of existential phenomenology. The question of the way existential phenomenological thinking can find expression in therapeutic practice remains in itself an open one. In this chapter, an overview is given of some of the main forms of existential therapy in order to provide a better context for what follows. It is important to have some grasp of this context in order to avoid thinking that it is possible to compare and contrast a unitary entity called existential therapy with a unitary entity called CBT. A discussion of the possibility of an existential-CBT dialogue requires some effort at defining where, as therapists, we are positioned regarding the various forms of existential therapy, as much as where we are positioned within the field of CBT.

Considering the field as a whole, the level of diversity among existential therapists may even be greater than that of CBT, especially so given the

CBT and Existential Psychology: Philosophy, Psychology and Therapy,
First Edition. Michael Worrell.

claim that there are as many forms of existential therapy as there are existential therapists. For the sake of brevity—and given that there are several excellent and detailed historical analyses available regarding the diverse forms of existential therapy (Cooper, 2003; van Deurzen *et al.*, 2019)[1]—the discussion here will focus on Daseinsanalysis, logotherapy, existential–humanistic therapy and existential phenomenological therapy.

Daseinsanalysis

> The highest aim of all psychotherapy is and remains the opening up of our patients to an ability-to-love-and-trust which permits all oppression by anxiety and guilt to be surmounted as mere misunderstandings (Medard Boss, cited in Friedman, 1991, p. 437).

Unlike many forms of therapy, such as psychoanalysis and person-centred therapy, existential therapy, like CBT, is somewhat unique in that it cannot be attributed to a single founding source. It has rather arisen in a variety of contexts at different times. Historically speaking, however, some primacy must be given to the school of existential therapy known as Daseinsanalysis. Daseinsanalysis is in many respects an attempt to engage with Freudian psychoanalysis via existential phenomenology in order to strip away what is regarded to be the unnecessary and distorting influence of Freud's abstract deterministic metapsychology while retaining many of his central clinical insights and recommendations for the practice of therapy. Associated with the work of two Swiss psychiatrists, Ludwig Binswanger (1881–1966) and Medard Boss (1903–1990), the approach of Daseinsanalysis remains an important contemporary school and practised primarily in continental Europe (van Deurzen et al., 2019).

Binswanger was a friend and contemporary of Sigmund Freud and maintained a long-term correspondence with him despite their considerable disagreements. Binswanger principally disagreed with what he viewed as Freud's natural science approach to understanding human beings, with its emphasis on a separate 'psychic apparatus'. In an attempt

1 True to form, there is even now a so called 'counter-tradition' within existential therapy, that seeks to disrupt and question the positions advanced by the 'traditional' forms of existential presented here (Bazzano, 2021).

to create a more holistic understanding of human beings, Binswanger drew upon the philosophy of Martin Heidegger and his description of human beings as Dasein, meaning being-in-the-world. Binswanger attempted to found a science of psychiatry based on a descriptive analysis of 'world projects' which included a phenomenological exploration and description of the structuring of the patients world. Binswanger, however, was also critical of Heidegger (who was in turn critical of Binswanger and dismissed his work as being based on a misunderstanding of his philosophy), thinking that Heidegger's analysis of interpersonal existence was deficient. Binswanger thus drew additional insights from the work of Martin Buber and others and argued that the most fundamental form of human existence is the 'we' or reciprocal love relationship (Frie, 1997).

Binswanger did not develop a specific form of psychological therapy based upon his insights. This task was taken up by Boss, who also benefitted from direct collaboration with Martin Heidegger, including running a series of seminars held by the philosopher with psychiatric and medical practitioners in Boss's home over a 10-year period (subsequently published as *The Zollikon Seminars,* Heidegger, 2001). The work of Boss is based firmly within the later philosophy of Martin Heidegger with its emphasis on human beings as a 'clearing' or openness towards Being. This rather poetic notion of human existence can be read as a further elaboration of the meaning of being-in-the-world. This, according to Boss (1963), provides a far more adequate understanding than Freud's notion of an individual psyche which is seen as separate from a world and other psyches. As Cooper (2003) notes, replacing the notion of a psyche, as well as related notions such as the unconscious and transference, with being-in-the-world has major implications for understanding the nature of psychological difficulties. For Daseinsanalysts, psychological problems are primarily described in terms of the extent to which the individual sufferer is 'closed off' from aspects of existence and the world (as well as open to other aspects).

Daseinsanalysis has attempted to replace Freudian meta-psychological models with a descriptive-phenomenological model. At the same time, however, Boss recommended retaining many of Freud's central procedures, such as the use of the couch and free association. Psychological problems, as well as being seen as ways of being closed to the possibility of relating to existence, are understood in terms of the effects of inadequate or abusive parenting. In a manner highly resonant with contemporary

Schema Therapy, where clients are seen as having experienced inadequate parenting that left them struggling to relate to the world in an open manner, the Daseinsanalyst will engage in a degree of reparenting, described as follows (Boss cited in Friedman, 1991, p. 437): 'In psychotherapy, the important thing is to let the patients first make up for the missing but at bottom indispensable experience of the protective and unshakable bestowal of care and love suited to the individual nature of the patients.'

Daseinsanalysis has much to offer existentially oriented practitioners as well as CBT therapists, including the incisive critique of many classical psychoanalytic concepts, as well as useful strategies for working with dreams. At the same time, there remain numerous unresolved controversies within the model. Daseinsanalysts, as well as other existentially oriented therapists who draw upon Heidegger, continue to be presented with the difficult issue of reconciling what has emerged regarding Heidegger's involvement with National Socialism in Germany and the extent to which National Socialism can be traced to aspects of Heidegger's philosophy (see Cohn, 2002, for a discussion of these issues). An additional challenge, and potentially a productive and constructive one, arises from the work of a group of American psychoanalysts who have attempted to develop what they have defined as a post-Cartesian psychoanalysis. While still expressing a fondness for Freud, the work of Robert Stolorow and George Atwood (2019) is an existential phenomenological reworking of psychoanalysis that, similar to Daseinsanalysis, draws principally from the philosophy of Heidegger. Unlike Daseinsanalysis, however, these theorists have dispensed with many of the Freudian recommendations for practice, such as the use of the couch in favour of an empathically attuned face-to-face encounter. Their work is particularly notable for the highly detailed, clinically focused descriptions of forms of therapeutic relation that can make sense of, and respond to, experiences of emotional trauma.

Logotherapy

> Logotherapy focuses on the search for the meaning of human existence. Such a search is an important undertaking in psychotherapy since the lack of awareness of life's meaning is among the most important causes of emotional frustration in our time (Viktor Frankl, cited in Friedman, 1991, p. 467).

The work of Viktor Frankl (1905–1997) is highly influential and perhaps the best known form of existential therapy. Frankl's work *Man's Search for Meaning* (1984), describing his experience in a Nazi concentration camp, became a best seller and remains an important introductory text for existential approaches to therapy. Despite his importance, in many respects, some of his central propositions are at odds with the principles of existential phenomenology. The term 'logos' is the Greek word for meaning, thus logotherapy may be rendered as meaning therapy. Like Daseinsanalysis, logotherapy was heavily influenced by psychoanalysis (Cooper, 2003). Frankl's main proposition, however, is that, contrary to the Freudian emphasis on instinctual drives, human beings have a primary drive towards meaning. Frankl founded what became known as the Third Viennese School of Psychiatry (following Freud's first and Adler's second schools). Unlike Daseinsanalysis, Frankl did not develop logotherapy on the basis of any one existential philosopher, however, he was influenced in varying degrees by the phenomenological philosophies of Scheler (who wrote on the phenomenology of values), Husserl and Heidegger, in addition to Binswanger's emphasis on the primacy of love (Halling & Nill, 1995). His approach stands in stark contrast to philosophers such as Sartre who argue that existence is, in a fundamental sense, meaningless and absurd. Instead, he argues for what is in essence a more spiritual–religious understanding, which asserts that meaning is *found* rather than constructed and that there is a sense in which it is possible to find a true or correct meaning in a situation.

For Frankl, psychological problems arise when people experience their lives as lacking in meaning, a situation he terms 'the existential vacuum'. In contrast to the more descriptively oriented practices of most other existential models, the logotherapist, according to Frankl, uses a range of often directive and educational interventions to help clients discover meaning in their lives. Such methods include the use of Socratic dialogue, metaphor and paradoxical intention. The aim of paradoxical intention is to assist the client in adopting a more responsible and accepting stance towards their psychological symptoms. In a manner strikingly similar to some intervention possibilities in CBT, a client experiencing social anxiety that is focused on a concern about sweating will be encouraged to deliberately expose themselves to a situation in which another person sees them sweating profusely (Frankl, 1988). Indeed, Frankl appears to make great use of the strategy of exposure; however, in doing so he appears to adopt a far more directive approach in contrast to the highly collaborative stance advocated in contemporary CBT.

A further strategy advocated in logotherapy is that of 'dereflection' (Cooper, 2003). According to Frankl (1988), a central factor in some psychological difficulties is the degree to which individuals maintain attention on themselves and their symptoms. In dereflection the client is encouraged to take a more external focus of attention. Again, as with exposure techniques, the strategy of dereflection finds an echo in contemporary CBT which attempts to reduce rigid internally directed attentional processes (Wells, 2000).

Logotherapy is distinct from other forms of existential therapy in its claim that it is possible for individuals to find the meaning of their lives, and that such meanings are found rather than constructed. It is also distinct in advocating for a more directly educational and interventionist stance on the part of the therapist. These more directive aspects have been seen by a number of existential writers as expressing a degree of authoritarianism that is at odds with other forms of existential practice (Cooper, 2003).

Existential–Humanistic Therapy

> It is about how you live with your emotions . . . it is about being helped to see that the change you seek is already within you. It is coming to recognise and appreciate the spark of something eternal that is your core (Bugental, 1999, p. 1).

Halling and Nill (1995) describe the existential–humanistic approach as having arisen from the impetus provided by the publication of the book *Existence: A New Dimension in Psychiatry and Psychology* in the United States by Rollo May et al. (1958). This book remains in print and continues to be essential reading for practitioners interested in existentially informed ways of working. This text introduced to American readers the writings of European existential therapists such as Binswanger, and also included chapters by humanistic therapists such as Carl Rogers. As Cooper (2003) has discussed, the existential phenomenology represented in this text also became mixed with the pragmatism and humanism characteristic of the US intellectual and cultural context. Additionally, the influence of psychoanalysis is apparent, and existential–humanistic therapists make frequent use of concepts such as resistance and the unconscious, although what these terms refer to becomes transformed. These approaches are therefore highly integrative and, in fact, one of the founders of the approach, James Bugental, referred to this approach as 'an all-American hash' (Hoffman et al., 2019). This mixing of philosophies and worldviews is so much a feature of the approach that existential–humanistic therapists are regarded by some European existential therapists as not practising existential therapy at all (Cooper, 2003)—this is despite the fact that several of its leading theorists, such as Rollo May (1909–1994) and Irving Yalom (1931–), are widely recognised as among the most influential of all existentially oriented therapists.

What is the essence of this tension between American and European existential practitioners? From the European perceptive, the issue centres around what is thought to be highly significant misunderstandings of several central propositions of existential phenomenology, which can perhaps be attributed to the influence of the philosophies of humanism and pragmatism.

Humanism

As Copson (2015) has discussed, a humanistic attitude and philosophy has found expression in a wide range of cultural domains for at least the last 2,500 years. Copson (2015) suggests that within academia, humanism can be traced to the period of the Renaissance and refers to attitudes that place primary value on human beings in contrast to gods and religion, and that affirm the importance of reason in the evaluation of evidence. At such a broad level, such a definition would incorporate therapeutic approaches such as CBT as instances of a humanistic outlook as much as those therapies explicitly identified as humanistic. The use of the label humanistic psychotherapy has, however, come to have a narrower definition, being applied to approaches that arose principally in American and Europe in the 1940s and 1950s, and grew to great popularity and influence in the 1960s and 1970s, that emphasised an essentially optimistic view of the natural capacity of human beings to develop and grow in inherently positive directions. Additionally, such views have emphasised the centrality of an individual experiencing a *self* that has depth and interiority and that can be regarded as a source of truth and authenticity. As Cain (2001, p. 10) states: 'Self-exploration, self-definition, reconstrual of the self, and the development of self-knowledge are the primary concerns of the humanistic therapist'.

Classical versions of humanistic therapy include the person-centred approach of Carl Rogers (1961), Gestalt psychotherapy (Perls et al., 1951) and psychodrama (Moreno, 1946/2019). At times, existential therapy has been classified as a form of humanistic therapy (Cain, 2001), and at other times existential writers (Spinelli, 1994) have sought to distinguish existential therapy as being substantially different from, and indeed a challenge to, humanistic assumptions.

In his discussion of existential therapy, and possibly expressing the influence of a more humanistic sensibility, Yalom (1980) sought to distance his own approach from what he saw as the unnecessarily gloomy and depressed outlook of the European existential analysts, whose writings he criticised as obscure and abstract. In contrast to the European emphasis on the limits of existence and the angst-ridden dilemmas of guilt and responsibility, existential–humanists emphasise such features as spontaneity, experiential intensity and individual freedom. In fact, the boundaries between existential–humanistic approaches and other humanistic approaches appear very fuzzy, with a range of therapies, such as Gestalt therapy (Perls et al., 1951) and focusing (Gendlin, 2003), making significant use of existential phenomenology without necessarily defining their approach as a form of existential therapy.

From the European existentialist perspective, it is argued that the existential–humanistic perspective fails to give fundamental importance to relatedness as an existential principal and, as a consequence, it tends to present a more individualist and subjectivist attitude (Spinelli, 1994). Thus, Bugental (1999) has described how, in existential–humanistic approaches, we find an emphasis on the client learning to turn inwards, to value their inner subjective experience and their embodied emotional experience, as the pathway to truth and authenticity. Bugental and other existential–humanistic therapists also employ the term 'resistance' to describe the avoidance of being in contact with this inner realm of emotional experience, and they use a variety of educational and experiential and directive strategies in an attempt to support the client to overcome such resistance.

Pragmatism

As Cooper (2003) notes, as much as the existential–humanistic therapies are influenced by European existential philosophy, they appear to be equally indebted to the philosophy of pragmatism as developed by American philosophers such as William James (1842–1910). In this, they share a philosophical kinship with contemporary forms of behaviour therapy such as Acceptance and Commitment Therapy (ACT). As the developers of ACT have emphasised (Hayes et al., 1999/2011), for pragmatists what is true is what works. Thus, a wide range of intervention strategies may be employed in both ACT and existential–humanistic therapy in the service of achieving positive outcomes. In existential–humanistic therapies, strategies—including role plays, experiential body-focused exercises and cognitive restructuring interventions—may all be employed in an eclectic manner. In comparison with many European existential therapists, existential–humanistic therapies have been far more willing to provide detailed descriptions of actual intervention strategies.

Possibly the foremost contemporary theorist in existential–humanistic therapy is Kirk Schneider (2008) who has developed a form of existential–integrative therapy that provides detailed descriptions for working directly with a wide range of client presentations. The pragmatic emphasis of contemporary existential–humanistic theories is such that it has facilitated a greater degree of dialogue with a number of therapists working within a CBT framework. For example, in Schneider's text on existential–integrative psychotherapy (2008), a case study is presented by Bunting and Hayes (2008) from the perspective of ACT, with ACT understood to express a range of principles consistent with those of the existential–humanistic perspective.

Rollo May and Irving Yalom

The writings of May and Yalom remain among the most accessible of all existentially oriented work. As Halling and Nill (1995) discuss, the work of May expresses the influence of his mentor, the theologian Paul Tillich (1886–1965). Tillich's most influential work was *The Courage to Be* (1980) in which he described the nature of existential anxiety and contrasted it with its antidote—'courage'. According to Tillich, speaking in a manner that appears to substantially resonate with the ideas of Functional

Analytic Psychotherapy and Acceptance and Commitment Therapy (see Chapter 9), an act of courage involves radical self-acceptance and self-affirmation rather than an attempt to deny or eliminate anxiety. Consistent with the orientation of existential–humanistic therapy, May viewed the self as a 'centre of experiencing' which, when threatened by non-being (e.g. following the loss of an important role or a central belief about the self or the world) will attempt to preserve centeredness by 'shrinking its world'. For May, existential–humanistic therapy involves the establishment of a genuine and authentic therapeutic relationship that provides a context within which clients may courageously attempt to expand their awareness and their potential for growth (May, 1981).

Yalom's (1980) work is particularly noted for its clear descriptions of client presentations that can be read as expressing the presence of a variety of existential concerns that centre around themes of death, freedom, isolation and meaninglessness. Yalom presents existential therapy as a form of dynamic psychotherapy that differs from psychoanalytic therapy principally in its understanding of the source of human anxiety and distress. Consider the existential theme of isolation. For Yalom, while many of the issues that clients bring to therapy concern and arise from their relationships with others, each human being is fundamentally and unavoidably experientially and psychologically unique and alone. Existential isolation arises from the fact that due to the unique and never to be repeated aspects of our thrownness into the world (derived from a combination of our genetic make-up, temperament, family, cultural context, etc.) our individual subjective experience is never completely shareable. While communication and dialogue remain possible, it is never possible for anyone, no matter how empathic they may be, to experience the world in the same way as another. This experience of existential isolation, while potentially a source of creativity and motivation, is also anxiety provoking. In his clinical work, Yalom takes an often highly directive and challenging approach to such issues and, in particular, examines the extent to which the difficulties of the client become apparent within the therapeutic relationship.

In summary, the existential–humanistic approach is a highly integrative and pragmatic approach that seeks to help clients respond creatively and positively to their experience of existential anxiety. It is characteristically optimistic and offers a wide range of intervention strategies for the therapist and client to work with. Reflecting its allegiance to a more humanistic worldview, it has also tended to emphasise an individually focused understanding of existence that highlights issues of self. More recent elaborations on this model have sought to find a degree of correction for this individualistic emphasis with an attempt at exploring the extent to which the model would be appropriate for various non-western groups which express a more collectivist understanding of the nature of self and which embody different understandings regarding the experience and expression of emotion (Hoffman & Cleare-Hoffman, 2011).

Existential Phenomenological Therapy

Contemporary existential phenomenological psychotherapy has experienced significant development over the past few decades via the work of a range of theorists who are loosely connected to the so-called British School of Existential Psychotherapy. There is a great deal of diversity within this school and no universally agreed upon understanding of how existential phenomenological principles are best expressed in therapeutic practice. There is nevertheless an agreed emphasis on the primacy of a descriptively focused exploratory process in which the therapeutic relationship is both the context and vehicle for therapeutic work. These emphases can be found in the work of R.D. Laing who, for many of these therapists, remains a source of inspiration as well as disagreement.

R.D. Laing and Ontological Insecurity

> In the context of our present pervasive madness that we call normality, sanity, freedom, all our frames of reference are ambiguous and equivocal (R.D. Laing, *The Divided Self,* 1960).

Stephen sits uneasily in the chair in front of me as he has done so during many previous sessions. It is clear that he has not washed for several days and is significantly, and worryingly (to me), underweight. He begins to tell me the exact same story of the development of his difficulties, in the exact same way, as he has in previous sessions. Stephen describes a process of having undergone an intense period of 'self-analysis' that he imposed upon himself following the ending of a romantic relationship.

Stephen, distressed at the loss of the relationship, decides that he needs to 'get to the bottom' of his concerns and questions regarding 'who I should be and how I should treat others. . .what is the right way to be?' He locks himself in his bedroom and begins a period of self-questioning attempting to arrive at a 'clear truth' only leaving his room briefly to use the bathroom or to eat (which he does infrequently). He barely sleeps and finds himself feeling more and more distressed. Eventually, after a period of over a month, he stated that 'the links between my synapses, the links between my neurons, they broke apart . . . they are no longer connected. . . . and I cannot feel or think as I should'. He has abandoned his efforts at self-analysis and now instead is preoccupied with this experience of disconnection. He often seems to me to be in contact with, and expressing, a range of emotions in session including humour and yet maintains that he no longer has access to the normal range of emotions, their intensity is blunted and the connection between emotions and the world has become severed.

However else Stephen's difficulties may be described, one vivid and apt description arises from the work of Scottish existential psychiatrist R.D. Laing (1927–1989) who would suggest that his concerns express the experience of a fundamental 'ontological insecurity'. Possibly the most impactful of Laing's writings, in terms of existential phenomenology, is his early work *The Divided Self: an existential study in sanity and madness* (Laing, 1960). The divided self was principally concerned with an attempt to understand the experience of individuals diagnosed as 'schizoid' or 'schizophrenic' from an existential phenomenological perspective. In contrast to approaches that viewed the behaviour and thinking of 'schizophrenics' as inherently irrational and incomprehensible, Laing sought to demonstrate that in fact such states of extreme psychological suffering could be understood as being the outcome of meaningful and intelligible acts (Cooper, 2003). In a widely quoted passage Laing (1960, p. 42) describes the individual's experience of ontological insecurity:

> The individual in the ordinary circumstances of living may feel more unreal than real; in a literal sense, more dead than alive; precariously differentiated from the rest of the world, so that his identity and autonomy are always in question. He may lack the experience of his own temporal continuity. He may not possess an over-riding sense of personal consistency or cohesiveness. He

> may feel more insubstantial than substantial and unable to assume that the stuff he is made of is genuine, good, valuable. And he may feel his self as partially divorced from his body.

Laing further outlines three types of anxiety that ontologically insecure individuals will experience. First is the fear of 'engulfment', which is the fear that their autonomy, their self, will be devoured by others. Secondly, they experience the anxiety of 'implosion', the fear that their inner sense of emptiness will be invaded by forces in the external world that will obliterate them. Finally, there is the anxiety of 'petrification and depersonalisation', the dread of being turned into an inanimate object. As van Deurzen-Smith (1995) notes, depersonalisation is also a response to the fear of engulfment or implosion as, out of terror, the individual disconnects from the world and others and experiences themselves as isolated and lifeless.

Laing's work was controversial, particularly when Laing became associated with the so-called anti psychiatry movement (Burston, 2000). van Deurzen-Smith (1995) has also argued that in his later work Laing tended to romanticize the experience of schizophrenia and that the experience of ontological security, far from being an experience restricted to those individuals who are diagnosable as such, is an aspect of existential anxiety present for all human beings. In addition to his compelling explanations for how severe forms of psychological suffering could be comprehensible and meaningful, Laing's impact can be seen to arise also from his emphasis on the nature of psychotherapy as being an inherently humane and non-technological way of being-with and relating to an other. This orientation to practice is clearly expressed in another frequently quoted passage in which Laing (1990, p. 45) states: 'Psychotherapy must remain an obstinate attempt of two people to recover the wholeness of being human through the relationship between them.'

There is no tradition of Laingian existential therapy in any organised consistent sense. Laing's work, however, has influenced a wide range of therapists and theorists who have developed their own understanding and models of existential phenomenological therapy. Subsequent to Laing, the development of a distinctive existential phenomenological perspective has been furthered by the writings of Emmy van Deurzen-Smith (1988, 1997), Hans Cohn (1997, 2002) and Ernesto Spinelli (1994, 2015), each of whom developed distinctive approaches to existential phenomenological therapy.

With existential phenomenological therapy, there is a sense in which each author, and indeed each therapist, is encouraged to begin again, to return to the things themselves, in order to develop their own unique perspective on the relationship between existential thinking and psychotherapeutic practice. Nevertheless, there are some important fundamental principles that unite the various perspectives into an identifiable approach. As Cooper (2003) has noted, the most central of these is the effort to develop an existential phenomenological approach to therapy that is primarily descriptive in focus and that seeks to divest the practice of therapy from any lingering notions of it being a quasi-medical intervention or technique. Thus, the word 'therapy' is often used in preference to 'psychotherapy', with therapy based on its original meaning of 'paying attention to the other or standing alongside the other' (Spinelli, 2015). In addition, according to this perspective, an individual's psychological difficulties are regarded as problems in living rather than instances of psychopathology or disorder. Possibly expressing its indebtedness to Laing, this perspective also tends to emphasise the centrality of the therapeutic relationship in which the possibilities of that relationship (as well as its limitations) are seen as the primary context and vehicle for whatever positive (as well as unpredictable) therapeutic outcomes may emerge. Any humanistic emphases on the inherent positive qualities of human beings and their capacity for spontaneity and joy are at most held very lightly, if at all, in favour of a more tragic view of life consistent with the writings of the existential philosophers. In contrast to the more pragmatically oriented existential-humanists, these perspectives also tend to de-emphasise any notions of therapeutic techniques or interventions in favour of an understanding of therapy as dialogue.

Emmy van Deurzen

> The existential approach to therapy is about learning to philosophise in the sense of asking important questions about what it means to be alive (van Deurzen & Adams, 2011, p. 11).

Emmy van Deurzen-Smith (1988, 1997) has developed a unique approach to existential psychotherapy characterised by an understanding of the nature of psychotherapy as a philosophical enterprise in which clients are challenged to think deeply and broadly about their assumptions, values and beliefs. van Deurzen-Smith (1997), in her text *Everyday Mysteries*, demonstrates how the writings of a wide range of existential philosophers (and other philosophers) clarify many of the issues that individuals struggle with—and how such writings can inform the focus of the existential therapist. van Deurzen's tragic-passionate view proposes that life is inherently challenging, difficult, unfair and precarious. Additionally, she describes human beings as inevitably challenged to respond to any number of inherent paradoxes and dilemmas. For example, a client's difficulties may be seen as expressing the dilemma of desiring connection versus autonomy, individual achievement and uniqueness. Neither end of this polarity is inherently more healthy, real or authentic, however, a client may engage in avoidance and self-deception by maintaining a wish or belief that it is possible for this dilemma to be resolved without pain, or that it may be possible to have it all.

van Deurzen's descriptions of her practice reveal a highly engaging, thoughtful, philosophical and, at times, directive and openly challenging style. She has described existential therapy as 'a tutorial in the art of living' (van Deurzen-Smith, 1988) in which the existential therapist challenges the client to live with greater awareness and ownership of the choices they are making. Therapy is thus presented as being an inherently educational enterprise in which the therapist, should they possess the requisite personal qualities, is present as a guide. van Deurzen-Smith (1988, p. 29) explains: 'Existential counselling is a philosophical investigation rather than a medical or a psychological one. The counsellor therefore functions as a mentor in the art of living. The accomplished existential counsellor is more like a sage than a brilliant technician or a cunning strategist.'

In many respects, of the theorists reviewed in this section, it is van Deurzen's approach that would appear to be the most amenable to comparison and integration with various CBT approaches. van Deurzen's challenging, educational and robust way of engaging clients to help them clarify their dilemmas in living, in order to freely and responsibly choose how to go forward in life, bears striking similarity to, for example, Acceptance and Commitment Therapy in which clients are vigorously challenged to 'show up, be present, reflect on "what do you want to stand for?" and commit to valued life directions'.

Hans Cohn

> It may seem as if the therapist has very little to offer—until we realise how rare it is in a relationship for one person to put him or herself entirely in the service of another, without giving in to the need to know and show it (Hans Cohn, 2002, p. 119).

The work of Hans Cohn (1916–2004) was primarily based on a sustained consideration of the philosophy of Martin Heidegger and the implications of this work for clarifying existential therapy. Cohn was originally trained as a psychodynamic therapist and, in a fashion similar to Daseinsanalysts, clarified his own approach to existential therapy principally in comparison and contrast to a Freudian psychodynamic perspective. Cohn (1999) was also a well-regarded poet and his published work on existential psychotherapy is characterised by a minimalistic and highly condensed style that managed to convey a great deal to the reader in a way that invites subsequent re-reading. Cohn, in a fashion comparable to Yalom (1980), outlines a basic existential model in which human beings can be said to struggle with and attempt to evade various aspects of existence itself. Following Heidegger, he highlighted how the relationship between the ontological and the ontical aspects of existence means there is no necessity for the therapist to confront the client with the ontological dimension or to directly interpret this in any causal or reductive fashion. As the ontological dimension is included within the ontical dimension, it remains the case that the existential therapist focuses primarily on the client's ontical everyday experience of being-in-the-world. Cohn's (1997) discussion of the ontological givens of existence includes the following list of existential challenges: being-in-the-world, being-in-the-world-with-others, thrownness, mortality, the unavoidability of choice, embodiment, spatiality, temporality, mood as attunement and sexuality.

Cohn's incisive writings are highly valuable for the way in which they elucidate the practice of existential therapy from a Heidegerrian basis. So, for example, Cohn challenges the frequently mistaken assumption that existential therapists do not work with the client's past but only focus on the here and now. For Cohn, this misconception is based on a misunderstanding of the existential meaning of time. Following Heidegger, Cohn (2002) argues that the present moment always includes the past as currently lived and future-directed—time, as lived time, is always multi-dimensional and cannot be understood in terms of clock time or as a series of measurable and separable 'nows'. Similarly, Cohn challenges the notion that existential therapists do not use interpretation and argues that a distinction can be drawn between analytic interpretation that seeks to explain a phenomenon in terms of underlying causal processes, and phenomenological interpretation that seeks to clarify phenomena as they are revealed by 'widening the context for understanding'. Cohn's (1995) discussion of the meaning of authenticity in Heidegerrian philosophy also clarifies the extent to which authenticity cannot be thought to be the achievement of a separate self that has somehow attained a heightened and superior state; rather, authenticity is understood in terms of the possibility, always precarious and never permanent, of a greater 'openness towards existence'.

Ernesto Spinelli

> The multitude of ideas of existential phenomenological thought and practice . . . point us towards a stance or attitude towards therapy that attempts to be an embodied expression of those ideas so that our aim is to breathe them rather than simply communicate them through words or techniques (Ernesto Spinelli, 2019, p. 70).

Pierre Hadot (1995) in his book *Philosophy as a Way of Life* argues that philosophy is a 'form of life' and that 'philosophical discourse' is not the same thing as philosophy. The question 'What is philosophy?' has occupied philosophers for many centuries. Its relevance here is in the question: In what way is existential phenomenological philosophy of direct relevance to the practice of therapy? Ernesto Spinelli's response to this question, as illustrated in earlier quote, is that the value of existential thought lies primarily in the possibility of the therapist coming to embody and express its principles in their manner of being with their clients. In a range of publications, Spinelli (1994, 2001, 2015) presents a deeply philosophical understanding of the possibilities and limitations of an existential approach to therapy based on the notion of it being primarily a way of being and relating to clients. Spinelli (2015) argues that the most distinctively novel possibilities offered by existential phenomenological thought do not lie primarily within the various themes or concerns that it addresses, such as death, freedom, choice and the like, but rather in *its way of addressing* such themes.

Drawing upon the work of a range of existential phenomenological philosophers, Spinelli suggests that an essential aspect of this embodied practice is the therapist's willingness and ability to remain open to the client in the way they currently express their existence. This view, consistent with the phenomenological injunction to become aware of and bracket preconceptions, requires the therapist to set aside any notions of behavioural change, improvement, or cure in order to more adequately enter into and describe the client's lived experience of being.

Spinelli's writing emphasises the highly demanding and challenging nature of working existentially *for the therapist*. A common challenge for therapists to consider, according to Spinelli, is 'What is it about my client's current way of being that I find difficult to accept and stay with?' He has further described and elaborated his understanding of what it means to 'be open' towards the client as a form of 'unknowing'. He explains (Spinelli, 2015, p. 115):

> The attempt to remain as open as possible to that which presents itself in the current and ongoing encounter and to treat the seemingly familiar, assumed to be understood or understandable, as novel, unfixed in meaning, and hence, accessible to previously unexamined experiential possibilities.

Somewhat provocatively, Spinelli (2015) has also suggested that this attempt at openness and un-knowing could be described as the therapist, at least initially, being willing to take up the role of 'idiot'. This role of *the therapist as idiot* serves to express the notion of not taking up the stance of expert change agent, as well as a willingness to seek to remain with the client as they currently are while opening up the seemingly obvious or taken for granted as worthy of reflection.

Spinelli (1994) has also maintained a strong focus on examining a range of ways in which therapists come to assume forms of power, based upon their theory-derived assumptions of the role of the therapist and the nature of therapy that can lead to both subtle and not so subtle misuses of power. Spinelli (1994) draws attention to the empirical research suggesting a high degree of equivalence between different forms of therapy and argues that it is an error to attribute the effectiveness of therapy to the impact of its specific technical interventions. Again provocatively, he has suggested, drawing upon the Disney cartoon of 'Dumbo the elephant', that in many instances the specific technical interventions function as 'magic feathers' for the therapist who is then more able to experience and express a greater degree of faith in the possibilities of successful therapy.

Summary

- Like CBT, there is no one existential therapy that finds universal agreement and acceptance among its practitioners. While there is a family resemblance that lies principally in the attempt by different therapists to draw inspiration from a range of existential phenomenological philosophers, each existential therapist is required to take up a position with or against these various perspectives to clarify for themselves and others where they stand.
- Important differences exist between continental European forms of existential therapy and US existential–humanistic therapy.
- Most forms of existential therapy emphasise a descriptive exploration of the client's experience of living.

Existential Reflections

In a small group of peers, consider the following questions:

- How often, in your practice, do larger questions around the meaning of life arise?
- Are there particular client presentations (such as depression) where this is more common?
- To what extent do you believe that CBT, of any particular orientation, is able to address these concerns?
- In what manner, if any, are discussions with clients regarding the meaning of life experientially different compared with discussions about other forms of belief?

5

Existential Practice

> *It is more like a game, an art, a drama, a conversation, than the application of a technique based on a theory.*
>
> —Heaton (1995, p. 5).

Chapter 4 demonstrated that existential phenomenological thought has found expression in a range of different therapeutic approaches that do not, taken as a whole, constitute a unified field. There are significant points of divergence and disagreement between these approaches regarding such fundamental questions as the aims of therapy and the role of the therapist. Some of these divergences can be traced to different emphases that can be found in existential phenomenological philosophy. Perhaps the most fundamental of these is the extent to which human existence is described in terms of the primacy of the individual versus the primacy of relation (Mackessy & Bazzano, 2021). This can be seen as expressive of a basic existential tension that exists between the effort or desire to stand out as a unique and separate individual versus the need or desire to merge and become part of a relationship or context with others. This tension appears to occupy the concerns of a range of existential therapists at pains to demonstrate how existential therapy is unique among therapies versus those who seek an integrative stance in which existential therapy is related to and in important senses like others. Like any existential tension worthy of the name, this tension is likely never fully resolvable and will remain as a 'given' to be responded to but never solved.

CBT and Existential Psychology: Philosophy, Psychology and Therapy, First Edition. Michael Worrell.

This chapter discusses further the basic principles of an existential phenomenological approach to therapy. Given the above, this description is limited to 'an approach' rather than 'the approach' and it is likely that my description will provoke as much (possibly more) disagreement from a range of existentially oriented therapists as it would agreement from others. This discussion of how existential phenomenological therapy might be expressed in practice will come nowhere close to being a manual as this is understood in some approaches to CBT. These principles and guidelines are drawn from the British existential phenomenological school, and especially from the work of Spinelli (1994, 2015), van Deurzen-Smith (1988, 1997) and Cohn (2002), although they will also be seen to be consistent with some of the views of a range of other existential perspectives discussed in Chapter 4.

Principles of Existential Phenomenological Therapy

What would it mean to identify fundamental principles for existential phenomenological therapy? The terms 'principle' here is being used in the sense of a foundational proposition upon which other propositions, ideas, hypotheses and theories may be constructed. The overall coherence of a theory can then be evaluated to the extent that its various propositions are consistent with these underlying principles. To give an example of how this works, Radical Behaviour Therapy, as developed by B. F. Skinner (1987) and others, used experimental research to uncover a set of principles of behaviour change, of which several were identified, including positive and negative reinforcement, extinction, punishment and stimulus generalisation. Readers inclined to assert that such principles are in fact out of date and applicable only to the behaviour of mammals such as mice, might like to engage in a thought experiment to explore the extent to which their behaviour (or that of their friends and family), with respect to the use of internet platforms such as Facebook and Twitter, can be understood with reference to such terms (Seymour, 2019). The invention of the 'like' button could be considered a Skinnerian dream, a digital 'lever' with global reach. Radical Behaviour Therapy advanced an approach to the conduct of science that emphasised the identification of basic principles of learning as opposed to the construction of more elaborate theories. Skinner (1987) was thus critical of cognitive psychology due to its emphasis on constructing more elaborate theories relying upon unobservable mediating factors. In fact, he provocatively suggested that cognitive psychology (along with humanistic psychology and psychotherapy) was an obstacle to developing a science of behaviour.

The use of the term 'radical' in radical behaviour therapy is instructive. Radical is here used not in the sense of 'extreme' but rather in the sense of 'consistent' or 'thorough'. For Skinner, the principles of operant conditioning also applied to the researcher or therapist as much as they did to the client or subject in an experiment. They applied to the context or environment of therapy, the context of a scientific laboratory and the behaviour of groups of researchers. There is an often-used cartoon showing two experimental rats talking to each other and one of them stating: 'man have I got that guy in the white coat well trained! Every time I press the lever he delivers food!'. Often this is used to portray the apparent naivete of the behavioural researcher when in fact it can serve to demonstrate exactly the point Skinner makes; in the experimental context the subject and researcher reinforce each other!

Existential therapists have often proposed that their approach is in some senses a radical approach to therapy. Usually, this radicalness is said to arise from the fact that it is a uniquely philosophical therapy rather than a psychological model (van Deurzen and Adams, 2011). This proposition is debatable. However, existential therapy may be radical in a similar sense to radical behaviour therapy, that is, its radicalness arises from the way in which its fundamental principles are consistently expressed both at a theoretical level and in the practice of therapy. Existential philosophers and therapists have identified a range of different dimensions, existential givens or themes and there is no generally accepted or finalised list of these. For example, Cohn (2002) considered sexuality to be an existential aspect of human beings and also considers aspects such as embodiment, 'spatiality' and time. Spinelli (2015), by contrast, has argued for a clarification of fundamental principles of existential phenomenological therapy that he identified as relatedness, uncertainty, and anxiety. These principles, he argues, underlie the way other issues, such as sexuality, can be clarified and explored from an existential phenomenological perspective.

The Principle of Relatedness

Spinelli (2015) suggests that, of all the various themes and existential dimensions that have been identified, relatedness or inter-relation is the most fundamental, as all other aspects and dimensions are understood through a relational lens. Thus, for example, how we live in space is understood in terms of its inter-relational expression rather than through objective notions of how space may be divided up and measured. Similarly, time is understood relationally, rather than in terms of 'clock time'. Existentially, we live space and time. It can be very challenging to maintain a relational perspective on phenomena as we are more used to seeing things from an objective and individualised stance. It appears that it is an aspect of the way language works that we tend to 'thingify' processes and to turn verbs into nouns. Issues and themes that have often been understood to express aspects of an individualised and separate self, such as freedom and responsibility, take on a very different emphasis when considered from an inter-relational standpoint. Choice, for example, is often understood to be an aspect of an individualised separate self. Existentially, choice is never fully an individual matter, the choices we make have their meaning and impact relationally and are never fully and solely owned by a separate individual.

In order to express something of the process-like, relational nature of existence, Spinelli (2015) introduced the term 'worlding', by which he means an attempt to express 'being-always-becoming'. Worlding refers to a pre-reflective process-like experience of being that is prior to any reflectively emerging separation of subject from object. This can be contrasted with what Spinelli describes as the 'worldview' which, for each of us, arises as a result of reflective awareness of being. When we as human beings experience existence reflectively we do so via the imposition of linguistically derived structural limitations that impose a degree of thing-like separation, or essentialising. In order to be able to reflect upon and communicate our experience of being, it seems, we necessarily do so via a process of 'thingification', which imposes limits and distinctions which can never fully capture or express the process-like nature of being itself. One of the most important results of such a process of construction is the self-construct. In existential phenomenology, the self is not regarded as a type of solid enclosed entity that can be viewed as in some way the source point or the generator of experience (Spinelli, 1994; van Deurzen-Smith, 1997). Rather, the self as such is open, process-like, incomplete and contextual. The self-concept, on the other hand, as a result of reflective processes, can be considered to be the attempt at solidification of the pre-reflective experience of being. Thus, the various core beliefs and rules for living, as identified by CBT, could be seen as aspects of the self-construct, although the self-construct need not also be seen as essentially cognitive as it may include more embodied ways of being that become fixed and identified as consistent with 'who I am' and 'who I am not'.

The Zen teacher Charlotte Joko Beck (1993) provides a metaphor that seeks to express a similar insight into the distinction between worlding and having a worldview. Beck asks us to consider whirlpools in an ocean. The whirlpool arises via a complex interplay of forces in the ocean. For a period of time, the whirlpool can be seen to arise and to maintain its structure. Human beings, according to Beck, are somewhat like whirlpools that arise only for them to then assert that their existence as whirlpools is fundamentally separate, self-sustaining and self-originating. Such whirlpools may experience themselves as separate and unique, not only from the existence of other whirlpools, but also from that of the ocean itself. Can the whirlpool be considered to be correct in its insistence of separateness? Is each not nevertheless unique?

From an existential perspective, while we experience our existence in terms of a solid reality in which separate and individual objects exists, the true nature of reality is in fact that it is in flux and in-process. Individual human beings, the self or I, and the individual actions of a person may be identifiable and describable; however, these descriptions are in essence abstractions and always ultimately partial attempts to thingify or objectify being-always-becoming. Our understanding of others also, in this perspective, becomes tentative and fragmentary, the otherness of the other always inevitably exceeding our understanding and resisting our attempts at prediction and control.

The Principle of Uncertainty

One of the central guiding aims of behavioural psychology has been the attempt to derive theoretical constructs and applied methods that will allow for the possibility of prediction and control. While not necessarily ruling out the possibility that forms of prediction and control may be achievable or even desirable in certain defined and limited contexts, the principle of existential uncertainty, by contrast, asserts that there remains 'an inescapable openness of possibility in any and all of our reflections upon our existence' (Spinelli, 2015, p. 22). Existential uncertainty arises as a consequence of the fundamental relational foundation of human existence. As a result of our thrownness, as Heidegger would have it, we can never fully determine or predict what circumstances and events may befall us, neither can we fully predict nor control how we will experience or interpret our experience within such circumstances in any final unshakable way. Consider the following unreliable reflections of one of my own experiences.

I am about to see a new client about whom I know little. A fellow member of staff takes me aside before I head to the waiting area. She wants me to prepare myself as my first client is a young woman who is very disturbed. Additionally, she is described as having a significant facial disfigurement that will make it difficult for me to look at her without a negative emotional response and that the client will be very sensitive to this. Once I have greeted my client in the waiting area and we have both seated ourselves opposite each other in the therapy room, I am able to view what I had anticipated to be a disturbing and possibly distressing facial appearance. To my surprise, my experience of my client's face could only be described as one of great vulnerability and gentleness. The fact of a disfigurement was clear, but how this could be seen as disturbing escaped me. My client was notably anxious and visibly shaking. She then experienced what appeared to me to be a panic attack for approximately 10 minutes during which she hyperventilated. I waited this out, with her stating clearly that the attack would be finished soon. Once it had, I asked her about what had just happened and what the trigger for this might have been. She replied: 'This morning, I opened the fridge . . . the milk was not where I thought it was . . . I know . . . it sounds mad . . . but . . . if I can't be certain of something as simple as this . . . how can I be certain of anything at all?'

The experience described above can be read as expressing a number of dilemmas in regard to the existential given of uncertainty. While my colleague's statements regarding what to expect regarding my new client were, with hindsight, easy to dismiss as unhelpful distractions and preconceptions that could have limited my openness to my client, at the time they were experienced by me as helpful, as giving me a sense of certainty and preparedness. My client's statements, on the other hand, expressed a deep anxiety regarding an experienced lack of certainty, an experience that seemed to plague her every interaction with her world. Thus certainty/uncertainty reveal themselves as potentially creative, engaging, limiting, freeing, disturbing and anxiety provoking.

To be clear, the principle of uncertainty is in no way suggesting that all is uncertain at all times. As Spinelli (2015) clarifies, there remain all manner of certainties and pre-conditions, including environmental, biological and psychological factors, that are required for reflection upon experience to be possible. The principle of uncertainty points, rather, to the inevitable openness that arises *within* such preconditions. Existential therapy also points us towards those inevitable givens of existence, such as death, time and other people, that are in no sense optional but that nevertheless reveal degrees of uncertainty through the very necessity that we must take up a response to these givens.

Existential Reflections on Uncertainty

In a small group of peers, recall a time when you worked with a client, preferably one where you felt that therapy was going well and that the client was progressing, whatever you considered that to be. Consider the following:

- What in your work with the client was experienced by you as potentially novel and unexpected?
- Were there any 'changes of course' that occurred after assessment and formulation that caused you to rethink and reconsider?
- If the overall outcome was as expected, what novel information did you encounter about your client and about yourself as therapist during the intervention phase? If the answer to this is not much, what might this suggest?

The Principle of Anxiety

Critics of CBT often wrongly assert that its various strategies and theories aim at the elimination or removal of anxiety. In fact, most CBT therapists would assert that anxiety is a fundamental aspect of human experience. Anxiety, in this sense, is viewed as a hardwired biological aspect of human existence. The principle of anxiety, as understood in existential therapy, views anxiety not simply in terms of a biologically driven aspect of our existence but as a fundamental constituent of our existence that arises as a direct consequence of the principles of relatedness and uncertainty (Spinelli, 2015). As discussed in chapters one and two, existential anxiety is not only concerned with disturbing and difficult direct experiences of anxiety, though it certainly includes such experiences; rather, the principle of anxiety asserts that anxiety underlies all of our responses to the givens of existence, such that instances of joy, creativity and engagement also express the manner which an individual has found to live with and respond to the lived experience of relational uncertainty. Thus, whatever orientation we may take towards anxiety—one of experiential openness and willingness, or one of avoidance and escape—existential anxiety remains.

Existential Reflection on Anxiety
In a small group of peers, consider the following situation that arose in my practice. I was seeing Sally, a mother of three young children and a beauty therapist, in a General Practice Surgery. She had been referred to me after experiencing panic attacks which, at their worst, had occurred three times a day, leading her to avoid work and social interaction. We worked together using CBT strategies for panic attacks. This was highly successful and within six weeks her panic attacks had ceased. However, over the next six months Sally made regular follow-up sessions in order to review her progress. In each of these sessions, she reported being panic free, yet she also spoke about a vague sense of unease. Every now and then she reported having a sense of diffuse anxiety, commenting: 'Why do I *have* to

experience this? I just don't think it's right that I should have to live a life where I have any anxiety at all!'

How might you respond to a statement such as this? In what way, if any, does the existential principle of anxiety relate to this statement in an informative way?

In summary, the principles of relatedness, uncertainty and anxiety have been proposed by Spinelli (2015) as constituting the fundamental principles of existential phenomenology. They provide the fundamental starting point from which a wide range of other existential themes and dilemmas, such as embodiment, meaning, time, change and the nature of psychological problems, can be considered.

The Nature of Psychological Problems

Existential therapists, as a whole, have tended to reject the notion that various forms of psychological distress and disturbance are best viewed as expressions of one or more diagnosable psychological disorders, such as exemplified in the various editions of the DSM or ICD. In this, they share common ground with a number of behaviourally and cognitive-behaviourally oriented practitioners who maintain that such categories, as well as having poor reliability and validity as separable and distinct forms of distress, are misleading as they appear to locate the source of difficulties *within* an individual. They also tend to frame the nature of psychological distress in terms of a medical category of illness and say nothing about the essential nature of these forms of psychological distress. In contrast to this, Existential Therapists seek to take as open and non-pejorative position as possible, and so forms of psychological distress are framed instead as problems in living. This attitude, however, should not be taken to indicate any minimisation of the distress that clients may be experiencing. In fact, a great deal of phenomenologically oriented research has been conducted to help gain a better descriptive understanding of the nature of a wide range of severe forms of psychological distress (Stanghellini et al., 2019). Rather than attempting a diagnosis of a specific form of disorder, existential phenomenological therapists attempt to place the client's presenting concerns and distress within the context of their overall lifeworld or worldview and the manner in which this can be seen to express the individual's response to the fundamental givens of relatedness, uncertainty and anxiety. In one sense, psychological difficulties represent attempted solutions as much as they do problems, and existential phenomenological therapy seeks to understand how these difficulties are expressive of attempted solutions and what might be at stake in any movement towards greater flexibility and change.

The Aims of Existential Phenomenological Therapy

Most forms of CBT, with the exception in some respects of ACT, view the primary aims of psychological therapy as assisting the individual client, couple, family or group to reduce or eliminate a variety of distressing psychological problems. Possibly the most challenging aspect of existential phenomenological therapy for CBT therapists (again with the possible exception of those aligned with ACT) is that it explicitly encourages the therapist to set aside the notions of improvement, cure, remediation of symptoms, and learning new skills. This is not to suggest that positive outcomes or new learning may not be the result of therapy, nor to suggest that the client is in some way required or encouraged to let go of any desire for change or to set aside any goals for therapy. Rather, what is being asserted is that, consistent with the phenomenological method described in Chapter 2, it is the task of the therapist to attempt, at least initially and during early sessions with clients, to identify and set aside any theory-based or professionally-based notions of what the nature of the client's difficulties may be, and what the aims and outcomes of any therapeutic dialogue should, must or will be.

Spinelli (2015), as discussed in the Chapter 4, described this attempt as one of un-knowing. This stance encourages the therapist to view presenting psychological difficulties as in some sense ambiguous. That is, psychological difficulties, as much as they may involve the client experiencing a great deal of distress and disturbance, can also be viewed as meaningful expressions of the client's manner of being, and potentially key components or expressions of the client's worldview. The potential modification of this worldview, as much as it may involve the lessening of psychological distress, may also involve trade-offs, tensions and new challenges that cannot be predicted and remain uncertain in their implications and impact.

The existential phenomenological therapist is required to take the client's presenting difficulties as meaningful expressions of their lived experience. Rather than attempt to seek the means by which the client can directly overcome these difficulties, the task of the existential phenomenological therapist is to attempt a dialogue with the client that allows for a rich and expanding description of the client's experience of these difficulties and what they may express in regard to the client's wider relations with self, other and the world. Paradoxically, it is through the client's greater willingness to say still with their experience, that possibilities of movement and change are felt to rise.

Authenticity as an Aim in Existential Therapy

One way in which the possible aims of existential therapy have been framed is in terms of the notion of authenticity. This is contrasted with inauthenticity which is generally regarded as a state in which we are absorbed into the concerns of everyday life, distracted and unaware and avoidant of contact with the givens of existence, such as being-towards-death, freedom, choice, responsibility, etc. The notion of authenticity being an aim of therapy has been a controversial one (Cohn, 1997). The difficulty is that it seems to set up a potentially better or higher way of being that can be strived for and maintained. Worse, it could be regarded as a permanent aspect of an individual, like a personality trait, in which people could be compared regarding their level of authenticity. This is in fact a poor understanding of the nature of authenticity, at least as understood within existential philosophy. Rather, following the work of Heidegger (1962) and others, authenticity is to be considered more like a temporary and potentially disturbing and anxiety-provoking form of attunement. It is a state (not a trait) of being open to existence, as well as a state of awareness of finitude and limitation. In this sense of greater openness, as well as the sense of embracing anxiety and moving forward, authenticity could be seen as a possible outcome of therapy, but in no way is this a predictable aim that can be deliberately brought about by specific interventions on the part of the therapist.

For the CBT therapist reading this description of the aims of existential phenomenological therapy, a likely reaction is that it may seem impossibly vague and woolly—two terms that within a CBT worldview are as equal in negative connotation as the terms gluttony and sloth would be for a medieval theologian. However, the broadness and apparent fuzziness of these stated aims are consistent with existential phenomenology's understanding of itself as being based upon a human science perspective that seeks a primarily descriptive rather than a causal or explanatory analysis of psychological problems.

The Therapeutic Relationship

Another claim for the radical nature of existential phenomenological therapy lies in the extent to which it asserts that psychotherapy is fundamentally relational. Consistent with the principle of relatedness, this perspective places primary emphasis on the relationship between the therapist and client as being the context and vehicle by which any positive therapeutic changes might arise. A range of existential therapists have asserted that the key to their approach is not an offer of technical means or expertise for overcoming problems, but a unique form of relational context in which problems in living can be disclosed and explored. This approach highlights various qualities of being that are crucial for enabling the clarifying therapeutic aspects of the encounter to emerge.

For existential phenomenological therapists, the relationship between client and therapist is a central and unique expression of a more fundamental relatedness. Consistent with its contextual human science approach, the existential phenomenological therapist attempts to explore the client's lived experience of their presenting difficulties, including how these are present (or absent) in the context of the therapeutic relationship. Assuming the therapist is able to embody a sufficiently adequate degree of relational flexibility, an attempt is made to enter into and descriptively explore the lived experience of the client from the client's own perspective. The therapeutic relationship itself then becomes, according to Spinelli (2015, p. 109): 'The microcosm through which the microcosm of the client's stance towards the possibilities and limitations of inter-relational being in the world is both explored and expressed'.

The task of the therapist can be described as an attempt to express and embody a degree of experiential openness and attunement to the client's experience and worldview that expresses an acceptance of that worldview as it is currently being experienced and expressed, rather than implying or attempting to find technical means to achieve a directive or educationally based alteration of that worldview. The notion of acceptance as an embodied quality of being is central and highlights points of potential contact with a range of CBT approaches. An attitude of acceptance is adopted in an effort to receive what is presented by the client as it is presented, without necessarily attempting to transform, interpret or change the meaning of what is presented.

This attempt within existential phenomenological therapy to describe the client's lived experience with a sense of acceptance could easily be interpreted by CBT therapists, who are more used to a directive and educational style of practice, as giving permission for a somewhat directionless and unfocused therapeutic dialogue. This would be a misrepresentation of the approach. In fact, adhering to a phenomenological approach requires a great deal of discipline and focus on the part of the therapist, and a number of theorists have provided frameworks to aid the process of exploration, description and dialogue.

Frameworks for Descriptive Exploration

Existential phenomenologists are much concerned with the issue of 'structure'. The givens of existence are said to structure our existence or, indeed, to provide the necessary structures for human experience to emerge and to be intelligible. In the domain of standard CBT (as will be discussed in Chapter 6), a key defining feature of the approach is the extent to which therapeutic work is structured. It may seem from the discussion above that, by comparison, existential phenomenological therapy is unstructured or indeed chaotic. It is true that, compared to standard CBT, a much looser and more open structure is favoured. It would be uncharacteristic of the approach, for example, to begin each session with an attempt to set an agenda and to evaluate the session at its completion with reference to the extent to which the agenda was covered. Nevertheless, various existential therapists have proposed structures for exploration that can aid the therapist in contextualising the client's presentation and the work of therapy as a whole.

van Deurzen-Smith (1988), building on the work of Binswanger (1963), has suggested that the descriptive exploration of the client's lived experience can be aided through reference to four different yet interrelated dimensions of existence in the world. These include

1) The 'Umwelt' or the physical environmental dimension that includes the client's embodied experience and the natural and physical-environmental context of a client's world.
2) The 'Mitwelt' or the social world of being-with-others, including interpersonal roles and relationships, as well as wider contextual aspects such as culture, class, race and gender.
3) The 'Eigenwelt' or personal or 'I' dimension that includes the experience of self, as well as self-concept and personality.
4) The 'Uberwelt' or spiritual dimension that includes values, meaning, philosophical outlook and religious of faith perspectives and practices.

For van Deurzen-Smith, this structure can provide the therapist with a map that allows them to contextualise a client's presenting problem within an overall view of their experience of living. Rather than a formulation as this would be understood in CBT, the resulting map allows for a far richer and more adequate description of what is at stake and what is expressed by a client's difficulties.

An alternative structure has been provided by Spinelli (1994, 2015), who suggested that it is possible to structure therapeutic exploration in regard to 'realms of encounter'. Spinelli's suggested structure focuses on the lived experience of self-in-relation and includes:

1) The 'I-focused' realm: the client's (and therapist's) experience of themselves within any given relationship. 'What do I tell myself about me in this current context?'
2) The 'You-focused' realm: the client's experience of the other (such as the therapist) being in relation to them. 'What do I tell myself about my experience of you in this current context?'
3) The 'We-focused' realm: the client's and therapist's experience of being in relation with the other. 'What do I tell myself about the experience of us in the current context?'
4) The 'They-focused' realm: the client's and therapist's experience of others in their respective worlds. 'What do I tell myself about others' experience with each other?'

Spinelli (2015) has further suggested that, due to the primary emphasis on the principle in relatedness in existential phenomenology, it is the importance given to his third and fourth realms of encounter that gives existential phenomenological therapy a distinctive contextual focus.

Both of the structures for description outlined above may provide the therapist with the means to contextualise and explore the client's presenting issues in a manner that is consistent with the principles of relatedness, uncertainty and anxiety. However, again, it is important not to mistake what is being presented here as equivalent to a framework for assessment and formulation. In most forms of CBT, an initial assessment and formulation is conducted as a necessary prelude to the intervention. To be sure, if conducted well, the assessment and formulation process is thought to be itself therapeutic in that it may challenge some of the client's unhelpful attributions regarding the nature of their difficulties as being insoluble and evidence of their personal defectiveness. However, in existential phenomenological practice, the process of description, as this unfolds in a unique and unpredictable relationship with the therapist, *is* the intervention. As Cohn (1997, p. 33.) has stated: 'The client you meet as the therapist is the client who meets you. There is no client as such. If two therapists meet the same client, it is not the same client.'

Having described both the philosophical background as well as its expression in existential psychology and a range of existential therapies, I now turn to a consideration of the range of CBT models that have been developed and the question of the extent to which these models both converge and diverge from the propositions of existential phenomenology.

Summary

- Existential phenomenological thinking is founded on the principles of relatedness, uncertainty and anxiety.
- The principle of relatedness has profound implications for a range of issues, such as the relationship between emotion and cognition, the nature of psychological problems, the process and dilemmas of change, the nature of the therapeutic relationship, and the possibilities and limitations of therapeutic dialogues.
- The clarification of these existential principles is useful when considering the potential relationship between existential phenomenology and various forms of CBT.

Existential Reflections

Spinelli (2015, pp. 111–112) has argued that: 'Acceptance requires of existential therapists the abdication of the assumption that the trained and expert professional who is the therapist can know and direct the means by which the client is to be helped'.

In a small group of peers, consider the extent to which the above claim is possible within a therapeutic engagement understood to be CBT. If you were to consider conducting a behavioural experiment in which you attempt to embody this proposal in your interactions with clients, what new possibilities might emerge? What might be lost or no longer possible while holding this view? What positive or negative consequences might follow from this stance if you were to attempt to generalise it?

Part 2

Cognitive and Behavioural Therapies

6

Beckian Cognitive Therapy

Aaron Beck has undoubtedly been one of the most influential researchers and theorists working in the field of psychological therapies in the twentieth and twenty-first centuries.

In his seminal work outlining the cognitive model of psychopathology and psychological therapy, Beck acknowledges the influence of the existential and phenomenological philosophies of Heidegger and Husserl as well as the contributions of the phenomenological studies of psychopathological experiences by Jaspers, Binswanger and Straus (Beck et al., 1979). Additionally, Clark et al. (1999) have stated that the philosophical perspective that most clearly captures the insights and concerns of cognitive therapy is existential phenomenology. As will be clarified further below, the influence of existential phenomenological ideas on the development of Beck's cognitive therapy can be seen in a variety of ways. However, cognitive therapy was never presented as being principally a working out, or direct application of, existential phenomenology and there remains a number of significant tensions and inconsistencies that have implications for the practice of therapy and may constitute important issues for dialogue and debate.

Beck's cognitive model was initially developed as a specific treatment for depression and, as has recently been clarified by Rosner (2018), was intended to be a contribution to psychoanalytic ego psychology, prior to the uneasy and never finally settled marriage between cognitivists and behaviourists. Beck's model of psychopathology and therapy has subsequently been applied successfully to a range of anxiety disorders

CBT and Existential Psychology: Philosophy, Psychology and Therapy,
First Edition. Michael Worrell.

(Clark & Beck, 2010) as well as personality disorders (Beck & Freeman, 1990), substance misuse (Beck et al., 1993) and psychosis and schizophrenia (Garety et al., 2001) in addition to being extended in scope to encompass couples (Epstein & Baucom, 2002) and families (Datillo, 2013).

Various attempts have been made to define the essence of cognitive behavioural therapy (CBT) and to clarify its distinctive principles and strategies. Salkovskis (2002, p. 3) for example, defined CBT as: 'A set of empirically grounded interventions implemented by individuals who understand themselves to be working as "scientist-practitioners"'. As noted in the introductory chapter, this definition points to potentially the most important feature of the family of cognitive behavioural therapies-their reliance upon an empirical-experimental approach that emphasises an interaction between theory building, empirical investigation and clinical practice. In an important article that attempted to define the essential features and ingredients of cognitive therapy as well as defend the model from a range of common critiques, Clark (1995, p. 155) offered the following quotation from Rush et al. (1977):

> Standard cognitive therapy is a structured, time-limited, problem-oriented psychotherapy aimed at modifying the faulty information processing activities evident in psychological disorders like depression. . . The therapist and patient collaborate to identify distorted cognitions, which are derived from maladaptive beliefs or assumptions. These cognitions and beliefs are subjected to logical analysis and empirical hypothesis testing which leads individuals to realign their thinking with reality.

This quotation is both useful and revealing in that it serves to emphasise some of the essential principles of the cognitive model as well as outlining a number of the defining procedural aspects of the therapy. In addition, the quote can be read as expressing a range of tensions and unresolved questions which will be discussed further below.

Principles of Cognitive Therapy

Beck et al. (1979) and Salkovskis (2002) have argued that it is not possible to define CBT simply in terms of its technical interventions. Rather, a wide range of interventions can be employed (and often these have been borrowed and adapted from other psychotherapies) to the extent that these interventions make sense in terms of the cognitive model and specific cognitive formulation of a particular client's difficulties. That is, it is the conceptual and theoretic aspects of the cognitive behavioural model that define it rather than simply the choice of intervention strategies or techniques. The discussion below draws principally from the work of Alford and Beck (1997) and Clark (1995) to clarify the necessary and sufficient ingredients for a therapy to be understood as an instance of cognitive therapy.

The Primacy of Cognition

As Clark (1995) has emphasised, the cognitive model views human beings as active participants in constructing their sense of reality. This can be seen to contrast with earlier behavioural and psychoanalytic models that seemed to express a view of humans as being more passive responders to either environmental or intrapsychic and unconscious forces. More broadly, the cognitive model describes both active and passive aspects of the human mind's processes of constructing meaning. Cognitive therapy uses an 'information processing' framework that proposes that all acts of perception and knowing are products of an active information processing system (at times Beck uses the term 'information processing apparatus') that selectively attends to the environment, filters and then assigns meaning to the information impinging on the person. Individuals experiencing emotional distress and disorder are seen as tending to think in rigid and distorted patterns and making cognitive errors that lead to deficits in their ability to process information accurately when encountering stressful or negative situations. This processing of information is seen as evolutionally adaptive. In this sense, distorted or biased cognitions are not regarded as being so primarily from an abstract or logical-rational perspective, but rather they are 'correct' or 'incorrect' only in relation to a specific goal or context (adaptation to an environment). Clark et al. (1999) also assert that, at best, all cognitive constructions, both those associated with distress and otherwise, are approximate representations of reality.

Beck and his collaborators have identified a range of cognitive structures, content and processes that are seen as the essentials of a 'generic cognitive model'. Often the term 'cognitive' is used in a very loose fashion. The term 'cognitions' has variously been used to refer to various forms of cognitive content such as automatic thoughts as well as 'the whole process of perceiving, assimilating, integrating, and interpreting external information' (Beck & Hollon, 1993, p. 80). Despite this variation in use and definition, a number of key concepts form an essential foundation of Beck's theory in both his original and later revised forms. These key concepts are outlined briefly below.

Schemas and Core Beliefs

In a narrower sense, schemas should not be regarded as 'cognitions' but rather as cognitive structures that when activated by external or internal events are involved in the processing of information and assignment of meaning. Schemas and core beliefs are seen as usually developing in early life, with negative core beliefs and schemas developing in response to negative events such as traumatic experiences with care givers or environmental deprivation. Schemas are regarded as a 'higher level' cognitive structures that act to determine both the content of what is thought as well as how the individual processes information (such as how attention is allocated and memories accessed). Maladaptive schemas are regarded as conferring vulnerability towards the development of psychological and emotional distress, Schemas may contain a range of related core beliefs which constitute rigid, absolute and generalised beliefs about the self, others and the world. Examples might include 'I am defective', 'others are rejecting and demanding', and 'the world is unsafe and unpredictable'. In his early work on depression, Beck described the 'negative cognitive triad' which consisted of the individual's negative thoughts and beliefs about the self, their interpretations of others and the world as well as their expectations and beliefs regarding the future. These three interrelated domains are also present in the cognitive analysis of other distressed states such as anxiety where the self is experienced as 'vulnerable' or 'unable to cope successfully', and the world or specific objects and people are experienced as threatening or dangerous and the future is experienced as foreshortened—'I am about to die of a heart attack', or agonisingly prolonged—'these awful feelings will persist forever'. The generic cognitive model proposes that schemas and their associated core beliefs are activated by stressful or significant events. Core beliefs and schemas then bias the way the individual processes information, producing emotional and behaviour responses that in turn further exacerbate and maintain the emotional distress as well as reinforcing these same beliefs and schemas in a vicious cycle.

Assumptions and 'Rules for Living'

In addition to core beliefs and schemas, the cognitive model includes the related concepts of 'assumptions' and 'rules for living'. These are understood as being conditional beliefs that function to direct the individual's behaviour. These conditional beliefs often reflect an individual's values and standards for how 'I should and should not be' as well as how others 'should and should not be'. As Dobson et al. (2018) discuss, conditional assumptions often can be seen to focus on the key issues of 'acceptance' (In order to be acceptable to others and myself I must always be polite and friendly) 'competence' (I must be seen at work as being on top of my game at all times) and 'control' (If you let others get close they will let you down, so it is best to keep yourself to yourself). Additionally, such rules for living can be seen as, at times, serving a protective function. So as long as the individual is able to keep to the dictates of 'who and how I should and should not be', the painful emotions, memories and images associated with the underlying core beliefs and schemas are kept 'off line'. Where the individual encounters situations that challenge their ability to conform with these assumptions, the underlying schemas may be activated, leading to the individual's consciousness being flooded with negative automatic thoughts and images that are consistent with the schema and core beliefs.

Negative Automatic Thoughts and Images

Negative automatic thoughts and images represent the most accessible and surface level forms of cognition. It is important not to confuse this with more rational and deliberate thought, such as that involved with completing a task, such as filling out a questionnaire. Negative automatic thoughts may well occur as the individual is engaged in such tasks, however, these are understood as often being on the peripheral edge of awareness, what in earlier psychodynamic language would have been regarded as the pre-conscious. Automatic thoughts are also understood as being more tied to the specific current context and to be less general and also more open to reality testing. At the same time, automatic thoughts are experienced by the individual as part of their phenomenal reality and so are often taken for granted as being obviously 'true'. Automatic thoughts are often seen as being closely associated with, and key drivers for, distressing emotion and as such are a key target for early work in cognitive therapy. Clients in cognitive therapy are taught how to more closely monitor and respond to automatic thoughts. Such cognitions may also be avoided and supressed by the individual due to their distressing nature as well as due to the client's beliefs regarding their meaning and their expectations of how others would respond to the open communication of such ideas.

Cognitive Specificity

A key principle of the research programme for cognitive therapy has been the 'cognitive specificity hypothesis'. Cognitive specificity refers to the idea that different patterns of emotional distress and behavioural difficulties arise from particular categories of meaning and that it is possible to separate and understand these patterns in reference to the underlying patterns of meaning. Thus, panic attacks may be differentiated from health anxiety by reference to differences in the underlying meanings and may also be more effectively treated by interventions that target these specific meanings rather than a more general meaning. In this example, they key difference between the experience and maintenance of panic attacks versus health anxiety, concerns meanings centred on the dimension of time. Panic attacks (in the cognitive model proposed by Clark, 1988) are seen as being maintained by catastrophic misinterpretations of the meaning and significance of bodily sensations as well as beliefs regarding the necessity of a range of 'safety behaviours' that for the individual are seen as means of preventing the feared catastrophe from occurring, but in fact function both to exacerbate and prolong the very same bodily sensations the individual fears, as well as preventing the disconfirmation of the catastrophic beliefs. Health anxiety by contrast is seen as being maintained by similar anxious beliefs regarding the significance of bodily sensations and the necessity of safety behaviours (such as reassurance seeking, bodily scanning and frequent medical visits) with the key difference that the catastrophic outcome is expected to occur in the near or more distant future whilst in panic it is expected and experienced as occurring imminently. A significant amount of clinical and experimental research has provided evidence for the role of beliefs as well as broader classes of cognitive process such as attention and memory in the generation and maintenance of different forms of emotional distress (Beck & Perkins, 2001).

Cognitive Mediation

Beck's cognitive therapy asserts that cognition has a central mediating role in relation to both behaviour and emotion. Additionally, where therapeutic interventions can be shown to have had a positive impact on a client's distress, whether these are specific to CBT or an alternative therapy, they will have done so via their effects on the modification of cognitive content and/or process. That is, all therapy is believed to work via the modification of cognition. Beck and Hollon (1993) and others (Clark, 1995) have been at pains to clarify that this proposition is not equivalent to proposing that cognition is directly or solely *causal* of emotion or behaviour in any simple linear fashion, as experimental evidence exists demonstrating that emotion and behaviour both have reciprocal relationships with cognition. Indeed, many so-called 'disorder specific' CBT models, based on Beck's work in depression, have been developed whose central features is a more precise rendering of the multiple feedback loops that exist between various aspects of cognition, affect, behaviour and environment (Clark & Beck, 2010).

A Focus on the Present

As Clark (1995) has asserted, a key feature of standard Beckian CBT, has been a focus on the present time frame for understanding and working with psychological distress and problems in living. This translates into an emphasis on the identification and modification of processes that are believed to be implicated in the maintenance of current psychological difficulties rather than a focus on more distal factors that may have been responsible for the origination of these difficulties. This does not mean that more distal developmental factors are completely ignored, however, as the various schemas and rules for living and conditional assumptions are said to have developed in response to experiences in early life including experiences with care givers and a range of environmental factors such as deprivation or trauma. Indeed, the model also includes the possibility of genetic and physiological vulnerabilities.

Cognitive Assessment and Cognitive Accessibility

Consistent with the behavioural tradition, standard CBT emphasises that cognition is capable of being accessed by both the therapist and client and, furthermore, that it is possible to measure cognition in a meaningful way. While cognitions are, in one sense, not directly observable by the therapist, standard CBT asserts that the client's self-report can be a reliable and valid means of accessing the cognitive content and process of most significance. At the same time, this focus on the client's consciously accessible experience of cognitive content and process, does not deny that there is a large amount of cognitive activity that may be outside of the client's awareness. Such out of awareness cognitive processing has been the subject of a great deal of experimental work from cognitively oriented psychologists (Mathews, 2006). This experimental work, however, has had little impact on the way practicing CBT therapists assess and intervene in cognition, and the standard model continues to insist that a focus on consciously accessible cognition is the royal road to change, and continues to reject any notions of 'deep' and fundamentally inaccessible cognitive structures as being the primary cause of psychological distress (Clark, 1995).

The Continuity Hypothesis

In one sense, while standard CBT focuses on distressing psychological experiences like depression, anxiety and psychosis, it does not represent a form of 'abnormal psychology', as the emotional and behavioural difficulties associated with psychopathology are understood to be based upon exaggerations of normal cognitive and behavioural responses which are themselves the product of the same processes of learning characteristics of all psychological responses. Thus, Alford and Beck (1997) propose a continuity between normal and abnormal responses and assert that schemas and meaning construction processes evolved to facilitate adaptation to the environment. In themselves, therefore, particular psychological states cannot be said to be either adaptive or maladaptive but are so only in relation to a given situation and the wider physical and social environment of the individual. In a related manner, standard Beckian CBT does not hold to the position that the definition of psychological health is the absence of all distortions of thinking or unhelpful beliefs. It is acknowledged that individuals who are not experiencing a distressed emotional response or behavioural dysregulation, may still experience a range of thought distortions.

In summary, these seven central propositions: the primacy of cognition and the centrality of information-processing, cognitive specificity, cognitive mediation, the accessibility or 'knowability' of cognition, the continuity hypothesis and a focus on the present time frame, serve to define the essential features of Beckian or standard CBT.[1] The manner in which a CBT therapist actually engages and works with clients can only be fully understood with reference to these same principles. Indeed, Clark et al. (1999, p. 74) state that these assumptions, which they further summarise as an emphasis on 'subjective consciousness, the centrality of the self and the proclivity for meaning construction' are both pivotal to the cognitive perspective and are in each case consistent with existential phenomenology. Prior to considering this claim, however this chapter will first also briefly consider Beck's more recent elaboration of the model that sheds further light on standard CBTs notions regarding the process of change in therapy. Additionally, the chapter will consider briefly the defining procedural aspects of standard CBT that may distinguish it from other approaches within the broad family of CBT approaches and other perspectives.

Revision and Expansion of the Generic Cognitive Model

Beck (1996) and more recently Beck and Haigh (2014) have proposed revisions to Beck's original generic CBT model that have added additional layers of complexity, to respond to some perceived shortcomings as well as to account for a wider range of phenomena. Beck (1996) noted that, in his original model, schemas appeared as individual cognitive structures and a more 'linear' model of schematic processing was

1 The defining principles of cognitive therapy have here been presented in terms of seven key assumptions. These have also been stated by Clark et al. (1999) in terms of 12 assumptions and Alford and Beck (1997) as 10 'axioms'.

proposed. In his revised model, Beck (1996) argues that schemas are themselves organised into more general 'modes'. Modes are understood as constituting suborganisations of the personality. Personality is here conceptualised in terms of interacting subsystems including cognitive, affective, motivational and behavioural subsystems, with each of these sub-systems in turn containing a number of schemas. Beck also differentiates between a number of different types of modes including primal modes, constructive modes and minor modes. Primal modes are seen as being concerned with meeting basic needs for security and the preservation of life. Constructive modes concern the ability to expand and to increase resources and to enrich relationships and engage in creativity. Minor modes are conceptualised as involved with the regulation of everyday activities and behaviours such as reading and recreational activity. These concepts thus introduce additional motivational elements into the model.

In applying this more complex model of modes and schemas to psychopathology, Beck suggests that each clinical disorder can be understood in terms of a specific primal mode that, when triggered, comes on-line, and draws upon its congruent systems to implement the goal of the mode (survival and self-protection for example). Once activated, a mode maintains itself via feedback loops within the overall system as well as the filtering of incoming information such that mode inconsistent information is selectively ignored while mode consistent information is retained and often amplified. Modes are not regarded as either adaptive nor non-adaptive in themselves but only with reference to the context in which the mode is activated. So, for example a threat mode being activated to a severe and exaggerated degree may be maladaptive in the context of a work meeting but adaptive in response to a natural disaster.

In the more recent update of the generic cognitive model, Beck and Haigh (2014) maintain the focus of the model upon the centrality of cognition and the role of faulty information processing and information processing errors and also introduce a number of additional concepts. Central for accounting for a range of findings within the broader field of cognitive psychology regarding the speed with which information processing and the assignment of meaning occurs, is the notion of dual information processing. Beck and Haigh (2014) suggest that the information processing system consists of two subsystems, an automatic or primary subsystem and a reflective or secondary subsystem. The automatic subsystem is characterised by the rapid processing of information particularly in regards to potential threats and gains or losses. The automatic system is rapid and may operate outside of awareness. It is also characterised by cognitive shortcuts or heuristics and is prone to making cognitive errors and demonstrating biases in processing. The reflective system, by contrast, is slower, more deliberate and under conscious control. The two systems are seen as working together and both are seen as evolutionary adaptive. Clark and Beck (2010) have applied this expanded model to a range of anxiety disorders and suggest, for example, that the experience of panic is characterised by a dissociation between the automatic and the reflective systems such that when in a panic attack, the individual has difficulty accessing memories and meanings that are more associated with the reflective system.

While processes associated with attention have always formed part of the basic cognitive model, additional emphasis is given to the role of attentional process in maintaining emotional and behavioural distress in the revised model. 'Attentional focus' refers to an automatic process of attending to both detail and context and, when this is under conscious control, can facilitate reflection and behavioural and cognitive change. When outside of awareness, rigid attentional focus may act to maintain distress. For example, in both panic states and health anxiety, the model highlights the role of exaggerated and rigid attentional focus on bodily sensations as a key maintaining factor for these difficulties.

Beck and Haigh (2014) provide additional theory regarding the process of cognitive change. This can be seen to draw upon the constructivist ideas of Piaget and others. The process of schema change is understood to occur via both 'assimilation' and 'accommodation'. Assimilation occurs when new information is incorporated into a schema without this resulting in significant change to the schema itself. Beck and Haigh (2014) suggest that a moderate degree of assimilation is necessary for adaptive functioning while too much assimilation may result from excessively 'permeable' schemas and may result in an overly loose, disorganised style of thinking.

Accommodation, on the other hand, is a process whereby new information is incorporated into a schema via a degree of alteration in the schema itself. Beck and Haigh (2014) suggest that schemas become 'denser' with repeated activation and are also reinforced by habitual repetitive behaviour that is consistent with the schema. Such schemas become highly durable and resistant to change. Should the individual encounter and sustain attention on information and experience which is schema inconsistent (such as through a behavioural exposure intervention in therapy) a degree of cognitive dissonance and accommodation may be the result. Accommodation in turn is said to lead to the 'energizing' of the schema. Energized schemas will then control subsequent information processing in either an adaptive or maladaptive fashion.

In summary, Beck's more recent elaboration of the generic cognitive model has introduced a greater degree of complexity and can be seen as a movement away from a simpler linear notion of schematic processing. The revised model is also an attempt to bring clinical cognitive therapy more in line with findings in the broader field of cognitive science. In what way however are these theoretical concepts expressed and utilised in actual practice? In the next session, basic procedural aspects of CBT are outlined. Here, it will be seen that CBT in many respects faithfully renders many of its central theoretical propositions in practice.

Defining Procedural Aspects of Standard CBT

One goal of standard CBT, is to help clients take on something of a scientific approach to the understanding and modification of their own experience and behaviour. In a process termed 'collaborative empiricism' the client is invited to work together with the therapist to learn strategies and tools to help them identify and modify specific cognitive content and processes, most centrally related to their presenting difficulties. Therapists from other, non-CBT, orientations tend at times to view this as evidence of a cold, overly rationalistic, therapist driven and controlling, process where, in a sense, the therapist acts as an editor of the clients' thoughts, seeking to fish out and eliminate instances of apparent irrationality or distortion in order to replace these with a more correct or rational understanding of reality, or even worse, helping the client to 'take their mind off the problem' (Loewenthal, 2008). In contrast, the actual experience of working within a framework of collaborative empiricism is well expressed in the following statement from Wills and Sanders (1997, p. 59):

> A spirit of collaboration gives a slow, reflective 'ping-pong' quality to sessions: the time that the therapist and client are speaking may be about equal; the therapist shares her thoughts about the client's thoughts, and asks for feedback. Whilst questions may be asked by both therapist and client, both work together, collaboratively and empirically, to find answers. The client's thoughts, feelings and behaviours are reflected on, not interpreted.

Therapy as Problem Solving and Psycho-education

CBT is primarily a problem solving therapy with explicitly psycho-educational aspects. That is, an important goal of all CBT interventions is to help the client to learn to be their own therapist. Rather than CBT interventions being applied *to* the client *by* the therapist, an openly collaborative, transparent and experimental stance is preferred. In addition to the solving of specifically identified and operationalised target problems presented at the commencement of the therapy, a major goal is to ensure relapse prevention by ensuring that the client has sufficient understanding and mastery of key CBT strategies to be able to apply these to problems experienced after the therapy has ended.

Assessment and Formulation

CBT commences with one or more assessment sessions which are designed to gather information about the client's current difficulties and their history with a particular focus on potential current maintaining factors (principally cognitive and behavioural maintaining factors such as behavioural avoidance and self-focused attention). The completed assessment will be followed by the collaborative construction of a formulation of the main presenting difficulties. This formulation, shared openly with the client and constructed with their active participation, hopefully provides a 'good enough' or adequate understanding of what had led to the development of particular difficulties and what the key factors are that can be targeted in therapy. The adequacy or otherwise of the formulation is reviewed during therapy and the formulation may be updated or revised in the light of new information.

As Kuyken et al. (2009) have stated, formulation in CBT aims at an understanding of a client's presenting difficulties through the use of CBT theory in order to arrive at explanatory inferences about both the causes and maintaining factors that will become the focus of treatment planning and intervention. Key to this approach to formulation is that it is concerned with both a causal explanation of client difficulties and the making of predictions regarding the most likely efficacious clinical intervention. In the contemporary practice of formulation, this most often results in the construction of a formulation diagram, or narrative, that will usually include the specification of: predisposing or vulnerability factors, triggering events, core beliefs, rules for living, automatic thoughts as well as a list of symptoms across mood, behaviour and physiology, in addition to the specification of a range of feedback loops or vicious cycles that act to maintain the current difficulties. The case formulation is intended to address the questions of 'why has this person developed this difficulty at this time?' and 'what will be the most efficacious intervention to achieve clinically significant change in these problems?'

Goal Setting

Consistent with its behavioural heritage, contemporary CBT practitioners place great emphasis on the precise definition and operationalisation of goals for therapy. Thus, a client attending with depressed mood and stating that they wish to 'feel happier', for instance, will be encouraged to consider and clarify what they mean by 'feeling happier' and to then set specific, observable and measurable goals related to this, such as restarting attending bridge club twice per week. Changes in psychological state are also usually closely monitored throughout the use of standardised measures such as the Beck depression inventory. The success or otherwise of the therapy is then evaluated with reference to these specific goals as well as the verbal and written feedback taken from the client regarding how they are experiencing the therapy and its impact upon their lives.

Socialisation

Also consistent with its emphasis upon psycho-education, collaboration and transparency, CBT therapists tend to actively 'socialise' clients into the structure of CBT. That is, they provide explicit information of how CBT 'works' including a description of its underlying model and a description of the types of demands CBT may make upon the client in terms of, for instance, the completion of homework tasks, giving the therapist feedback, and bringing items to include on the agenda for each session. CBT therapists may also be explicit about what the available evidence is that a CBT approach is likely to be effective or not with a particular class of difficulties, based upon published research.

Structuring

Standard CBT tends to be a short-term structured therapy, although longer term CBT may be offered for more complex presentations. A typical course of CBT lasts from 12 to 24 sessions with follow-up sessions to ensure the maintenance of gains. The CBT therapist approaches each session in a structured fashion. There is a shared plan or agenda for each session that the therapist encourages the client to take an active part in co-constructing. A key skill for successfully working from a CBT standpoint, is to successfully manage the degree of structure necessary to allow focus to remain on the most central issues and goals, but also to have enough flexibility to allow for a more open dialogue that allows room for the unexpected. The structuring of sessions also requires that the therapists ensure that they gain frequent feedback from their clients regarding their experience of each session and the progress of therapy as a whole.

Specific Cognitive and Behavioural Intervention Strategies

Standard CBT is characterised by specific cognitive and behavioural interventions that target the cognitive content and processes identified in the client's formulation. Thus, the use of thought records, behavioural experiments, imagery rescripting techniques, behavioural rehearsal and role play will be used with a view to changing specifically identified beliefs. Increasingly, specific packages of CBT have been developed into manualised forms of therapy focused on specific diagnostic groups.

Homework Tasks

CBT involves the co-construction of therapeutic tasks or homework that the client carries out between sessions. In certain respects what happens between sessions in the client's normal environment is seen as more important than what happens during sessions themselves. While earlier versions of behavioural therapy may have stressed homework tasks in terms of behavioural rehearsal or exposure to feared situations, in CBT, homework tasks are understood primarily in terms of the particular cognitive variables which they are designed to clarify or challenge (Bennett-Levy et al., 2004). Thus 'behavioural experiments' may be designed, the function of which is to allow the client to gain new experientially based information that may assist in the process of change. Frequently, this will involve some aspect of behavioural change, such as dropping avoidance behaviours and to directly approach a feared object or situation. The key interest and target is the resulting change in cognition rather than a shift in behaviour.

In summary, the procedural features of CBT can be seen as coherent expressions of its underlying philosophical and conceptual model. Some of its procedural aspects, such as the strong recommendation to start each treatment session with the setting of a clearly negotiated and specific agenda, are also reflections of its focus on identified clinical problems. Thus, agenda setting appears particularly useful when working with depressed clients who may feel that therapy will be hopeless and also experience the full 'therapeutic hour' as itself overwhelming. Agenda setting helps to counter these concerns and potential obstacles by proposing that there will be specific outcomes pursued during the session which are of great relevance to the client and that the length of the session is limited.

Some Unresolved Questions

While some critics, influenced to varying degrees by existential phenomenology, have challenged CBTs emphasis on experimental procedures and in particular the use of randomised control trials as the principle, if not sole, method of demonstrating therapeutic effectiveness, an equally crucial area of tension concerns the empirical status of cognitive mediation as well as the related issue of standard CBTs theory of change. That is, a key issue concerns 'what' is it that is responsible for the beneficial results of CBT, and, 'how' should the nature of this change be characterised?

The Status of Cognitive Mediation

As discussed, while Beck's model has undergone some significant elaboration, what has remained consistent is a focus on the hypothesis of the primacy of cognition and the related notion that positive therapeutic change is achieved via change in cognitive content and process. A number of authors, however, have raised questions about the empirical status of the hypothesised role of cognitive mediation, and the emphasis on the use of rational–logical strategies to change thoughts. Hayes (2004), for example, has argued that the empirical literature contains three significant anomalies that are as yet unresolved: Firstly, component analyses that attempt to understand the specific contributions of various aspects of complex intervention packages such as CBT (that include a range of cognitive, behavioural, emotional and environmental interventions) have not shown that the specifically cognitive interventions provide any added value to the results of therapy. Secondly, CBT has sometimes been found to be associated with rapid early improvement in symptoms measures, that appear to occur before the implementation of any specifically cognitive interventions. Thirdly, measured changes in cognitive mediators have not been demonstrated as preceding changes in symptoms.

In a review of the available literature on component analyses and cognitive mediation, Longmore and Worrell (2007) concluded that there was little evidence that cognitive interventions significantly increase the effectiveness of the therapy, and in addition, that there is little empirical support for the role of cognitive change as causal in symptomatic improvement. Beck and Haigh (2014) have argued that, since the date of that review, new empirical findings have emerged which do support the hypothesised role of cognitive mediation, at the same time; however, Hollon and Beck (2013, p. 425) have concluded: 'For many disorders, the extent to which the underlying mechanisms of change are cognitive in nature remains unclear'.

It is possible that as further research is conducted, with more sophisticated designs and statistical methodology, that more substantial evidence for cognitive mediation across different psychological problems will be obtained. At present, it remains the case that this is an open question.

Rationalism and Realism

In addition to the empirical anomalies and inconsistencies that have been identified, the logical-rationalist approach to the modification of cognition has also been criticised at a theoretical level by several researchers who have proposed multi-level cognitive architectures, that are seen as providing a more adequate description of human information processing and the nature of change. Brewin (2006) for example, drawing on contemporary cognitive science, has proposed that human cognition consists of multiple memory systems that give rise to multiple self-representations. Rather than correcting or eliminating faulty or incorrect representations, he argues, successful therapy assists the client to develop new self-representations that compete in memory for activation and control of information processing with the pre-existing (but not eliminated) representations.

Brewin (2006) is clear that his account differs substantially from that of standard CBT as its underlying philosophy is explicitly constructivist rather than rationalist. That is, it does not require the assumption that clients' thinking is in any way inherently irrational of distorted or that the new alternatives introduced in therapy are themselves inherently more rational or reasonable, or even physically possible. Rather, the alternative self-representations developed in therapy only need to be more positive, memorable and attention grabbing, in the context of cues that previously triggered negative self-representations. Brewin's proposition also appears to be supported by newer developments within standard CBT that attempt to utilise the therapeutic potential of imagery.

For example, Wheatley et al. (2007) describe the use of a form of imagery rescripting for distressing memories in depressed individuals where positive therapeutic change is achieved without any use of logical-rational challenging of automatic thoughts. Indeed, the positive mental images that are created in therapy are distinctive often by their inherently irrational and fantastical natures.

In a similar fashion, Teasdale (1997) has contrasted propositional meanings, which are semantic and declarative, with implicational meanings which are implicit, holistic, more closely tied to emotion and which reflect the 'felt sense' of experience. Teasdale argues that implicational meanings are often the most central focus for therapeutic interventions; however, these forms of meaning 'do not have a specific truth value that can be assessed' (Teasdale, 1997, p. 152). Therapy, for Teasdale, needs to focus on the clients 'actual way of being' (Teasdale, 1997, p. 150) rather that attempting to challenge and change irrational beliefs, as engaging in primarily rational–logical analysis will merely focus upon semantic, declarative meanings and will not engage emotion.

Many of the contemporary debates within CBT centre around the extent to which the therapeutic practice of CBT is best characterised as being 'rationalist' and 'realist' versus 'constructivist'. A number of CBT therapists have sought to re-establish CBT on a more thoroughly worked out constructivist philosophical basis. As will be discussed further in Chapter 8, this discussion is complicated further by the fact that there is no easy black and white differentiation of theories into constructivist or rationalist/objectivist.

Summary

- Standard 'Beckian' CBT was developed in a way that acknowledged influence from earlier existential phenomenological perspectives.
- The central focus on meaning is a clear point at which the two perspectives meet, as is the focus on the present and an emphasis on therapeutic explorations that stay with consciously assessable forms of meaning and experience.
- Beckian CBT appears to have both elements of a more rationalist objectivist stance as well as more constructivist elements. Over time, there has been a greater emphasis on the constructivist elements as well as greater complexity.

Existential Reflections

In a small peer group, consider the following issues for reflection and dialogue:

- To what extent does it make sense to you to identify and challenge, 'cognitive distortions'? In what way, if any, do you see a limitation on your ability to identify and challenge these in a meaningful way?
- Is Beckian CBT more rationalist or more constructivist? If these were placed on a continuum, where would you place your own practice? What challenges, losses and gains might arise from shifting towards either polarity?
- What is your perspective on the necessity of structure and psycho-education in conducting therapy?
- To what extent do you agree with the position that all positive therapeutic changes are achieved via a change in cognition? If the word cognition is changed to the term 'meaning' what difference does this make for you?

7

Schema Therapies—The Depths of Meaning

I am sitting in a large training room that is almost full. Present are a group of senior clinical psychologists, all trained and experienced in CBT, many of them with years of experience in working with some of the most challenging presentations of psychological distress. The reason for our meeting is an audience with the primary developer of 'Schema Therapy', Dr. Jeffrey Young. Dr. Young is attempting to induct us into the relational dimensions of schema therapy. He has asked for a volunteer, an individual to play the role of therapist while he plays that of client, a distressed client diagnosed as 'borderline'. Most of us shift uneasily in our chairs being unwilling and anxious to expose ourselves to the potentially critical gaze of our colleagues and Dr. Young. Eventually, one of our most experienced and highly regarded colleagues, a colleague with many years of experience in working with severe trauma, volunteers. In the exercise, Dr. Young, role plays a client with a high degree of emotional and behavioural realism, and begins describing a dilemma in which the client has felt ashamed by an interaction on social media and is angry, distressed and wanting to retaliate in some fashion. The therapist's task is to respond directly and simply to the client's request for help and clarification. Dr. Young states he will stop the interaction at any point at which it feels to him that the therapist is 'playing the professional role, or is not directly present and available'. In the ensuing dialogue, Dr. Young stops the interaction frequently, each time asking

CBT and Existential Psychology: Philosophy, Psychology and Therapy,
First Edition. Michael Worrell.

the therapist to 'drop the role and be present'. Intriguing to witness, the therapist eventually feels her way into the interaction, her embodied expression indicating a willingness to let go and pay attention as well as a willingness to be present and be affected.

Several theorists, still very much working within what would be regarded as a 'second wave' cognitivist framework, have substantially expanded consideration of the role of schemas in the generation of psychological distress. In so doing, these theories have also expanded the way in which the role of the therapeutic relationship and the role of emotional factors are considered within CBT. This expanded emphasis on relational and emotional factors has considerable significance for a consideration of the potential relationship between CBT and existential phenomenology.

As was seen in the discussion of the development of Beck's Cognitive Therapy, the concept of a cognitive schema was present and important from the beginning. For Beck, a Schema was defined as 'a cognitive structure for screening, coding, and evaluating the stimuli that impinge on the organism' (Beck, 1967, p. 283). Subsequent theorists have made substantial and extended use of this concept; however, debate continues regarding the exact definition of a schema and the difference between this concept and the related notion of core beliefs (Riso & McBride, 2007). There is, additionally, no widely accepted or unified Schema school within CBT but rather a range of different schema-focussed models. It should also be noted that this increased emphasis on schemas is not without controversy. James (2001), for example, has argued that trainee and inexperienced therapists should be dissuaded from a focus on working with schemas and that the apparent interest and attraction to working with deep structures should carry a 'health warning'.

In this chapter, two different schema-focussed models are considered in terms of their relationship to existential psychology. The first is 'Schema Therapy', that was developed specifically to expand the ability of CBT therapists to work with more challenging client presentations such as personality disorder and chronic depression. The second concerns Robert Leahy's Emotional Schema model which, as the title indicates, offers a considerably expanded and elaborated understanding the nature of emotional factors in therapy.

Young's Schema Therapy

Jeffrey Young and colleagues developed ST as an expansion of what he refers to as 'traditional CBT' so that it would be more effective when working with clients who present with longer term, more entrenched and complex, characterologically based difficulties. Young et al. (2003) argued that traditional CBT makes a number of assumptions about clients that are often violated when clients present with more entrenched difficulties. Firstly, traditional CBT assumes that clients will be willing and able to comply with the requirements of a standard treatment protocol. Young et al. (2003) suggests that this also assumes that clients will be motivated to reduce symptoms, build skills and to focus upon and solve current life problems. Young argues that in many cases these assumptions are not met and that clients can struggle to comply with the role demands of standard CBT. Instead, they may present as highly ambivalent about change, as being unwilling or unable to complete between session homework tasks and to be highly ambivalent or reluctant to use self-control strategies and instead seek to gain more direct emotional consolation or support from the therapist.

Secondly, according to Young et al. (2003), traditional CBT assumes that with relatively brief psychoeducation and direct instruction, clients will be able to report on specific cognitions and emotions. Many clients with longer-term complex difficulties, however, do not meet this assumption and experience great difficulty in reporting on cognitions or emotions or separating the two. Instead, such clients engage in a great deal of cognitive and emotional avoidance and they may be highly motivated to avoid staying with, and communicating, highly distressing memories, thoughts and emotions. Such avoidance has become habitual and is in itself highly resistant to change.

Thirdly, Young et al. (2003) argue that traditional CBT assumes that clients will be able to directly change distorted cognitions and unhelpful behaviour through rational-logical strategies such as empirical analysis, logical discourse, graded behavioural exposure tasks and experimentation. Young argues that, for many clients, this is not the case and that their distorted cognitions and behavioural patterns are highly resistant to change, even after months of sustained intervention. Young argue that for many such clients their distorted cognitions and unhelpful behaviours are ego-syntonic, that is, they are experienced as central to the client's identity and that 'to give them up can seem like a form of death- a death of part of the self' (2003, p. 4).

Traditional CBT, according to Young (1990), also assumes that clients are able to relatively easily engage in a collaborative therapeutic relationship, without that relationship itself being experienced by the client as challenging or difficult, and thus a barrier to focussing upon clear intervention strategies and tasks. Young argues that clients with long-term characterological difficulties often struggle to actively collaborate with the therapist and that these difficulties mirror the difficulties that they experience with others outside of the therapy. Such clients may approach the therapist in a highly dependent fashion, attempting to get emotional needs met through the relationship with the therapist or alternatively present as distant and hostile. Young argues that for such client's interpersonal difficulties and conflicts are the core problem.

Finally, Young (1990) suggests that traditional CBT assumes that clients will present with problems that are readily operationalised in terms of discrete and often measurable goals and targets for intervention. In many cases, according to Young, this assumption is not met, as such clients present with difficulties that are often vague, chronic, pervasive and difficult to meaningfully translate into discrete goals for intervention. Instead, these clients present with difficulties across many domains of their life and may experience their life as a whole as empty, or as having 'failed'.

In order to construct a form of cognitive behavioural therapy more adequate to such challenging presentations, Young drew upon theoretical and technical strategies from a wide range of sources such as that Schema Therapy should be considered a form of integrative therapy. Young (1990, Young et al., 2003) integrated insights and ideas from Attachment Theory (Ainsworth & Bowlby, 1991), elements from the Object Relations Theories of Winnicott and others, in addition to the experiential and emotion focussed interventions from gestalt therapy, such as imagery and role play strategies. Young has described how the emphasis on the use of experiential interventions stemmed from his own experience of engaging with such strategies. He reported that 'in about ten sessions of Gestalt Therapy, I learned more about myself than I had learned in a year with the cognitive therapist' (Edwards & Arntz, 2015). At the same time, Beck's cognitive therapy remains a significant and indeed primary source and inspiration for Schema therapy. Schema therapy maintains the use of structure, psychoeducation, the use of homework strategies as well as central conceptual ideas regarding the role of distorted cognition and information processing.

Both Young's Schema Therapy and Beck's model rely upon notions of schemas and Modes. There are similarities as well as differences in the way these terms are used in each model. For Young, schemas, and especially what he refers to as 'early maladaptive schemas' are seen as being at the core of personality difficulties and having had their origin in early 'toxic' childhood experiences' Young et al. (2003) defines an early maladaptive schema as a:

- Broad pervasive theme or pattern.
- Consisting of memories, emotions, cognitions and bodily sensations regarding self and self-other relations.
- Developed during childhood and adolescence.
- Elaborated throughout the life course.
- Problematic and dysfunctional for the individual to a significant degree.

Of some significance is that within Young's model, a client's behaviour is not itself regarded as part of a schema, rather behavioural responses, often maladaptive compensatory or coping behaviours, are seen as being 'driven' by the activated schema. Schemas are regarded as being the core of an individual's sense of self, they are seen as self-perpetuating and highly resistant to change. They are also seen as often operating outside of the client's awareness and triggered by events that are in some fashion processed as being schema relevant. Once triggered, such schemas are associated with high degrees of emotional and behavioural dysregulation.

Universal Human Needs

Young et al. (2003) have also suggested that the origin of schemas lies in the frustration of a number of core emotional needs in childhood. Such needs are seen by Young as universal aspects of human experience and development. These needs include:

1) Secure relationship attachments that provide safety, stability, nurturance and acceptance.
2) Autonomy and sense of competence and individual identity.

3) Freedom to express valid needs and emotions.
4) Spontaneity and play.
5) Realistic limits and self-control.

Young and his collaborators have also suggested that the individual's innate temperament may interact with the childhood environment to produce schemas. Moreover, they have integrated a neurobiological perspective drawing upon the work of LeDoux (1996) on the biology of traumatic memories. Young et al. (2003) suggest that, based upon LeDoux's (1996) work on the role of brain physiology, it can be hypothesised that when an individual encounters a current environment that is reminiscent of a childhood trauma, the emotions and bodily sensations associated with the event are activated by the amygdala unconsciously, or, where the individual is conscious of these states, the emotions and body sensations are activated more rapidly than cognition. They suggest that the activation of emotions and body sensations is automatic and likely to be a permanent feature of the individual's life, however the degree of activation can be lessened (but not eliminated) to the extent that a process of 'schema healing' is achieved. They further suggest that the fact that emotional and cognitive aspects of traumatic experiences are stored and located in different brain systems, may explain why schemas are resistant to change via more rational-logical cognitive methods and why more directly relational and emotion-based interventions are necessary for such clients.

Young (1990) originally identified 18 specific early maladaptive schemas which were grouped under five domains that in turn reflected the five hypothesised core emotional needs. While a full listing of these schemas is beyond the scope and purpose of this chapter, the five domains can be specified as: Disconnection and rejection, impaired autonomy and performance, impaired limits, other directedness (including subjugation and self-sacrifice) and over vigilance and inhibition. Young et al. (2003) regard 'schema healing' as the ultimate goal of therapy. The process of schema healing however is seen as long and often arduous. They argue that individual will often resist the process of schema change as:

> Patients resist giving up schemas because the schemas are central to their sense of identity. It is disruptive to give up a schema. The whole world tilts. In this light, resistance to therapy is a form of

> self-preservation, an attempt to hold onto a sense of control and inner coherence. To give up a schema is to relinquish knowledge of who one is and what the world is like (2003, p. 32).

Schema Modes

Central to the most recent elaborations of schema therapy is the notion of schema modes. This concept has some parallel and overlap to Beck's notions of modes as well as some differences. Young et al. (2003) define schema modes as moment to moment emotional states and coping responses. As such, in Young's model modes can be seen as referring to psychological *states* while in Becks model modes more closely resemble psychological *traits*. More precisely, a mode has been defined as

> those schemas or schema operations—adaptive or maladaptive—that are currently active for an individual . . . An individual may shift from one dysfunctional schema mode into another; as that shift occurs different schemas or coping responses, previously dormant, become active (Young et al., 2003, p. 40).

The process of mode shifting has also been referred to as 'mode flipping' and may occur highly rapidly in response to changing contextual factors. In therapy it may appear as if an entirely different 'self' has appeared. Modes are seen as parts of the self that have not been integrated into a stable sense of identity. Edwards and Arntz (2015) acknowledge the degree to which the concept of modes and mode flipping have parallels in a range of different psychotherapeutic perspectives including transactional analysis and gestalt therapy. Young et al. (2003) proposed 10 schema modes grouped together into four categories:

1) Child modes—seen to be universal and innate and including 'vulnerable child' and 'angry child' modes.
2) Maladaptive coping modes—including 'compliant surrender' and 'detached protector' modes.
3) Maladaptive parent modes—including 'punitive parent' and 'demanding critical parent'.
4) Healthy adult modes—understood as the functional part of the self and where a goal of schema therapy is seen as assisting the client to achieve and maintain this psychological state.

As the Schema model has been extended to encompass a wider range of severe psychological disorders, a greater number of modes have been proposed. For example, Lobbestael et al. (2007) have described 21 specific modes. Young et al. (2003) also proposed that the concept of schema modes can be used to understand both borderline personality disorders as well as more severe forms of dissociative identity disorder where the key differentiating factor is the number of modes involved and the degree of dissociation between modes.

Limited Reparenting and Empathic Confrontation

Schema therapy uses a wide variety of assessment and intervention strategies. Consistent with standard CBT, it retains the use of such features as collaborative formulation, psychoeducation, session structure and the use of homework tasks. Often the degree of session structure is much looser and more flexible, reflecting the operation of schemas and schema modes during and between the sessions. Additionally, rational–logical strategies to correct thought distortions may also be used; however, these are not regarded as primary. Rather, the schema therapist uses a range of imagery based and experiential strategies such as role play and chair work, borrowed from other therapeutic orientations. Many of these are difficult to easily categorise as belonging within a more logical–rationalist model of correcting information processing. Perhaps the most distinct feature of Schema therapy, however, is the requirements that it makes of the therapist to provide a particular form of relational experience for the client. The therapeutic relationship in schema therapy is regarded as a key driver of change itself. More specifically, schema therapy asks of therapists to provide both 'empathic confrontation' and 'limited reparenting', as well as retaining many of the features of the more collaborative stance of traditional CBT.

Empathic confrontation describes a therapeutic stance that incorporates both an understanding and validation of the client's experience, as this is being disclosed in the therapy, as well as a robust and clear highlighting of a need for change. Young et al. (2003) emphasise that empathic confrontation is not a technique but rather an authentic relational stance that requires a 'true emotional bond'. The therapist needs to genuinely care for the client in order for this stance to be effective. This stance is primarily employed to encourage the client to work actively against their schemas and to break behavioural patterns and establish new modes and schema inconsistent patterns. Empathic confrontation is described as always starting with a careful and accurate description and acknowledgement of the client's phenomenal reality or truth, followed by attempts at reality testing and the correction of cognitive distortions or schema driven behaviours. Crucially, the schema therapist is reliant upon forming an alliance with the client against the schemas, so that the confrontation is with the schemas rather than being experienced as against the client.

Limited reparenting is perhaps the most challenging and novel aspect of schema therapy. This refers to the therapist intentionally using the therapeutic relationship to partly meet the client's core childhood emotional needs. Like empathic confrontation, limited reparenting is not itself regarded as a specific technique but rather is viewed as a central aspect of the desired therapeutic stance. Young et al. (2003) emphasise that this limited meeting of core emotional needs also happens within the normal ethical boundaries of a professional therapeutic relationship and what is on offer approximates missed emotional experiences. The schema therapist endeavours to work as a form of 'good parent' who is able, within limits, to meet the client's basic emotional needs as well as model what an effective adult mode functioning looks like. The form that limited reparenting takes is seen to be modulated and planned according to the assessment of the client's modes, schemas and core needs. So, for example, a client for whom 'demanding standards' is a key schema, the therapist will emphasise ways of relating to the client that encourage spontaneity and appreciation for the clients being, separate from any emphasis on performance, achievement or failure. Additionally, they may attempt to relate to the client in a way that expresses an appreciation of the experience of the relationship itself over any emphasis on 'getting things done'. By contrast, when the therapist encounters a client in 'angry child mode' the therapist may allow and validate a degree of emotional expression of frustration whilst also encouraging more adaptive ways of getting needs met in relationships outside the therapy. Schema therapists will also work to set clear limits on the 'detached protector' mode so that greater access is possible to the 'vulnerable child mode'.

Schema therapy can be seen to make a range of relational and emotional demands on therapists that go well beyond that described as consistent with standard CBT. This includes a great deal of flexibility in responding to moment-to-moment changes in a client's modes during a session as well as a greater willingness to emotionally invest in the relationship with the client. As Rafaeli et al. (2011, p. 115) state:

> Schema therapists allow themselves to be real people, not detached clinicians, in the therapy relationship. As a consequence, delivering limited reparenting successfully is often quite challenging, as the degree of both skill and empathy required is high. To meet this challenge therapists must be well acquainted with their own schemas and coping styles.

Leahy's Emotional Schema Therapy

A recurring issue throughout the various forms of cognitive behavioural therapy has been the nature of the relationship between thought and emotion. In the earlier versions of Beck's cognitive therapy, emotion is most often presented as being an outcome of cognitive content and process. As this model has progressed in application to a wider range of psychological difficulties, various feedback loops between cognition and emotion were identified which opened up the possibility for examining the ways in which emotion, once activated, in turn influenced cognition. In Beck's latest formulations, emotion appears as itself constituting an important 'system' having a range of reciprocal interactions with cognition but with cognition retaining its primacy. The work of Robert Leahy (2015) on developing a theory of Emotion Schemas has further extended this consideration of the complex relationship between cognition and emotion. This model is of particular relevance to the current discussion, as Leahy makes substantial use of insights from existential phenomenology and reaches a number of conclusions that can be read as consistent with existential phenomenology. Leahy's work (2001, 2015) represents a highly creative extension of standard CBT, that substantially moves towards a more constructivist perspective.

Leahy's model of emotion schemas remains essentially a cognitive model, although, as noted above, it moves towards the constructivist end of the rationalist–constructivist continuum. The model also bears some resemblance to a range of other third wave CBT models such as Acceptance and Commitment Therapy and Dialectical Behaviour

Therapy (see Chapter 9). Additionally, the model has some resonance with 'Metacognitive therapy' (Wells, 2000) that highlights the role of individuals' meta-cognitions, or their 'beliefs about beliefs' and beliefs about the way the mind does, or should or should not work, and the interaction between these metacognitions and unhelpful efforts of cognitive control and avoidance. Leahy's model constitutes a metacognitive theory of emotion that proposes that people respond to their emotions as objects of perception. Thus, individuals' beliefs about the meaning and significance of emotion, as well as their use of a range of adaptive and non-adaptive strategies of emotional regulation, are seen as key in understanding and treating a wide range of psychological difficulties.

Emotional schema therapy is focussed on individuals' beliefs about 'good' versus 'bad' emotions, shame about emotional experience, beliefs about the duration and controllability of emotions, tolerance for mixed and unclear emotional experience, beliefs about the uniqueness and difference of one's own versus others' emotions and beliefs about the need to express or avoid expressing the experience of emotion. In addition, the model focuses upon identifying and altering a range of problematic emotional regulation strategies that clients may use such as rumination and worry, avoidance, suppression, substance use, etc. Such emotion schemas and emotional regulation strategies are viewed as being relevant across a wide range of forms of psychopathology and as such the model is essentially transdiagnostic rather than specific to a particular type of psychological difficulty such as personality disorders. Additionally, the model is presented as an enhancement and extension of current CBT perspectives and as particularly relevant when working with more complex presentations, or where clients are found to be more highly avoidant and difficult to engage with more directive strategies such a behavioural exposure.

Leahy (2015) argues that western culture and philosophy can be seen to have maintained a polarised view of the primacy of the rational versus the primacy of emotion. Leahy traces the emphasis on rationality to the philosophy of Plato who in *The Republic* used the metaphor of a charioteer who attempts to control two horses—one that is amenable to direction and the other which charges off, out of control. Emotion was viewed by Plato as equivalent to the out of control horse, and seen as an impediment to the pursuit of virtue. This emphasis on the superiority of rationality was also maintained by Stoical philosophy, a direct source of inspiration for the developers of cognitive behavioural therapy. By contrast, Leahy (2015) also identifies a range of philosophies and movements within western philosophy and culture that he views as maintaining the 'primacy of emotion'. These include the Greek tragedies of Euripides, the Romantic movement and also existential philosophy. These philosophies and movements, according to Leahy, can be seen to embody a more 'tragic' view of life that recognises that suffering is inevitable and that a well-lived life includes the willingness to experience both intense positive and negative emotional states. Leahy's Emotional schema model can be read as an attempt to rebalance CBT so as to include a greater place for the primacy of emotion and a more tragic world view without losing sight of its foundation in rationality and an essentially optimistic view of the possibilities of individuals living flourishing, meaningful lives. Central to this is Leahy's assertion that therapy is not in essence about 'feeling Good' or feeling happy:

> The emotional schema model suggests that the goal is not 'feeling good', but the capacity for feeling everything. . . This model argues for the inclusion of emotions- even 'disparaged' emotions such as anger, resentment, jealousy, and envy- and for the acceptance of those emotions as part of the complexity of human nature (2015, p. 8).

In addition to expanding the CBT perspective on emotion, by arguing that individuals often respond to their experience of emotion as an object of perception according to deeply held and often rigid beliefs about the significance, appropriateness and meaning of emotions, Leahy's model extends the CBT understanding of what emotion *is*. Leahy (2015) has, like Young, constructed a model of schemas that is in important respects integrative. Of particular importance to the Emotional schema model are insights and concepts drawn from Emotion Focussed Therapy (Greenberg & Paivio, 1997), which is itself an integrative model drawing upon attachment theory, gestalt therapy, person-centred therapy and systemic therapy. The key insight taken from emotion focussed therapy is that emotion can itself be seen to 'contain' meaning. Furthermore, Leahy (2015) can be seen to draw upon the existential phenomenological insight regarding the intentionality of emotion. That is, emotion cannot be understood without understanding its context and that context is always one in which emotion is intentional and directed towards a world: 'There is an "aboutness" to emotion- a person is sad about being alone, angry about being insulted. . .Emotions have targets' (2015, p. 30).

The Solution Is the Problem

In a fashion strikingly reminiscent of existential therapists such as May (1983) and Yalom (1980), Leahy (2015) argues that often the 'problems' that clients bring to therapy such as difficulties with a phobia or obsessive and compulsive rituals or depression, can be better regarded as attempted 'solutions' to the 'given' aspects of existence. Drawing directly on the philosophies of Heidegger and Sartre, Leahy suggests that:

> individuals struggle with their freedom of choice, often having difficulty with the 'given' that is arbitrarily part of their everyday lives, while recognising that the choices people face often involve dilemmas or tradeoffs that are emotionally difficult. Choice, freedom, regret, and even dread, are viewed as essential components of life in this model, and these 'realities' cannot simply be eliminated by cost-benefit analysis, rationalization, or pragmatism (2015, p. 10).

Applying the emotional schema model to the anxiety disorders, Leahy (2007) argues that each different form of anxiety disorder can be seen as an attempted solution to the problem of unavoidable anxiety. So, for example, in the case of social anxiety, individuals may be hypervigilant for indications of their own bodily arousal and signs of negative evaluation from others, and rely on strategies of escape and avoidance as well as safety behaviours such as over-preparing for conversations and avoiding eye contact. Leahy suggests that 'Each of these "solutions" *constitutes* social anxiety- thereby making the solution the problem' (2007, p. 38).

Emotional schema therapy maintains the use of a great many of the interventions that characterise traditional CBT including Socratic dialogue, collaboration, psychoeducation and behavioural experiments. The therapist is explicit that the aim of therapy may not be to 'get rid' of unpleasant or unwanted emotion but rather to explore the possibility that the client's theories and strategies for avoiding and controlling emotional experience are more constitutive of the problem than the emotion itself. Leahy (2015) outlines seven primary themes which characterise the model and its application:

1) Painful emotions are universal—the goal of therapy is not to eliminate these and to replace them with happiness. The goal of therapy is to assist the client to achieve 'a more complete life- one in which painful emotions have their place, are recognized as part of being human, and as emotions that may reflect the values that are important to the individual' (Leahy, 2015, p. 23).
2) Emotions evolved to alert us to the presence of danger and to indicate what is important to the individual—they are adaptive and functional.
3) Implicit schemas about emotion determine the impact of an emotion on the escalation and maintenance of itself and other emotions.
4) Problematic schemas, including catastrophising about the significance of an emotion, believing emotions do not make sense, viewing emotions as out of control and permanent rather than temporary, viewing emotion as shameful and unique to the self and being best kept to the self rather than expressed.
5) Emotional control strategies such as suppression and avoidance may act to confirm and maintain the negative emotional schemas.
6) Expression and validation of emotion in therapy and life may help to normalise, universalise, differentiate emotions and challenge the veracity of negative emotional schemas.
7) Learning to stay with and acknowledge painful emotion can be important in building resilience and supporting a client towards greater self-efficacy and a more complete meaning in life.

Working with the Therapeutic Relationship and Therapist Schemas

Both in his work on the emotional schema model as well as theoretical work on resistance to change in therapy (Leahy, 2001), Leahy has emphasised the importance of the therapeutic relationship as well as therapists having some awareness of, and ability to work with, their own schema-based vulnerabilities. Leahy (2001) has suggested that the psychodynamic notions of transference–countertransference are equally of relevance to CBT therapists and has suggested that these phenomena are best conceptualised in terms of therapist–client schema matching and mis-matching. Leahy challenges CBT therapists to consider how their own emotional schemas may become activated in therapy with clients and be expressed in terms of thoughts such as 'my patient's negative feelings just go on and on'. Additionally, he argues that therapists with negative schemas about emotion may view therapy as something to be applied in a mechanistic fashion, in which the goal is to rid the client of symptoms. As a result, he suggests, such therapy will appear and be experienced as robotic, superficial and overly technique focussed and characterised by an over concern with session agendas and specific treatment protocols. Specific problems and obstacles in therapy, traceable to the therapist's beliefs and difficulties may include:

- A failure to elicit and stay with client emotion,
- over-emphasis on rationality and problem solving,
- labelling clients as 'irrational',
- leaving too little space for emotional expression and exploration,
- superficiality and failing to adequately explore a variety of emotions present in an experience,
- suggesting explicitly or implicitly that the goal of therapy is to feel better,
- implying that painful feelings are problematic and
- implying that there is a solution to every problem.

Leahy suggests that to work more effectively with clients and to assist them in achieving a more meaningful life, that includes allowing the presence of negative emotion, it is essential that the therapist is aware of and challenges their own beliefs regarding this domain of experience. It could also be argued that his contributions to CBT, presented as extension and refinements of the CBT perspective on emotions, also identify and challenge a range of more rationally focussed assumptions that are key features of the traditional model and not just beliefs that individual therapists bring with them to the model.

Unresolved Questions

Schema therapies have substantially enhanced and extended the CBT perspective. As noted earlier, however, there is yet to emerge an agreed upon and widely adopted schema school. Additionally, while advocates of both Schema Therapy and Emotional Schema Therapy have argued that these models can be readily combined with more traditional forms of CBT, this notion remains controversial with other authors concerned that the apparent attraction to deep cognitive structures and 'deep change' may distract attention away from the more empirically validated strategies that target behavioural maintenance processes and more surface level cognitive content and process, associated with defined psychopathological categories. While evidence is emerging for the effectiveness of Young's Schema Therapy for personality disorders (Bamelis et al., 2015) it remains the case that evidence is yet to emerge supportive of the specific and unique effectiveness of explicitly schema-focussed intervention strategies.

Summary

- A variety of schema focussed models have been advanced that significantly enhance and expand the traditional CBT model.
- These models provide a more complex view of the nature of emotion and the challenges of achieving significant psychological change.
- The therapeutic relationship is seen as central in these models as a vehicle for change and as often implicating the therapist in a personally direct and real way.
- Schema focussed models suggest that therapists, in order to work effectively, need to develop and maintain an awareness of their own schema-based vulnerabilities.

Existential Reflections

Considering your currently preferred model, reflect on the following:

- In what way does the schema-focussed therapy notion of 'limited reparenting' fit with or challenge your current view of the therapeutic relationship
- In what ways does Leahy's use of existential ideas to promote a more 'tragic view of life' challenge or fit with your sense of the possibilities and limitations of therapy?
- In what ways does an emphasis on the 'trade-offs' and downsides of change as emphasised in the models reviewed here, challenge or affirm your theory of change?
- In what ways does the schema therapy perspective on the significance of emotion support or challenge your more typical stance towards this question?

8

Constructivist, Narrative and Postmodern CBT

There are no facts, only interpretation.

—Friedrich Nietzsche.

While CBT is often characterised by its concern to identify key or even 'hot cognitions', nevertheless it has not escaped attention that clients usually present in therapy with a range of stories or narratives regarding their lives, and how the problems that bring them to therapy are situated in these narratives. The notion of 'narrative', while addressed in most forms of psychotherapy, is one that has been a particular focus of a range of constructivist and the so-called postmodern approaches. This chapter reviews a range of narrative and 'post rationalist' forms of CBT, that have developed on the basis of views and arguments that are related to those found in existential phenomenology.

Constructivism has had a wide influence within the fields of psychology and psychotherapy. This influence spreads well beyond that of the cognitive and behavioural psychotherapies and there are constructivist forms of psychoanalytic (Hoffman, 1998) and systemic therapy (Anderson & Goolishan, 1992) in addition to those associated in some fashion with CBT. McLeod (2004) states that constructivism and social constructionism are themselves integrations of diverse strands of thought including the social phenomenology of Schutz (1972), the hermeneutic philosophy of Gadamer (2004) and the post-structuralism of Bakhtin (1973) and Foucault (1980). There is no single identifiable school of constructivism. Adding to the complexity, constructivism and

CBT and Existential Psychology: Philosophy, Psychology and Therapy,
First Edition. Michael Worrell.

constructionism are often conflated with 'postmodernism' which is itself highly diverse (Stam, 2001).

Mahoney (1991) defines constructivism as a family of theories that share the following assertions:

1) That human knowledge and experience entail the (pro)active participation of the individual.
2) That there is a structural and functional primacy of abstract (tacit) over explicit and concrete processes in experience.
3) That learning, knowing and memory as phenomena reflect the ongoing attempts of body and brain to organise and endlessly re-organise, their own patterns of action and experience.

Mahoney (2003) states that constructivism has played an increasing role in contemporary dialogues in areas as diverse as neuroscience, ethics, government, politics and spirituality. Proponents of constructivism argue that the approach has a long and diverse history within western and non-western culture. Mahoney (1991, 2003) for example, traces core themes of constructivism to the ancient Taoist philosophy of Lao Tzu (sixth century BC) and the Greek pre-Socratic philosopher Heraclitus (540–475 BC). Both Lao Tzu and Heraclitus described the virtue of living with the 'flow' of nature as well as the notion that opposites coexist and require one another for meaning to emerge. Additional key philosophical sources for constructivism, according to Mahoney (1991, 2003), include Giambattista Vico (1668–1744), Immanuel Kant (1724–1804), Arthur Schopenhauer (1788–1860) and Hans Vaihinger (1852–1933).

Vico is seen by Mahoney (2003) as of particular significance, in that he challenged what he saw as the flaws in the philosophy of Descartes that led to the separation of mind and body and the quest for absolute certainty via a disembodied reason. Vico, by contrast, stressed that human understanding is a process of construction that takes place in social and historical contexts. Additionally, he asserted that thinking expresses metaphors of the body and that fantasy, imagination mythology and etymology are important resources for self-understanding (Mahoney, 2003).

The Personal Construct psychology of George Kelly (1955) is generally regarded as foundational for the development of a constructivist perspective in psychology and psychotherapy. Kelly's theory of 'personal constructs' was highly influential across diverse forms of psychotherapy including Beck's cognitive therapy as well as humanistic forms of psychotherapy (Hoffman, 2009). In Kelly's model, constructs are dichotomous or bi-polar in nature as well as being dynamic. Beck and Haigh's (2014) model exhibits strong resonance with Kelly's discussion of constructs exhibiting features of being relatively permeable as well as degrees of tightness and fluidity or looseness. Kelly described people as acting like 'personal scientists' and being active in constructing theories of self and world. Kelly's approach to psychotherapy emphasised the role of the therapist in collaborating with the client to challenge the client's way of constructing their understanding of self, others and the world, and possibilities for action in the world. Kelly emphasised the highly idiosyncratic nature of the constructing process. For example, where a client has constructed themselves as 'depressed' the bi-polar opposite of this construct may not be 'happy' but instead 'irresponsible' or 'amoral'. The therapist's role is to understand both sides of this construct in order to more creatively and sensitively explore possible ways of developing new constructs and new possibilities for action. Kelly (1973) developed 'fixed role' therapy, which as an intervention bears striking resemblance to that of behavioural experiments in CBT. In a fixed role intervention, the client is assisted to create a character or role that embodies constructs, beliefs and ways of behaving that are in clear contrast to their usual way of construing self and other. The client is then invited to try out this new role in action to experience and consider how other and the world respond to this new role.

Central to all perspectives within the broad field of constructivist therapies is the issue of 'epistemology'—that is, the question of *how* we come to know what we know and how me make and justify claims to truth. Constructivists generally start from the position that rather than there being an 'outside' objective reality that is accessible to description and knowledge, people play an integral and active role in creating (or co-creating) 'constructions' of reality. Science and scientific practice, from within these perspectives, is often viewed as being less about a unique discovery of objectively true laws of nature, and more about theory building and meaning creation (Leitner & Epting, 2001).

Forms of Constructivism and Constructionism

Mahoney (1991) notes that in the social sciences the term 'constructivism' has been used to refer to both those perspectives that highlight the active constructing and interpreting processes of an organism/individual within a context, as well as those perspectives that emphasise the extent to which social contexts, and social practices construct and constrain the experiences of individuals and groups. Leitner and Epting (2001) distinguish between three broad groupings of constructivist theories that differ in terms of the central question of the relationship between human knowing and construing and the status of an external objective world. The first group of 'radical construction*ists*' (which can be distinguished from other Constructi*vist* approaches) appear clearly aligned with what would be regarded as a 'postmodern' worldview. An example of this form of theory is the language-based perspective of Efran et al. (1990) that draws in particular on the philosophy of 'structure determinism' of the biologists Maturana and Varela (1987). Maturana and Varela's (1987) analysis of living organisms refers to the notion of 'auto-poesis'. This entails the proposition that all living systems are self-creating, self-organising entities. Reality, which cannot be objectively known and described, is fundamentally 'a purposeless drift' (Efran et al., 1990, p. 23).

More broadly, these language focused theories are based upon the philosophical writings of a number of 'post-existentialist' and post-structuralist philosophers such as Derrida, Foucault, Deleuze and Lyotard (Van Zyl, 2018). In these models, the status of an external objective reality appears to very significantly recede and there is no valid way in which we can come to know the nature of reality outside of the meanings that we have constructed. At times, the world as such does not appear to exist in any fashion outside of the effects of the construction of meaning via language. Language appears to take on an independent constructional role with reality and individual experience being determined by the operation of language. Language, however, also loses any role as the conveyor of truth, rather, there are multiple 'languaged' realities. In these more radical versions of constructivism, meaning appears to become disembodied and its direct link to affective aspects appears to be lost. Psychology becomes reduced or dissolved into critical social theory. Polkinghorne (2004, p. 62) has argued that the postmodern versions of social constructivist theory have contended that people are not the centres or originators of meaning or action but are understood instead as 'performers playing roles written for them in the social discourse'. Defenders of various constructionist and postmodern positions, however, have argued that critics have seriously misread their positions and that they do not espouse philosophies that argue for the non-existence of any external reality outside of language (Gergen, 2001).

Efran et al. (1990) have also disputed that the focus on language entails a neglect of emotion, embodiment and action and argue instead that what they refer to as language incorporates embodied and emotional action in the world.

O'Donohue (2013), discusses the relationship and impact of postmodern philosophy on theories of science. He suggests that while it is difficulty to precisely define postmodernism, a key feature of these philosophies is a rejection of modern enlightenment views of objective scientific knowledge claims to describe features of the real world. Reality as such is not mirrored in the human mind as cognitive representations or scientific theories, but rather is constructed by the human mind in a manner that is highly influenced by various ideologies of culture, tradition, gender and race. Scientific knowledge claims, in these views, are often seen as being aspects of efforts at social and political control. Scientific practice is seen as an oppressive practice that 'privileges' specific forms of knowledge and knowing at the expense of other ways of 'local knowing'. Several theorists have, for example, criticised the notions of evidence-based practice in psychological therapies from just such a viewpoint (Van Zyl, 2018). These philosophies, and the psychologies inspired by them, regard the 'deconstruction' of texts and 'psy-practices' as a key task, as this can expose hidden ideologies, contradictions and political motivations. A key concern of postmodern philosophies such as Jacques Lyotard, has been the identification and challenge of a range of 'meta-narratives' such as 'progress' and 'history'. The use of 'reason' is itself seen as an aspect of a failed meta-narrative. The claims of existential phenomenology itself have also been rejected on the basis of being representative of just such a meta-narrative (Hoffman, 2009).

As Frie (2013) has argued, the dilemma facing theorists who wish to promote a postmodern version of psychotherapeutic practice, is that these perspectives so often appear to collapse individual lived experience into a linguistic, or as is discussed further below, a social-cultural context. This deletion of the individual agent has been argued to constitute an extreme form of relativism and nihilism. Without some foundation upon an experiencing, acting agent in the world, the therapeutic process would seem to lose any validity and meaning (Frie, 2013).

The second group of constructivists identified by Leitner and Epting (2001) are referred to as 'social constructivists'. Rather than emphasising the primary role of language itself, these theorists emphasise instead the meanings that a particular culture provides and disallows for its members. A 'social construct' in these theories refers to an artefact, a human made concept or practice, arising from a particular social group (O'Donohue, 2013). These theories would also be seen as belonging and expressing a postmodern worldview. An individual person, for the social constructionists, comes to be defined and constrained by the meanings available in the culture. Theorists such as Gergen (1991) have describe the way in which the self becomes 'saturated' with a wide range of different social constructions. This analysis suggests that the self in postmodern culture has lost coherence and unity and that individuals have multiple selves that interreact with the multiple and saturated selves of others. In a manner similar to the radical constructionists, social constructivists at times appear to reduce psychology to sociology and there is a loss of the connection between social constructions, provided now by an all pervasive and determining cultural practices that operate largely outside of the awareness of persons, and embodied being and affectivity.

Leitner and Epting (2001) also propose the existence of a middle ground between radical and social constructivists that they term 'critical constructivism'. In this position, a real world is assumed to exist independent of the meaning construction process. Meaning is constructed or rather co-constructed in the interaction between the individual and the world and others. The attempt of the critical constructionists is to avoid reifying either the individual person of the social/cultural realm but to focus on the dialogue between the two as the ground for the creation of meaning. CBT approaches that have been informed by constructivism would appear to be situated most appropriately within this group. As will be discussed further below, some constructivist theorists such as Guidano (1991) and Mahoney (1991) do make room for and outline various forms of 'selfhood processes' while the self seems to disappear completely in the radical constructionist accounts. It should be noted however, that the categorisation and differentiation of various forms of constructivism itself remains contested. In the sections that follow this chapter discusses the contributions of several CBT theorists who have sought to reconstitute CBT along constructivist lines. Key to this has been the problematic contrast between what is understood as rationalist and post-rationalist models of CBT.

Safran's Integrative, Interpersonal, Emotion-focussed Perspective

The work of Jeremy Safran and colleagues (Safran & Muran, 1990; Safran & Segal, 1996) has consistently attempted to broaden the scope of CBT. This work has included, but is not restricted to, issues and perspectives that fall within a postmodern worldview. Safran and Messer (1998) argued for a pluralistic/postmodern approach to psychotherapy integration with an emphasis on clarifying points of similarity and difference through dialogue. Safran's work to open up CBT to a wider variety of perspectives has focussed principally on the following domains:

- The introduction of a more interpersonally focussed understanding of cognition and emotion.
- Understanding the therapeutic relationship as a key driver of change and as a setting in which the client's difficulties with living may be effectively disclosed and challenged.
- Incorporating a greater focus on emotion such that the primacy of emotion is asserted alongside the primacy of cognition.

Safran's early work was principally concerned with integrating a more interpersonal perspective into CBT drawing upon the work of Harry Stack Sullivan (1953). This work was intended as a refinement of CBT rather than the creation of a new model. Safran (1990) argued for an elaboration of the concept of schema to include the idea of 'possible selves' which refers to an individual's ideas of what they could become, what they would like to become, and what they may be afraid of becoming.

Additionally, Safran has argued for what is referred to as an 'ecological approach' to information processing as an alternative to the dominant metaphor of mind-as-computer. Safran (1990) argues that the dominant information processing paradigm fails to account for the fundamental difference between the way in which computers process information and the way in which persons acquire knowledge of themselves and the world. Human information processing appears to occur much more in the form of action and interaction within a social environment. Accordingly, it is not possible to understand cognition independent of emotion and action in a world. Cognition, emotion and action cannot be separated, as acting in the world and acquiring knowledge of the world are the same process.

An approach to investigation that attempts to understand the nature of cognition by temporarily bracketing off action and emotion is bound to come up with a distorted understanding of the phenomena of interest. Cognition, emotion and behaviour are in reality fused (Safran & Greenberg, 1998, p. 114).

Safran (1990) also argued for integrating insights from Attachment Theory and proposed that interpersonal schemas allow individuals to maintain relatedness with others. From Sullivan's (1953) and Safran's (1990) interpersonal perspective, an individual's fundamental sense of security in the world is a function of the individual's sense of 'potential relatedness' to others. Additionally, Safran hypothesises that interpersonal schemas are partially encoded in the form of procedural knowledge that people experience as a 'felt sense'. Thus, in order to work more effectively at the level of interpersonal schemas, it may be necessary to work directly with emotion and expressive behaviour. Safran and Segal (1996) argued that CBT therapists should embody a therapeutic style that includes the possibility of 'meta-communicating' with the client about the reactions the client evokes in the therapist and providing feedback about the nonverbal behaviours that evoke these reactions. The here and now of the therapeutic interaction is regarded by Safran as a key focus on assisting the client to understand and change unhelpful cognitive-interpersonal cycles. In this perspective, the separation of technical and relational factors becomes artificial as all technical interventions can be understood as themselves expressions of relational possibility.

Safran and Greenberg (1998) draw upon the propositions of emotion theory in a manner that challenges standard CBT's insistence on the primacy of cognition. Key to this perspective is that emotion is itself a form of meaning. Emotion has adaptive evolutionary functions and provides the experiencing individual with information about their tacit values and standards. Furthermore, as the experience and expression of emotion is impacted by anticipated interpersonal consequences, the quality of the therapeutic relationship becomes a key mediator of change.

Safran's critique of the information processing model used by standard CBT, as well as his and his colleagues' suggestions for a more emotionally focussed and embodied understanding of cognition, has significant resonance with the existential phenomenological perspective advanced by Hubert Dreyfus (2016). Dreyfus has been an ardent critic of the mind as computer metaphor and the limitations of this model for the prospects of the field of artificial intelligence. Drawing on the philosophy of Heidegger, Dreyfus has long argued that it is not possible to adequately account for skilled action, such as that of an expert tennis player, by reference to the notion of internal, cognitive, 'if-then' rules. Skilful action in the world is for Dreyfus the epitome of human intelligence. Here though, such intelligence is regarded as a bodily attunement to the world and its 'affordances' for action rather than the possession of a complex internal cognitive representation of the world. This is not to assert that representations do not exist as such, but that rather that representation most often occurs when skilful action in the world has broken down or has met some obstacle that requires reflection.

Guidano and Liotti's Developmental-constructivist, Post-rationalist Cognitive Therapy

Guidano (1991, 1998) and Guidano and Liotti (1983) have advanced versions of cognitive therapy heavily indebted to Attachment Theory, constructivist philosophy and aspects of existential phenomenology. Guidano (1998) explicitly contrasts what he regards as a 'post-rationalist' cognitive therapy with rationalist (standard) CBT that he positions as inevitably being focussed upon 'control':

> the therapeutic relationship established in rationalist and objectivist psychotherapy cannot become other than an instrument- a more or less authoritarian instrument- for the reestablishment of a rational, realistic and otherwise socially dictated order (Guidano, 1998, p. 100).

Guidano argues that, for the constructivist, rationality is inherently relativistic. There is no 'gods eye view' from which a therapist is in a position to judge the irrationality or otherwise of a client's thoughts. Guidano's post-rationalist cognitive therapy focusses upon the gaps and incongruities that inevitably exist between the individual's ongoing, embedded, acting, experiencing 'I' and their sense of self that continually emerges from abstractly self-referencing this ongoing experience—the observing and appraising 'me' (alternatively phrased as the self as subject 'I' versus the self as object 'me'). Guidano emphasises that the experiencing I is always ahead of and not equivalent to the reflecting Me.

Guidano and Liotti (1983) drew upon attachment theory as a resource to help theorise the difficulties and distortions that arise in the ability of the reflecting Me to adequately capture the experiencing I. These authors regard 'normal functioning' as being equivalent to a personal meaning organisation that is capable of evolving towards greater complexity via assimilation of contradictions in experience and construction. In psychotherapy, the experience of emotion is regarded as central in promoting reorganisation of self-constructs and emotion schemas. Guidano (1991) described a range of awareness-centred interventions, designed to increase the client's capacity for self-observation. This includes, for example, the 'moviola technique' in which the client is encouraged to review emotionally charged scenes in their life and to 'zoom in' and 'zoom out' and to alternatively adopt subjective and objective perspectives on these scenes. Therapy may also involve a reconstruction of the client's history of 'affective relationships' helping them to understand the pathway they took to their current manner of constructing meaning.

Key to Guidano and Liotti's (1983) constructivist perspective is an understanding of the nature of resistance to change as being essentially about the inherent need for individuals to maintain the coherence and stability of their current meaning constructions. Those constructions that are more 'core' to the sense of self are highly resistant to change and, as such, resistance is seen as essentially expressive of self-protective efforts at maintaining coherence and identity rather than expressing poor motivation or non-compliance. Guidano and Liotti (1983) argued that core beliefs and tacit knowledge of self-world relationships develops from various attachment experiences in childhood. Their version of post-rationalist CBT involves inviting the client to focus upon key moments in their developmental history in order to support the development of a richer narrative.

Mahoney's (2003) version of constructivist psychotherapy also focuses on 'deep' tacit core organising principles and uses a wide range of strategies to assist clients in increasing their awareness of these. He describes strategies such as the 'life review' which focuses on the elaboration of a life narrative as well as 'mirror time' which is a mindfulness-based intervention involving the client being able to become aware of, and stay with, emotions, memories and thoughts that arise as they view their own face in a mirror for a specified period of time.

Key to the therapeutic application of these constructivist principles is a preference for a more unstructured therapeutic process, a lessened focus on highly specified treatment targets and a focus on the therapeutic relationship and the accessing and exploration of emotional embodied experience as key processes of change. Additionally, in contrast to an attempt at the identification and 'correction' of cognitive distortions these approaches advance what they refer to as an 'almost reverential' appreciation for clients meaning making processes.

Narrative CBT

The notion of narrative or story has become central for a range of therapists and theorists both within and outside of a postmodern philosophical position (McLeod, 2004). A key proposition for a wide range of narrative approaches is that a fundamental property of the human mind is that it constructs and co-constructs narratives or stories. McLeod (2004) states that from a social constructionist perspective, therapy can be understood as a cultural practice where people who are experiencing problems in living are able to construct and re-construct a sense of agency, personal identify and belonging. A number of CBT therapists such as Rhodes (2014) and O'Conner (2015) have integrated aspects of narrative psychology and therapy into an enhanced CBT model. Rhodes (2014) is clear that in doing so he also draws upon the philosophy of 'critical realism' in that he asserts the existence of a 'mind independent reality' and that with clients it is important to assume an everyday notion of 'truth' as in 'what really happened'. Rhodes argues that the adoption of a broadly constructivist perspective does not prevent an attempt at objectivity or examining evidence claims and exploring client's real contexts and experiences such as the lived experience of racism or poverty.

O'Conner (2015) states that narratives serve a range of purposes. These include (a) expressing how an individual makes sense of experience, (b) how these experiences are represented to themselves, (c) justifying the client's perspective through rhetoric and reason, (d) contextualising the problem in surrounding events, (e) defining an 'episode' of experience with a beginning, a middle and an end, (f) positioning the individual in a certain type of relationship with the world and (g) not representing all aspects of an experience. A key difference between a narrative approach to problems versus a standard CBT approach, according to O'Conner (2015), is that the narrative approach treats the story as the basic account of the problem, including its cognitive content, without reducing this to specific individual key cognitions. Narrative analysis is also used to reveal various 'positionings' that may occur between an individual and 'the problem' with narrative interventions focussing upon examples and contexts where the problem is absent or successfully resisted.

O'Conner (2015, p. 107) gives an example of a successful narratively focussed intervention of a client moving from a position of 'I'm a bizarre person.' To 'I'm a person who has bizarre thoughts, but I can have influence over them'. This also illustrates a key narrative move of 'externalising the problem' so that the nature of the problem is seen less as an aspect of the self, and hence internal and fixed, and instead as an external entity that the client can take up a variety of stances towards and gain resources from others (including the therapist) to take up a more resilient or defiant stance.

Polkinghorne (2004) has argued that many therapists who adopt a postmodern and constructivist understanding of narrative in fact operate from a more existential stance that recognises the personal realm, lived experience and people as creators of meaning. The process of narrative therapy, for Polkinghorne (2004) is founded upon an existential view that people do have a capacity to revise and re-author restrictive narratives that may well have been assigned to them by their cultural positioning.

A Postmodern and Post-rationalist CBT?

Several theorists, drawing on a range of postmodern philosophies described above, attempted to describe what they regard as a form of post-rationalist CBT. Often these models have been described in contrast and opposition to standard CBT that is positioned as rationalist and objectivist. Neimeyer (1999) outlines what he regards to be the key epistemological differences between objectivist and constructivist approaches to psychology. Below in Table 8.1, drawing upon Neimeyer's (1999, p. 14) analysis, is a delineation of the main assumptions and propositions advanced by each.

Neimeyer (1999) argues that in addition to the above distinctions, it can be seen that both objectivist and constructivist models of therapy

Table 8.1 Contrasting Assumptions Between Objectivist and Constructionist Approaches.

Basic assumption	Objectivist/rationalist	Constructivist
Nature of knowledge	Representation of the external world	Construction and co-construction
Nature of truth	Correspondence between representation and external world	Multiple and contextual. Coherence theory and truth by social consensus
Goals of science	Discovery of natural laws via hypothetico-deductive and experimental methods	Creation of 'local knowledge' via a multiplicity of methods
Nature of mind	A reactive map of external events and relationships-mediational	Proactive plans for organising activity
Basic unit of meaning	The schema: assimilating events on the basis of similarity. Cognitions as self-other-world assumptions and rules. Modes as organisations of schemas	The construct: defined by difference and distinction. Constructions are hierarchically arranged in a self-organising fashion
Language	Mediates social reality	Constitutes social reality
Emotion	Outcome of change-emotion modified via changes in behaviour and cognition	Key to change- to be respected rather than controlled. A form of meaning itself
Goals of therapy	Correction of cognitive distortions and errors. Education. Therapist as change agent	Promotion of meaning making co-construction and new possibilities, and 'new stories' for action and 'resistance'

have adopted Kelly's (1973) metaphor of the 'personal scientist'. The key difference, he argues is that objectivist models, such as Beck's CBT, have adopted a more 'modernist' conception of science while constructivist theories have adopted a version of this metaphor that characterises science as emphasising the inherently fictional nature of all theories and hypotheses. As has been touched upon previously however, the black and white distinctions presented in Table 8.1 fails to do justice to the development of standard CBT over time. Several features of Beck and Haigh's (2014) revised model of generic CBT would seem equally at home on the more constructivist end. Thus, CBT emphasises that individuals are active in their constructions of reality, and rather than emphasising cognition as isolated self-statements, contemporary CBT emphasised the organisation of cognition into higher level schemas and modes as well as emphasising the extent to which schemas are about the prediction of action. Equally, Beck appears to have adopted a more constructivist criterion of truth in terms of his emphasis that there is no unbiased view of reality to be had, and that cognitions can only be regarded as distorted in relation to a particular context. At the same time, other aspects of this differentiation would appear to hold, in particular the modernist emphasis on achieving a greater and more adequate approximation of reality via a progressive science.

The characterisation of standard CBT as highly objectivist and rationalist has been maintained by a range of contemporary authors such as Winter (2008). However, this characterisation, and implied critique of standard CBT, has never been accepted. Indeed, Mahoney (1999, p. 54) writes that when he first began to outline what he saw as the essence of this differentiation of therapies into constructivist versus rationalist, 'I was surprised to learn that virtually every cognitive therapist I knew considered himself or herself to be constructivist rather than rationalist in preference'.

The debate regarding the extent to which CBT and related approaches such as Rational-Emotive Therapy, should be regarded as rationalist versus constructivist, was conducted with particular heat by Ellis (1992) and Wessler (1992). Ellis (1992) argued that RET should be considered fundamentally constructivist, and in fact more thoroughly constructivist than most other forms of therapy. Wessler (1992) by contrast argues that RET, as well as Beck's CBT, could be viewed as either rationalist or constructivist depending upon where one looked. Wessler argued that Ellis' RET was rationalistic in its practice while Becks CBT could be seen as constructivist in both therapy and practice 'but perhaps not enough to please ardent constructivists' (Wessler, 1992, p. 624). Similarly, Rosen (1993, p. 407) argued that 'Beck's model smoothly integrates realism and constructivism without doing violence to either . . . it appears that both rationalist and constructivist epistemologies can coexist in the same practice model'.

Dobson and Dobson (2009), writing from a standard Beckian CBT perspective, have argued that CBT endorses the general philosophical perspective that can be termed 'the realist assumption'. This assumption is that there is an independent 'objective reality' that exists separate from our beliefs and assumptions about it. Additionally, individuals can come to have a more accurate set of beliefs (or representations) about the nature of this external reality and to some degree the extent to which an individual's internal representations correspond to the nature of external objective reality is an indicator of good mental health.

The debate regarding whether traditional CBT should be regarded as rationalist and objectivist versus constructivist was particularly acute in the late 1990s. It can be argued that some of the insights of the constructivist psychotherapists have been integrated into some of the formulations of more mainstream CBT therapists such as the work of Robert Leahy on emotion schemas described in the Chapter 7 as well as his earlier work on providing a richer understanding of resistance to change in CBT (Leahy, 2001). Additionally, influential theorists within standard CBT such as Mooney and Padesky (2000) have presented guidelines for clinical practice that directly draw upon more constructivist perspectives. Mooney and Padesky (2000) emphasise the importance of drawing upon client creativity, working with the development of 'future possibilities' and supporting willingness in both therapist and client to stay with, tolerate and embrace experiences of ambiguity and doubt. Blenkiron (2010) has also outlined how the use of stories, metaphor and narrative can be integrated within a standard CBT perspective.

The debate regarding the extent to which standard CBT is best understood as constructivist versus rationalist has resurfaced more recently in the context of the expansion of the provision of standard and manualised forms of CBT in public health settings. Winter (2008), for example, has repeated and reemphasised the claim CBT is inherently rationalist and objectivist. In response, Mansell (2008) has argued that CBT is neither rationalist nor objectivist.

Clark et al. (1999) argued for what they referred to as a 'moderate realism'. They stress, for example, that the notion of cognitive distortion should not be taken to an extreme. That is, they argue that it is misleading to characterised the difference between psychological distress and disorder versus health in terms of the presence or absence of cognitive distortions or bias:

> Cognitive theory, then, does not assert that information processing is distorted in psychological disturbance but is accurate or unbiased in non-clinical states. Instead, cognitive theory states that all information processing is at best a biased approximation of reality. . . . this assumption also challenges the belief that there is only one correct way to formulate a human understanding of the phenomena of interest (p. 64).

Furthermore, Clark et al. (1999) argue that when they refer to objective reality they do not do so in the usual understanding of that term, and that in fact in many respects their perspective 'overlaps' in important ways that of more constructivist versions of therapy. Thus, they stress that:

> In social contexts where phenomenological realities intersect, there are multiple personal realities as well as an objective physical reality or context within which the subjective realities interact. These 'realities' are equally valid in the sense that they are part of what exists (1999, p. 61).

Chiari and Nuzzo (2010) argue that in fact both the information processing model and versions of constructivist thought and ecological cognitive models, such as that advocated by Safran, share an ontological view that they label as 'limited realism'—that is, both of these models claim that human knowledge is always limited and incomplete, and that from the beginning mainstream cognitive models have rejected the notion that there ever could be an exact correspondence between cognitive representations and an external real world. Clark et al. (1999) also argue that standard CBT does in fact adopt the 'modest realism' of theorists such as Held (1995):

> Cognitive theory and therapy acknowledge that there is an independent reality that does not originate in the knower . . . and that general laws and meanings can be attained through reason, science and technology (Clark et al., 1999, p. 62).

The debate between constructivists and moderate realists continues (Held, 2018; Raskin and Debany, 2018) although this is now conducted mostly within the specialist journals devoted to constructivist thought. It was argued above that CBT therapists such as Leahy (2001), Mooney and Padesky (2000) and Blenkiron (2010) have adopted several important constructivist ideas, particularly as these converge upon issues of resistance to change, the importance of client creativity and the use of narratives. This however has not led to a shift in standard CBTs self-definition as being a process focussed upon the identification and modification of cognitive distortions. Clark (1995) has argued that some of the concepts and therapeutic interventions advocated by the cognitively oriented constructivists appear to push the model into a more psychodynamic direction and stretch the boundaries of what can rightly be understood as CBT. He also argues that the concepts of deep, tacit structures seem to re-introduce ideas of an unconscious as well as advocating a therapeutic stance that is at significant divergence from the collaborative present focussed, problem-solving stance of standard CBT.

It could be proposed that existential psychology provides a more suitable philosophical grounding for CBT than that afforded by postmodernism and constructivism. Key to its appeal may be in its analysis of lived human action in the world. To explore such possibilities further, however, it is necessary too to review the work of a contemporary form of CBT that can rightfully claim to be an existential CBT, that is acceptance and commitment therapy. It is to this, and related models that generally fall within the so-called third wave of CBT that we now turn.

Summary

- A variety of attempts have been made to construct constructionist and 'post-rationalist' versions of CBT.
- These approaches draw upon philosophical perspectives that are derived from existential phenomenology and other sources.
- These approaches tend to challenge the separation of cognition and emotion and behaviour and to dispute the primacy of cognition.
- As forms of therapeutic practice, they tend to stress a less structured and explicitly educational way of working with clients as well as emphasising the centrality of the therapeutic relationship as a vehicle for change.

Existential Reflections

Consider the following questions in conversation with peers:

- To what extent is your own therapeutic practice based upon constructionist or postmodern ideas?
- If you are influenced by such ideas, what do you consider the implications of this to be for any notion of 'therapist as expert change agent'?
- Do you consider it possible, desirable, or undesirable to draw upon both rationalist and constructionist ideas in your practice?
- To what extent do you believe that there are, in contrast with some post-modernist perspectives, universal aspects of human existence?

9

Mindfulness, Acceptance and the Third Wave of CBT

Control is the problem, not the solution.

—Hayes et al. (1999/2011, p. 115).

Attending a training in acceptance and commitment therapy is in many ways significantly different from a regular CBT training event. In one of my first experiences of such training, held by one of the developers of the approach, Professor Stephen Hayes, we are challenged directly to 'show up, be present and move towards what we value'. In an initial experiential exercise, said to be an excellent means of gaining some sense of 'the essence of ACT' we are challenged to firstly consider the extent to which 'maintaining the possibility of intimacy' is a key value for us as professionals. Many, including I, responded in the affirmative. As an experiential exercise intended to allow us to experience, in a rich and direct way, the processes of mindfulness as well as experiential avoidance in the face of values consistent behaviour, we are asked to make sustained eye contact with the person sitting next to us while sitting quite close and directly facing each other. We are urged to maintain eye contact and to become aware of any uncomfortable or unpredicted psychological phenomena that may 'show up'. We are also invited to 'let these be' and to maintain eye contact. This continues for a 15-minute period. The exercise is extraordinarily challenging. The overall atmosphere of experiential immediacy reminds me strongly of the gestalt therapy groups I had participated in years before. Welcome to the third wave of CBT.

CBT and Existential Psychology: Philosophy, Psychology and Therapy,
First Edition. Michael Worrell.

A number of authors have commented upon the potential for dialogue and convergence between a range of mindfulness-based approaches and existential phenomenology (Claessens, 2010; Felder et al., 2014; Hickes & Mirea, 2012; Nanda, 2010). These authors have highlighted that the practice of mindfulness, with its emphasis on the capacity of both therapist and client to 'stay still' with experience, as it arises and changes, has affinity with the descriptively focussed practice of phenomenology. In this chapter, the principal versions of mindfulness-based CBT approaches, as well as other so-called 'third wave CBT' approaches, and their potential connection with existential psychology, are discussed.

Mindfulness-Based Cognitive Therapy (MBCT)

A variety of mindfulness-based CBT approaches have been developed for working with a range of clinical presentations. Many of these approaches trace the origin of the concept and practice of mindfulness to ancient Buddhist philosophy and practice as well as western religious and philosophical traditions (Williams & Kabat-Zinn, 2013). Unsurprisingly, there are a wide range of meanings associated with this term and important areas of difference between western psychological concepts and ancient Buddhist understandings. Variously, mindfulness has been understood as a 'state', a disposition or 'trait' as well as a set of skills. Bishop et al. (2004) identify two components of mindfulness as a state. The first of these is the intentional self-regulation of attention so that it remains focussed upon present moment experiences (thoughts, feelings and physical sensations) as they arise and change. The second component concerns attitudinal qualities of openness, acceptance and curiosity to whatever is encountered in awareness. Dispositional mindfulness, as opposed to a momentary state, is a general tendency to adopt a mindful state consistently over time. The skills approach to mindfulness concerns a range of strategies including formal sitting meditation, 'body scan' and breath awareness exercises that may be taught in a range of therapies both in individual and group formats.

Mindfulness-based cognitive therapy (MBCT) arose from the work of Kabat-Zinn (1982) who developed a mindfulness-based treatment for individuals experiencing chronic pain. On the basis of the positive empirical results for this programme, Segal et al. (2002) developed

Kabat-Zinn's methodology into a disorder specific intervention focussed upon the reduction of the risk for relapse of depression for individuals who are currently in remission. This work has since been extended to include both individuals who are currently depressed as well as individuals diagnosed with bi-polar disorder as well as other problems (Baer, 2014). Crane (2009, p. 3) suggests that the therapeutic possibilities of mindfulness may be extensive as they: 'enable us to see and work with the universal vulnerabilities and challenges that are an inherent part of being human'.

MBCT for depression is linked to a cognitive science account of the nature of depression and depressive relapse. In many respects, it constitutes an evolution of an essentially Beckian CBT perspective. Its most distinctive feature within this framework is that, during this intervention, no attempts are made to segregate cognitions as either rational or irrational, distorted or accurate, and there are no strategies employed that target the direct change of cognitive content or attempt to eliminate unpleasant emotions or sensations. Instead, MBCT advocates the development of an approach orientation alongside the development of self-compassion. Usually delivered in a group format over a six- or eight-week format, MBCT includes direct instruction in mindfulness practice and experiential exercises such as 'the three-minute breathing space' as well as the use of walking meditation and the development of a sustained daily practice of formal seated meditation (Crane, 2009). Considerable importance is attached to the notion that MBCT therapists must be able to embody the approach in their work with clients. That is, they are expected to have developed and sustained a personal mindfulness practice as well as being able to convey a mindful way of being in group and individual sessions. Fennel and Segal (2013) have noted the extent to which MBCT presents a strikingly different therapeutic stance for CBT therapists to embody. Specifically, they note the extent to which the adoption of a mindful stance involves (at least temporarily) letting go of an agenda to achieve change, explaining (Fennel & Segal, 2013, p. 133):

> CT is intentionally designed to 'fix' things and does it very well. This is perhaps the most difficult transition for cognitive therapists learning MBCT to make: intentionally not 'fixing' can at first feel like doing nothing, rather than doing something equally valid

> but different. … mindfulness-based interventions explicitly discourage attachment to particular desired outcomes, and encourage willingness to allow things to unfold in their own time and to tolerate uncertainty and 'don't know mind'.

The potential resonance between mindfulness and the open, accepting and descriptive stance of existential phenomenology seems clear. Indeed, Owen (2013) has suggested that mindfulness could be employed as a method to assist in teaching trainees about phenomenological practice.

Dialectical Behaviour Therapy

Dialectical behaviour therapy (DBT) was originally developed as a treatment for individuals diagnosed with borderline personality disorder (Linehan, 1993). The approach has subsequently been extended to other difficulties characterised by emotional dysregulation such as substance misuse, binge eating and bulimia, depression in older adults, bipolar disorder, violence and aggression and work with highly conflictual couple relationships (Lynch et al., 2007). Linehan (1993) proposed a biosocial theory of personality disorder that hypothesised that the core difficulties seen with this group of clients stemmed from two primary factors. Firstly, these individuals present with a biologically based dysfunction of the emotional regulation system and secondly their social environment is invalidating, punishing the expression of positive behavioural skills and reinforcing the use of more negative ones. The DBT therapist is encouraged to view the, at times, disruptive and distressing nature of the client's behaviour as being a natural response to environmental contingencies (Lynch et al., 2007).

Linehan (1993) describes DBT as drawing its principles from behavioural therapy, dialectical philosophy and Zen practice. Dialectical philosophy emphasises inherent tensions as well as the synthesis of opposites. The primary dialectic is that between acceptance and change. Linehan's (1993) original work with clients presenting with borderline personality disorder found that a therapeutic stance founded either on purely a change agenda or on acceptance was experienced by clients as invalidating. DBT attempts to embody a therapeutic stance that presents a balance and synthesis of acceptance and change.

DBT is a structured intervention, often delivered by a team of therapists based within a specialist unit, that focuses on the reduction of rates of suicidality and acts of self-harm. The treatment consists of four elements: individual therapy, attendance at group-based skills training sessions, telephone consultations with the therapists and group consultation meetings with all involved professionals. The treatment is divided into stages whereby the initial stage focuses on reducing highly negative and at times dangerous behaviours such as self-harm and later stages focus on improving well-being and being able to operate, for example, from a position of 'wise mind'. DBT seeks to improve clients use of four domains of skill: mindfulness, distress tolerance, emotional regulation and interpersonal effectiveness (Linehan, 1993). In DBT, mindfulness includes both the capacity to be present to 'what is' as well as the capacity to find 'skilful means' and a middle path between extremes or polarities. The dialectical stance of DBT has some resonance with existential therapy's focus on universal existence tensions or polarities such as acceptance–change, individuality-belonging, etc., although the existential approach often emphasises that such tensions must be lived and that at times no apparent 'synthesis' may be possible.

Metacognitive Therapy MCT

Metacognitive therapy (Wells, 2000) is based upon a model (termed the 'self-regulatory executive function model') proposing that psychological problems arise from, and are maintained by, a perseverative thinking style called the cognitive attentional syndrome (CAS). The CAS is described as consisting of dysfunctional coping strategies that represent an attempt to manage distressing cognitions and emotions and include worry, rumination, threat monitoring, self-focussed attention, thought control strategies, avoidance and reassurance seeking (Wells, 2000). The model proposes that the CAS arises from the individual's beliefs regarding the nature and significance of thoughts i.e., their metacognitions. These can include both positive and negative metacognitions. Examples of positive metacognitions include 'worry is necessary to prepare and respond to danger' and examples of negative metacognitions may include 'my worry is out of control and will cause me harm'. The aim of MCT is to assist the client to identify and challenge both positive and negative metacognitive beliefs and to adopt a more flexible thinking style.

It is possible to exaggerate the extent to which MCT belongs within a 'third wave' domain. While the model clearly advances the perspective that it is often ineffective and unnecessary to directly target, and attempt to change, negative thoughts, it nevertheless argues that it is important to identify, challenge and alter unhelpful metacognitive beliefs suggesting these may be targeted via strategies of Socratic dialogue and behavioural experiments in a manner consistent with Beckian CBT approaches. At the same time MCT also includes a range of attention training and mindfulness focussed interventions that are designed to assist individuals to change their relationships with cognitions and to promote a more flexible cognitive style. The attention training strategy developed by Wells (2000) is an auditory task that invites clients to engage in selective attention, divided attention and attentional switching. The aim of the intervention is to assist clients to reduce self-focus and to improve client's flexible control of attention. Another strategy, 'detached mindfulness', asks clients to become aware of trigger cognitions and to let go of or detach from them by taking a step back and refraining from perseverative thinking or rumination. Detached mindfulness techniques may include a free association task where the therapist reads out a series of words to the client and where the client is asked to let their mind go without attempting to control any thoughts or emotions that arise in response. Clients may also be asked to mentally observe their thoughts as if these thoughts were 'leaves on a stream' and to watch them pass and distinguishing between thoughts and reality (Wells, 2000). Such techniques are also used as strategies to challenge the client's metacognitive beliefs regarding the uncontrollability of worry or the necessity of attempts to do so.

Compassion-Focussed Therapy (CFT)

Compassion-focussed therapy (CFT) has evolved as an integration and extension of Beckian CBT, developments in neuropsychology/neurophysiology, evolutionary psychology, Attachment Therapy and Archetypal Psychology (Gilbert, 2010). While not constituting a Buddhist psychology, CFT nevertheless borrows extensively from Buddhism.

Specifically, Gilbert (2010) discusses how MBCT draws primarily from Theravada Buddhism with its on mindfulness practices while CFT borrows from Mahayana Buddhism which emphasises the practice of meditation exercises that are compassion focussed. Self-compassion is defined as ability to soothe oneself with kindness and non-judgemental understanding in times of emotional distress (Gilbert, 2010). Gilbert (2010) further describes compassion as involving being open to the suffering of self and others in a non-defensive and non-judgmental manner. Additionally, compassion involves a desire to act to relive suffering, beliefs regarding the causes of suffering as arising from universal aspects of what is it to be human, as well as compassionate behaviours towards self and others.

CFT was initially developed to address difficulties that clients experience with shame and self-criticism. Gilbert (2010) argues that while many clients, who are highly self-critical and shame prone, can learn strategies to identify and challenge their distorted cognitions, the alternative cognitions they generate exist in a self-to-self dialogue that remains highly self-critical. That is, the self-critical client judges and criticises themselves for having negative cognitions, thus ensuring that cognitive challenges have limited, if any, impact on emotional change. Gilbert (2009) proposes an affect regulation model in which three interrelated systems are identified: a threat and self-protection system, a drive and resource seeking system and a soothing and connection system. Gilbert (2009) proposes that each system has an evolved function related to basic motivations for survival, achievement and relationship with others. Within this model, psychological problems are seen as in part being due to imbalances between these three systems and most often, in the case of shame prone and self-critical individuals, as a result of an under activation of the affiliative/soothing system. A central aim of CFT is to assist clients to develop the affiliative/soothing system as a means of regulating the threat system. Gilbert and Irons (2004) suggest that people who are highly self-critical may lack access to memories of being cared for and soothed and therefore experience difficulties accessing and sustaining feelings of warmth, compassion and reassurance. This may be particularly so for individuals with traumatic backgrounds or for people whose attachment relationships were highly threat focussed.

CFT seeks to increase the client's access to a 'felt sense' of compassion through the adoption of specific skills such as 'compassionate thought balancing', mindfulness and compassionate acts towards self and others as well as the use of experiential interventions such as 'soothing rhythm breathing, 'perfect nurturer imagery' and 'compassionate flow' (Gilbert, 2010). Gilbert also states that the therapeutic relationship plays a central role in CFT, where, compared to a standard CBT approach, greater emphasis is placed on providing space for reflection as well as emotional experience during the session rather than a focus on goal achievement. Similar to the MBCT, and consistent also with existential therapy, CFT places emphasis on the importance of the therapist being able to embody mindfulness in their manner of engaging with themselves and clients, Gilbert (2010) argues that the CFT therapist must be an active participant in compassion focussed practices, and be able to embody these in their interactions with clients rather than being present as a deliverer of 'technologies'.

Behavioural Activation (BA)

Behavioural activation (BA) is a structured treatment approach that targets depressed mood and behavioural withdrawal or avoidance (Kanter et al., 2009). BA can be seen to exist in first, second and third wave versions. In its original form, BA arose from a behavioural analysis of depression, which emphasised the utility of altering environmental contingencies of reinforcement. In its early form, pleasant event scheduling and mood monitoring strategies were used to help clients widen their behavioural repertoire to an extent that these would then be shaped and maintained by naturally occurring contingencies in the client's environment.

Subsequently, strategies of BA were incorporated into Beck's cognitive therapy for depression. These strategies, consistent with a cognitive formulation, emphasised that positive changes were primarily driven by the effectiveness of BA in challenging a client's negative predictions as well as beliefs about coping. More recent versions of BA have described the intervention from a contextual behavioural science perspective (reviewed in more detail below). In these versions (Martell et al., 2001) the process of change is understood as one of assisting the client to move from an avoidant and withdrawn behavioural pattern to an approach orientation but without any direct attempts to challenge or alter private experience such as depressive cognitions or emotions. The approach includes strategies to assist clients to overcome avoidance of private experience and it is assumed that increases in activity levels will in turn increase contact with response-contingent reinforcement that will in return result in reductions in depressed mood.

Functional Analytic Psychotherapy (FAP)

Like acceptance and commitment therapy, and contemporary versions of behavioural activation, functional analytic psychotherapy (FAP) (Kohlenberg & Tsai, 1991) is derived from a radical behavioural perspective. Unique amongst CBT perspectives, FAP focuses principally upon the role of the therapeutic relationship. That is, the therapeutic relationship is seen as the primary vehicle of change and is the focus of its specific interventions and conceptual analyses. FAP has evolved as both a stand-alone therapy as well as an adjunct or enhancement to other therapies (even where these therapies may not themselves adhere to a radical behavioural perspective). FAP proposes that the therapeutic relationship shares many functional similarities with relationships in the client's wider social context and, as such, most often the concerns that the client brings to therapy will also be present and be expressed within the therapeutic relationship. The primary focus of FAP is on clients' 'clinically relevant behaviours' (CRBs), which are defined as the client's in-session behaviours that parallel those occurring in their wider social environment. The role of the FAP therapist is to respond contingently to CRBs in order to reinforce and shape a more effective behavioural repertoire in the domain of interpersonal and self-to-self relating. FAP therapists emphasise the creation of an 'evocative, attuned, authentic and mutually vulnerable therapeutic relationship, which becomes the vehicle for client growth and transformation' (Tsai et al., 2019, p. 55).

Kohlenberg and Tsai (1991) describe the process of FAP in terms of five guidelines for therapist in-session behaviour that maximise possibilities for responding effectively to client behaviour. Guideline one is to become aware of CRBs as they are occurring. Guideline two is the option to evoke CRBs. This may include the use of structured 'evocative' interventions such as an 'emotional risk log' a 'loss inventory' and non-dominant handwriting exercises and other experiential interventions (Nelson et al., 2016). Tsai et al. (2019) also describe how the nature of the therapeutic setting will itself frequently evoke CRBs such as invitations for self-disclosure, session time limits, therapist mistakes, homework suggestions and the power differential. Of particular importance is the therapist's ability to shift the conversation from a focus exclusively on content (such as on events that occurred between sessions) to a focus on process, and specifically, the process of ongoing and changing relational experience during the session. An example of this focus might include a therapist question such as 'How are you usually like when starting a new relationship? How is that similar to and different from how you are starting this relationship with me?' (Tsai et al., 2019). Guideline three is to positively reinforce CRB2s as they are occurring. Guideline four is to observe the potentially reinforcing effects of therapist behaviour in relation to the CRBs and finally guideline five is to provide functional interpretations (explorations regarding how the clients behaviour 'works' or is related to its consequences) in an effort to support the generalisation of positive changes.

In addition to these guidelines, FAP includes a framework that clarifies the extent to which, in this perspective, whatever emerges within the therapeutic relationship implicates the person of the therapist. Kohlenberg and Tsai (1991) explored the extent to which FAP provided a behaviourally based alternative to phenomena understood within psychodynamic therapy according to notions of transference and countertransference. While agreeing that these relational phenomena are indeed the focus of FAP, these authors emphasised the extent to which the responses of the client, in most instances, reflect responses to the actual presence and behaviour of the therapist (and vice versa). That is, the relationship is to be understood as real and as implicating the therapist and their learning history and context, as much as the learning history and context of the client.

Maitland et al. (2017) describe what they refer to as the awareness, courage and love (or ACL) framework. Within FAP, 'awareness' refers to being awake and in contact with what is happening in the present moment within a relational context, which includes awareness of self, the other individual and the process occurring between the two. Maitland et al. (2017) argue that the therapists need to assess both their own and their client's awareness in terms of: present-moment body sensations, cognitions and emotions; values, needs, goals and sense of identity, as well as awareness of the impact of their own behaviour upon others.

'Courage' is defined functionally to refer to the behaviour of self-disclosing or 'moving towards' another person despite aversive experience such as shame, caution, uncertainty and anxiety. Again, because courage is functionally defined, there is no set identifiable form of courageous behaviour that remains so across contexts. Thus, courageous acts may include gestures, statements, body language, remaining silent, or acts of clear and assertive self-disclosure. 'Love' is defined principally in terms of responsiveness to instances in which an individual has behaved courageously. Within the ACL framework, awareness, courage and love are defined as mid-level terms that identify functionally important classes of behaviour. These terms also apply to the therapist, who is challenged to make themselves vulnerable and emotionally available to clients. Rather than a more distanced or even collaborative stance, in order for FAP therapists to be effective in evoking and shaping CRBs, their responses to clients must be genuine and the therapeutic relationships created are intended to be emotionally intense, alive and 'real'. Responses from therapists that are overly professional, distanced or calculating are held to be less likely to function as effective reinforcers of client engagement and change.

The emphasis in FAP on the centrality of the therapeutic relationship as the context within which the client's difficulties can be disclosed and explored, has substantial resonance with existential therapy, as does the emphasis that whatever does or does not emerge implicates the being of the therapist. A key difference emerges, however, with respect to FAP's emphasis on using interventions that are deliberately goal-directed or improvement-seeking.

Acceptance and Commitment Therapy (ACT) and Contextual Behavioural Science

> The reality of our own death and the responsibility to make ongoing, purposeful choices are central to our work in acceptance and commitment therapy (Walser, 2019, p. 75).

Acceptance and commitment therapy or 'ACT' represents the evolution of a radical behavioural approach to the study of complex human behaviour (Hayes et al., 1999/2011). As well as being stated as one word, 'ACT', which emphases the focus on action and engagement, the acronym also serves to express the three core themes of the approach: 'accept' thoughts and feelings (but not literally), 'choose directions'—clarify values and 'what really matters in life and what you and to stand for in life' and 'take action'—making commitments to behaviour change and moving forward in those directions.

ACT is distinctive within CBT for its emphasis on the importance of clarity regarding philosophical assumptions as well as the existence of an ongoing dialogue and debate regarding questions of philosophy and the philosophy of science. A consideration of some of its philosophical assumptions clarifies the extent to which ACT draws close to some key propositions of existential phenomenology. In fact, Herbert et al. (2016) states that the roots of ACT lie within both behaviour therapy and the existential psychotherapies. It is also through a consideration of these basic assumptions, however, that serves to clarify the extent to which ACT and existential phenomenology remain fundamentally different projects.

Functional Contextualism

ACT is based upon a contemporary radical behavioural account of human language and cognition that has further developed the contextual aspects of B. F. Skinner's behaviourism. Hayes et al. (1999/2011) describe the philosophy of functional contextualism as deriving from the Pragmatism of William James as well as other influences. In functional contextualism, the basic unit of analysis is the act-in-context, with the hyphens serving to emphasise that this must be understood in terms of a whole event including its historical and situational context. Parts or elements (such as a specific behaviour of an individual) are only abstracted in accordance with a specific purpose or goal of analysis. Thus, contextual analyses are viewed as being inherently relational. Again, drawing upon the work of Skinner, ACT emphasises that 'behaviour' refers to anything that an organism does within a context. Thus, thinking, feeling, intending, understanding, etc., are all examples of behaviour. This also includes behaviour which is not publicly observable and thus the so-called 'inner' phenomena such as thinking are as much a legitimate focus of study as overt motor behaviour. This is in stark contrast to earlier and alternatives forms of behaviourism that sought to restrict analysis to the publicly observable motor actions of an individual or organism.

Functional contextualism emphasises the role of analytic goals in determining the 'truth' of an analysis (Biglan & Hayes, 2016). This has been termed the 'pragmatic truth criterion' and is set in opposition to the 'truth as correspondence' perspective that underlies more mechanistic versions of CBT such as Beckian CBT. In contextual behavioural science approaches, truth is defined in the sense of successful working. Function refers to both the issue of the consequences of action (in relation to a goal) and the sense of how a particular behaviour works. In ACT, a frequent question posed by the therapist may be 'And that behaviour is in the service of. . .?'

In addition to its emphasis on a philosophically derived conception of the nature of truth, ACT has also engaged in some debate and dialogue around questions of the nature of reality or being. That is, functional contextualism takes up a particular perspective on the nature of ontology. Hayes (2016b) and others have argued that functional contextualism is based on an 'a-ontological' stance. That is, in contrast to mainstream truth as correspondence models, ACT does not assume that its theoretical statements and terms correspond to a reality as it actually is. The goal is not to discover and map out how the world really is, but rather to determine how well any concept, or any therapeutic intervention, works in a given context. In this sense, ACT emphasises that all scientific knowledge is necessarily contextual or local and that truth claims are limited in nature (Herbert et al., 2016). On the question of the nature of reality itself, there has been some debate between those contextualists who argue that any such statements are outside the bounds of contextualism and those who argue for the necessity of assuming the existence of an 'independent, textured, substratum' that can never be known fully as it really is, but is nevertheless a necessary assumption in order for the activities of scientists and therapists to make sense (Herbert & Padovani, 2015).

Of some importance to the conduct of psychological therapy, ACT also asserts that the behaviour of therapists and researchers must also be included in the analysis. A psychotherapeutic theory, such as ACT or Beckian CBT, has a function in terms of organising the activities of therapists and is not true in any objectively real sense. Truth is a matter of pragmatism, and a psychotherapeutic theory is true to the extent that it is effective in supporting the attainment of its specified goals. Hayes (2016b) asserts that the goals that are chosen by a researcher or by a therapist and client together, can only be stated and owned and that the results of any particular analysis or therapeutic intervention do not in themselves justify the choice of that goal. That is, the amassed evidence base that ACT can be effective does not in itself justify its stated goals.

Following Skinner, the stated goal of contextual behavioural science, of which ACT is an expression, is 'The prediction and influence of behaviour with precision scope and depth' (Hayes, 2016a, p. 20). This clear specification of goals is of great importance for the current exploration of the relationship between existential psychology and CBT. Hayes (2016b) acknowledges that ACT, as a form of functional contextualism, overlaps with other forms of contextualism that he labels 'descriptive contextualisms'. Existential psychology is a clear example of a descriptive contextualism. Descriptive contextualism, while sharing many core assumptions of functional contextualism, starts from a different goal. As we saw, as a form of human science, the goal of descriptive contextualism is understanding, as opposed to the search for the means to exert influence or achieve predictive precision. This difference in chosen goal has some profound implications for the conduct of therapy and will be explored in more depth in subsequent chapters.

Language and Relational Frame Theory (RFT)

> *Language is the House of Being.*
>
> —Martin Heidegger.

Bunting and Hayes (2008) state that language is at the centre of the capacity of human beings to suffer. Furthermore, they state (Bunting & Hayes, 2008, p. 228): 'The core existential issues of meaning, isolation, freedom and death are unique to human beings because they are related to language processes'.

ACT is based upon a contextual behavioural theory of the nature of language and cognition referred to as relational frame theory, or RFT (Hayes et al., 1999/2011). The essence of RFT is that language is based on the learned derivation of relations between events based upon arbitrary cues. In contrast to animals that can be shown to learn primarily through direct environmental contingencies, humans, by virtue of possessing language, can learn that any event can be associated with any other event, even in the absence of having been directly associated. Dahl et al.

(2013) provide a useful example of the types of relational frames of interest to RFT in the domain of interpersonal relationships. These authors state that, according to RFT, all frames have three characteristics. Firstly, there is mutual entailment whereby a relation in one direction entails a relation in the other direction. Thus, if John is told 'Sally is more outgoing than Mary' then he will also derive the relation 'Mary is less outgoing than Sally' without having been directly trained to learn this relation. The second characteristic is combinatorial entailment, whereby two relations combine to entail further relations. Thus, if John is told 'Sally is more outgoing than Mary' as well as 'Mary is more outgoing than Josephine' then he will derive both that Sally is more outgoing than Josephine and that Josephine is less outgoing than Sally. The third characteristic is transformation of stimulus functions via relational frames. Here, according to the example provided by Dahl et al. (2013), if John is attracted to extroverted women and has a choice of meeting Sally, Mary or Josephine and has learnt the previous relations, we can predict that he is much more likely to choose Sally even though he has not met any of the three. According to RFT, the functions of the stimuli 'Sally' Mary' and 'Josephine' have been transformed through relational frames.

According to RFT, language can potentially turn any event into a source of psychological distress, e.g., a momentary happy mood may remind the individual that their mother has died and is not present to share the mood thus leading to sad emotions arising (Hayes et al., 1999/2011). RFT argues that learning via derived relations offers evolutionary advantage; however, it also brings with it some inevitable downsides. Principally, this is where a problem-solving frame of mind is brought to bear in domains where direct problem solving is ineffective. Thus, individuals are seen as attempting to use strategies of experiential avoidance and attempts to control private experience, such as distressing emotions and cognitions, that are ineffective and paradoxically lead to the maintenance and exacerbation of those same phenomena.

Acceptance and Commitment Therapy and a 'Tragic View of Life'

While the technical vocabulary of RFT is likely to be grating or alien to those interested in existential and phenomenological perspectives on human existence, the application of RFT to the clinical domain, via ACT, leads to some surprising additional points of convergence. Hayes et al. (1999/2011), in their original presentation of ACT, distinguish between what they refer to as the assumption of healthy normality versus the assumption of destructive normality. Hayes et al. (1999/2011) argue that the psychological mainstream (including CBT) has bought into an essentially medical model, that assumes that the natural state of human existence is one of health and, by corollary, the experience of abnormality, in the form of psychological distress, is a form of disease. That is, the common assumption amongst clients as well as therapists is 'I am meant to be happy- and if not, there is something wrong that can and should be fixed'. ACT, by contrast, asserts that psychological distress and difficulty are inevitable aspects of human existence, principally due to the manner in which language works and the extent to which we become entangled in language. This perspective, as well as wider empirical and theoretical concerns, have also led ACT therapists to dispute the reliability and validity of psychiatric diagnostic systems. In contrast with Beckian CBT, which has embraced an agenda of developing specific interventions for defined disorders (and thereby reinforcing and maintaining the notion that such disorders exist), ACT adopts a more transdiagnostic approach that challenges the taken for granted assumptions that psychological distress is understandable in terms of a disease model. In this, ACT and existential psychology find clear common ground.

Psychological Flexibility and the Goals of Therapy

As stated above, the goal of functional contextualism is 'prediction and influence with precision, scope and depth'. However, in the domain of clinical ACT work this is somewhat paradoxically presented as not being in the service of eliminating psychological symptoms such as panic attacks, obsessions or low moods. Rather, the very attempt of individuals to control and to eliminate psychological symptoms is seen as the very source of additional distress. ACT is described as often commencing with a review of all the unsuccessful or partly successful attempts the individual has made to control or eliminate unwanted emotions, thoughts or behaviours. Arriving at a state of 'creative hopelessness' is intended as a potentially productive, although inherently uncertain, context that might allow for something genuinely different to emerge (Hayes et al., 1999/2011).

The central aim of ACT has been described as the effort to support psychological flexibility which has been defined as: 'contacting the present moment fully as a conscious human being, and based on what the situation affords, changing or persisting in behaviour in the service of chosen values' (Hayes et al., 2006, p. 639).

Hayes et al. (2006) proposed what they term a 'hexaflex' model that specified the interrelated processes they view as active in supporting flexibility as well as those processes that result in psychological inflexibility. The six processes identified in the model are labelled by what are referred to as 'mid-level terms', that point the therapist and client towards relevant domains, but that do not in themselves exist in any objectively real sense, that is, these terms are regarded as functional.

The treatment targets of ACT are the processes of language and cognition that are held to limit psychological flexibility. Two key processes are experiential avoidance and cognitive fusion (Hayes et al., 1999/2011). Experiential avoidance refers to an individual's unwillingness to remain in contact with aversive private experiences, as well as their efforts to control and eliminate these experiences. Cognitive fusion refers to a situation in which an individual takes the context of their own thoughts literally. That is, they are fused with verbal rules and less in contact with currently existing environmental consequences. Thus, an individual is guided by the content of thoughts and beliefs in potentially destructive ways, rather than being guided by direct experience. Like other third wave therapies described in this chapter, ACT is more interested in assisting the client to notice the process of their thinking, and how this functions, than in assisting them to alter the content of their thoughts.

ACT specifies six main processes that are the targets of its intervention strategies: acceptance, defusion, self-as-context, contact with the present moment, values and committed action. Acceptance strategies are promoted as alternatives to experiential avoidance. Acceptance is understood to involve and active awareness of and capacity to stay with private events that may be triggered by an individual's history without attempts to change the frequency, intensity or form of those experiences. Acceptance is not understood as being an end point in itself but is rather a process that supports increases in value consistent living (Hayes et al., 1999/2011).

Cognitive defusion strategies are intended to alter the way the individual relates to their thoughts. Rather than attempting to change or challenge the content of thoughts, defusion interventions allow a sense of distancing from thoughts. Examples of defusing strategies include asking the client to report their thoughts in the form of 'I am having a thought that. . .'. Similar to mindfulness strategies discussed earlier, ACT includes a range of strategies intended to support the client's capacity to remain present. Greater contact with the present moment is again intended to allow the client's behaviour to come under greater influence of currently existing contingencies in the present situation.

Self-as-context is a particularly important concept with potential relevance to existential perspectives. Within ACT, a sense of self is held to emerge from relational frames such as I versus you, now versus then and here versus there (Hayes et al., 1999/2011). The process of language is described as allowing for the formation of a 'transcendent sense of self' or an observer perspective. Self-as-context is seen as important as from this perspective an individual is able to become aware of the flow of their experience without becoming entangled and fused with the content of experience. The self in this perspective becomes more like a place or location where psychological phenomena show up, rather than a thing like entity.

Values are defined as chosen qualities of purposeful action that can be distinguished from goals. Goals are defined as being like a specific destination such as 'arriving in Perth Australia'. A value, on the other hand, is more like a direction, as in 'travelling east' where, by definition, there is no final point at which it can be said you have arrived. Thus, a value of compassion can serve as an orientating direction but is never finished with or fully arrived at (although it remains possible that a different value can be chosen). Committed action incorporates many of the traditional behaviour change strategies that feature strongly in different CBT models and strategically any behavioural method may be used in an ACT therapy as long as this is in the service of psychological flexibility.

Values and Psychotherapy

In an important and in-depth critique of Behaviour Therapy, Woolfolk and Richardson (1984), argued that a major shortfall of the approach is its inability or apparent unwillingness to deal with the domain of values.

These authors also argued that behaviour therapists stray outside of their own evidence base whenever they state that the therapy simply follows the values and goals as stated by the client. That is, there is no specific evidence base to guide the therapist or client in regards to the specification of values and treatment goals. ACT can be seen both to substantially agree with this critique as well as having generated processes for addressing this shortfall. As noted above, ACT has been clear that the specification of its own goals cannot be said to be justified by its evidence base, the goals of ACT are regarded as chosen rather than pre-given or inevitable. In relation to the process of therapy, ACT has suggested that frequently it is often more useful to frame the work in terms asking the client: 'What do you want your life to be about? What do you want to stand for?' In an important sense, ACT can be seen to value 'valuing' itself and has developed a range of strategies to assist clients in engaging with this essentially existential question of meaning. Rather than promoting specific forms of rational values, the client is instead supported to clarify their values as far as this is possible, and to take active steps towards valued ways of being, whilst at the same time being willing to be open to unpredicted, and at times aversive, psychological and interrelational consequences without necessarily taking these 'literally'.

ACT and the Therapeutic Relationship

The philosophy and strategies of ACT have a range of highly significant implications for the nature of the therapeutic relationship. As noted earlier, functional contextualism requires that the therapist (their feelings, thoughts and behaviours during sessions) be included within the analysis, as the same processes and contingencies will be operative on them as with the client. Hayes et al. (1999/2011, p. 279) emphasised that the therapist is confronted with many of the same dilemmas in the process of living as the client and as such, in order to be effective, the ACT therapist must be willing to enter into a relationship with the client that is 'strong, open, accepting, mutual, respectful and loving'. This relationship is further described as one of 'radical respect' in which no assumption is made that the client should or must change specific behaviours. For example, when working with a client who is agoraphobic, there is no assumption that the client must at some point start getting out of their house. The ACT therapeutic relationship is further described as non-hierarchical. A key sensitivity is the possibility that the client will attempt to comply with the therapist's stated or implied rules for how they should be. As such, a much less structured therapeutic stance is attempted and a greater reliance is made of indirect strategies such as metaphor and experiential interventions. In presenting a metaphor or story to the client, for example, there is no concern that the client needs to understand or respond to a correct understanding of the intended meaning. At the same time however, the relationship is also described as being "directive and invasive" (Hayes et al., 1999/2011, p. 275). This directivness focuses upon the introduction of a very wide range of experiential strategies which are favoured over intellectual discussion or other strategies that may support cognitive fusion and entanglement.

It would seem that, for all the apparent closeness to existential phenomenology, ACT is at the same time quite far from the existential phenomenological emphasis on the centrality of descriptive understanding. It may be that at the lived, applied level that the differences between the approaches emerge. While for existential phenomenology the emphasis remains on the therapist attempting to divest themselves from the role of change agent, within ACT it can appear that this role remains, albeit in a now more paradoxical and at times indirect manner.

Summary

- Third wave, mindfulness and acceptance-based CBT approaches have been developed that have some striking areas of contact and agreement with existential phenomenology.
- These approaches encourage therapeutic explorations that assist both therapist and client to 'stay still' with experience.
- ACT, in particular, is an approach that has emphasised the importance of clarity in regard to philosophical assumptions and has developed as a form of pragmatic contextualism that shares many assumptions in common with descriptive contextualism.
- Important differences remain, in particular those arising from the broader goals of prediction and control.

Existential Reflections

In a group of peers, consider the following questions and issues:

- To what extent do you find the propositions of third wave CBT consistent with or a challenge to standard Beckian CBT?
- In what ways, if any, does the third wave CBT emphasises on embodying the approach, be it via mindfulness, compassion or 'showing up and being present' challenge, conflict, support or agree with your current stance on CBT?
- If you adopt a non-CBT stance to therapeutic work, how does the presentation of third wave CBT presented in this chapter alter or confirm your views regarding the nature of CBT?

10

CBT and Existential Psychology—Convergence and Divergence

Contemporary cognitive behavioural therapy is now so diverse that it can encompass, as suggested by Woolfolk and Richardson (2018), both 'Beck and the Buddha'. For the individual practitioner of CBT this diversity can be both a strength and a challenge. While some CBT therapists may seek to work exclusively from one of the available frameworks, the possibility of a more integrative or pluralistic approach also arises. It is not uncommon to encounter CBT therapists who have trained both in standard CBT and ACT, for example, but with little apparent concern regarding the philosophical incompatibility between the two perspectives. A pragmatic preference for 'what works' being the decisive factor rather than any attempt at conceptual consistency. As the previous chapters have demonstrated, existential themes and concerns have arisen across differing forms of CBT. In this chapter, the points of convergence and divergence between differing versions of CBT and existential psychology are brought together.

Standard CBT—Points of Convergence

It was noted that Beck, from the beginning of his work on cognitive therapy, identified a range of existential therapists as important precursors to his approach. Indeed, he has stated that the philosophical perspective most in keeping with cognitive therapy is existential phenomenology (Clark et al., 1999). A range of authors from within a broadly existential

CBT and Existential Psychology: Philosophy, Psychology and Therapy,
First Edition. Michael Worrell.

perspective have affirmed this and have also suggested that it is through the development of cognitive therapy that issues close to the hearts of existential phenomenologists have been brought within a more mainstream academic framework (Moss, 1992). Consistent with this, Fewtrell and O'Conner (1995) have argued that cognitive therapy can be understood as a structural phenomenological approach to the content of conscious experience. The 'continuity hypotheses' of CBT, which assert that psychopathological responses are expressions of essentially normal processes of learning and adaptation, is also consistent with an existential phenomenological position. Indeed, an existential perspective has the potential to substantially deepen and enrich this hypothesis. For existential therapists, the issues that clients bring to therapists reflect their struggles and dilemmas arising from aspects of existence. That is, the very same aspects of being-alive-with-others that both therapists and clients alike contend with.

Additionally, and in contrast to alternative psychoanalytic or earlier mechanistic behavioural models, existential therapists and CBT therapists both tend to focus upon what the client currently has access to, in awareness, and is able to report upon in regard to their experience and its meaning, rather than relying on more experience distant concepts of an unconscious or notions of stimulus-response contingencies. Both perspectives assert that while a good proportion of human cognition may occur outside of awareness, it is both appropriate and fruitful to focus attention upon aspects of experience that the client is able to become aware of during therapeutic work.

Beck's concept of the cognitive triad can also be seen to demonstrate the existentially grounded nature of meaning in that it includes the interrelated domains of self, world, and future. A more existentially informed explication of the cognitive triad would expand the notion of 'the future' to include the broader dimension of 'time' as depressed and anxious thinking not only focuses on the domain of the future but often dwells on the remembered past in the form of rumination, for example. Nevertheless, it would seem clear that the notion of a cognitive triad as an essential structure of meaning, is highly compatible with a range of existential frameworks that seek to provide a structure for therapeutic exploration.

In addition to a focus on meaning as content, in both CBT and existential phenomenology, meaning is seen as a result of processes of construction and interpretation. As Spinelli (2005, p.199) has stated: 'like phenomenological psychologists, CBT theorists increasingly view persons as active agents who derive meaning from the world via inference and evaluation'. Both CBT and existential phenomenology emphasise that people are active in their construction of meaning and that their processes of meaning construction are often subject to systematic forms of bias and limitation. These sources of bias express a range of species given as well as culturally given limitations. Both perspectives emphasise that while a 'real' world can be assumed to exist separate from our interpretations of it, we cannot have direct unmediated contact or knowledge of this world, and that human reality always remains an interpreted reality (Spinelli, 2005).

As Edwards (1990) has noted, cognitive behavioural and existential approaches both emphasise that therapy has an important educative aspect. CBT explicitly frames one of its most central aims as assisting clients to learn to be their own therapists and also uses a range of explicitly educative interventions and strategies. Existential psychotherapies, taken as a whole, appear more ambivalent about an explicitly educational focus in therapy. Some existential therapists openly affirm the importance of the therapist serving as a model and educator in therapy. For example, van Deurzen-Smith (1988) has characterised the process of existential therapy as 'a tutorial in the art of living'.

Other existentially oriented therapists, most notably Spinelli (2015) have argued that, while existential therapy will often involve important forms of client learning, such learning as occurs cannot be pre-planned or controlled by the therapist, and in fact the possibilities for learning are more likely to the extent that the therapists can successfully set aside any agenda of providing directive educational interventions. Arguably, though, if existential therapy is characterised as a form of human science enquiry, then the therapist can be seen to model and embody a human science approach to descriptive exploration that the client is invited, although not instructed, to experiment with.

Related to the use of directive and explicitly educative and change-oriented strategies, is the issue of the extent to which the processes of seeking cognitive change are consistent with the principles of existential phenomenology. As noted earlier, a defining aspect of Beckian CBT has been the focus on logical-rational examination of clients' beliefs and assumptions. However, it has also been argued that the practice of CBT as related to cognitive change exceeds this definition. That is, while logical rational discussion often forms an important aspect of such explorations, an equally common and often essential aspect are a range of interventions that could be characterised more adequately as assisting the client to examine the contrast and coherence between their beliefs and their own lived experience. Such explorations are not in essence rational or logical but often deeply experiential and exploratory. Similarly, the use of behavioural experiments and other exposure-based interventions are often more directed at the generation of new experiential possibilities, which then become the subject of joint reflection and consideration by client and therapist, rather than a direct attempt by the therapist to change the client's mind. (Padesky, 1993). As Edwards (1990) has noted, the fundamental CBT principles of collaborative empiricism, guided discovery and Socratic questioning are intended to assist clients to attend to all of their lived experience and to use this as the basis for cognitive change rather than attempting to appeal to some external abstract criterion of the rules of logic as the primary basis for achieving cognitive change.

Points of Divergence

While it can be argued that in the practice of CBT the client is considered to be, to some extent, free and able to engage meaningfully and choicefully in the dialogical process of therapy, at the level of theory is it the case that the human being is still viewed in essentially mechanistic and deterministic terms? Beck quite clearly speaks of a 'cognitive apparatus' and seeks to establish an explanatory model of human action. Although some, such as Gilbert (2009), have argued that CBT does not in itself constitute a science of mind, in attempting to base its theory building and research programme increasingly on forms of cognitive psychology that advocate a view of 'mind as computer', nevertheless it can be seen that CBT does make a range of assumptions about the nature of human being that are essentially mechanistic as well as based on a 'correspondence theory of truth'.

A number of phenomenologically oriented researchers and theorists have argued that perspectives that rely upon notions of 'information processing' and analogies of the mind as being 'computer like' are unable to give complete or adequate accounts of meaning in human terms. As Safran (1998), from *within* a CBT perspective, notes, the information-processing approach has been criticised for its view of persons as disembodied computing machines rather than as active agents in the world. Inherent to information processing models is that emotion, thought and action are considered independently. While contemporary CBT models stress a highly interactional view with multiple feedback loops between thought, emotion, action and the world, a view continues to be maintained that it is possible to meaningfully separate these aspects of human experience.

Cognitive psychology has been criticised for introducing 'black box' thinking whereby increasingly complicated functions are 'boxed' in increasingly elaborate descriptions of cognitive process and content. The difficulty remains that many of the functions attributed to the unobservable black boxes appear to only be enactable by a more complete and whole human being. Thus, how exactly do schemas actively select and assimilate consistent information and reject or avoid inconsistent information—how exactly do they know that the information is consistent or inconsistent?

Additionally, as can be seen with Beck and Haigh's (2014) more recent model, to better account for a range of phenomena, the model has become increasingly complex, such that we now have a model of modes where the range of functions and processes carried out by a mode appear more consistent with that carried out by a whole embodied human being. Safran (1998) argues that one of the major difficulties with information processing models is that once efforts are made to identify hypothetical stages and structures of information processing, an infinite regress is created. Where a model identifies various stages, processes and structures of information processing, a question eventually arises as to 'who or what is the agent that eventually acts upon this information in the final stage?'

Williams (1987) in a critique of the adequacy of cognitive psychology, argues that 'meaningfulness' in human terms requires an understanding of 'possibility', openness and choice within context, and that this fits very awkwardly within a cognitive model of 'logical operations'. Williams (1987, p. 218) states that: 'the language of cognitive psychology seduces us into thinking that it is more humanistic and less deterministic and mechanistic than it truly is.'

Fewtrell and O'Conner (1995) argue that the phenomena encountered by practicing therapists are often both complex and experiential and cut across the boundaries of concepts that, within the available cognitive models, are regarded as distinct. Most notable by its absence, from an existential phenomenological view, is the central place of 'embodied lived experience'. Nowhere is this complexity more apparent than in the area of the relation between cognition and emotion. While in CBT, the primacy and causally mediating role of cognition is emphasised, any move towards making specifically cognitive processes primary is resisted in existential phenomenological accounts. To be clear, existential phenomenological accounts of emotion also emphasise the intrinsic role of processes of interpretation and construction. However, in seeking to maintain an essentially descriptively focussed stance that opens up experience rather than attempting to create an explanatory-causal account of experience, existential phenomenology tends to provide descriptions that emphasise all human action as irreducibly 'embodied', emotional and always already within and inseparable from an inter-relational context.

Consider Heidegger's (1962) treatment of the human experience of 'mood'. For Heidegger human beings always find themselves in one mood or other and the nature of this mood can be seen to be revealing of how human beings find themselves and the world as being. In a depressed mood the self and the world and the dimension of time may be experienced all together at once as dark, limited and heavy. This experience of mood is not itself reducible to specific cognitions. Rather, meaning and cognition appears to arise secondarily from this more global and primary embodied mood state. Existential accounts appear particularly enlightening when dealing with emotion states that are experienced as 'all pervading' or like an atmosphere such as dread, angst and boredom. These analyses, however, seem less compelling when dealing with a context specific, time limited, emotional reactions such as a 'spark of anger' or indeed joy. Here, it would seem that a great deal of the work completed by cognitive researchers on the range of emotional experiences in psychopathological states may be open to phenomenological reanalysis and description.

It has also been argued that, to date, CBT models have given a rather restricted and limited treatment of meaning as compared to existential and other models. Brown et al. (2008) for example, have argued that while CBT is centrally concerned with meaning, paradoxically meaning as such has seldom been addressed. Brown et al. argue that in following the research programme of 'cognitive specificity' that is, the project of attempting to delineate the specific types of meanings associated and potentially determinative of distinctive diagnostically defined groups, broader and more abstract forms of meaning centrally concerned with issues of 'meaning in life' or 'loss of meaning in life' has been neglected. As Brown et al. (2008) go on to demonstrate, however, there is nothing within the more basic CBT principles that prevents it from addressing these broader, transdiagnostic or indeed existential levels of meaning and, a consideration of the way these issues have been addressed in existential phenomenological approach to therapy may prove most fruitful for the further development of CBT.

In summary, standard cognitive therapy and existential phenomenology appear to converge on the centrality of meaning and processes of meaning construction and interpretation. There are significant differences that arise, however, due to CBTs alignment of its project with that of cognitive psychology where an analogy has been maintained of 'mind as computer'. From an existential phenomenological perspective such an analogy, contains a number of significant limitations as well as potentially introducing a number of distortions when addressing the nature of meaning as it is humanly lived.

One of the potentially most difficult issues to address when examining the relationship between CBT and existential thinking is that related to the concept of an 'inner' world of cognitive processing and cognitive contents and an 'outer world' of other people and objects. Any model based upon the analogy of mind as computer introduces notions of input and output with internal operations being separate from interactions and events in the outside world. In fact, though, this notion of there being an inner world or indeed an inner self itself forms part of the taken for granted assumptions of western culture, what phenomenologists would call the 'natural attitude'. Phenomenological analyses have strongly challenged the adequacy of this taken for granted distinction between the inner and outer worlds and, in a manner that brings it close to some forms of radical behaviourism, asserts that there is no inner world as such but rather we are always 'Being-in-the-world'.

A related and no less important issue is that of the extent to which cognitions and meanings can be viewed as being 'distorted', 'biased' or 'incorrect'. As discussed above, for Beck, the cognitive apparatus is prone to making errors and mistakes that lead the individual to a distorted 'inner representation' of reality. In this model, the role of the therapist becomes one of teacher, who assists the client in learning strategies for identifying and correcting these thought errors so that a more realistic view of reality is possible. This model has been understood as being representative of both a 'realist' and 'rationalist' philosophy as well as being based on what is referred to as the correspondence theory of truth. This view of the nature of truth is that there exists an objective 'outside' reality that the human being creates internal cognitive representations of. The truth of these representations is said to consist in the degree to which they correspond to the nature of the external reality.

As we saw, Beck does not appear to adhere to an extreme version of this and in fact maintained what he refers to as a 'moderate realism' and it could be argued that he also adheres to a moderate form of the correspondence theory of truth. At the same time, Beck assets that he does not advocate that an absence of psychopathology is equivalent to an absence of distorted thinking and that a particular belief can only be seen to be distorted by reference to a particular context as well as the client's goals. Again, there is a level of agreement with existential phenomenological perspectives that maintain that any particular individual's constructed meaning can be at significant variance with those of others. At the same time, however, existential thinking disputes the notion that any individual's interpreted reality can be 'more real' or correct than another's as we do not have direct and unmediated access to an objective reality.

From an existential perspective, it could be argued that maintaining the notion of distorted thinking or thought errors itself increases the likelihood of distortions and biases arising in any attempt to descriptively clarify and explore a client's lived experience of being. Related to this, the assumed role of teacher or coach that the CBT therapist adopts, is also seen as a source of potential bias in this endeavour, as such a stance is likely to work against the therapist's and client's ability and willingness to 'stay with' and 'open up' the clients experience as this is disclosed. The phenomenological method explicitly requires the therapist to initially identify and set aside any notions of thought errors or distortions in order that a more adequate entry into the meaning world of the client is possible. To be clear, such a stance is not equivalent to arguing that the forms of cognitive bias identified by CBT therapists do not exist or are unimportant. As noted, phenomenological researchers have themselves demonstrated the multiple ways in which human perception is subject to consistent and identifiable forms of bias (Spinelli, 2005). Additionally, this does not mean that the therapist in existentially informed practice does not attempt to challenge or open up the client's world view to other possibilities. Rather, it is asserted that this task is likely to be facilitated by the therapist at least for some time, setting aside any notions of cognitive distortion or indeed any project of direct cognitive restructuring.

A related area of concern is the understanding of the nature of psychological change within standard CBT. As was seen in Chapter 6, Beck's early work emphasised a linear and rational model based upon the correction of unhelpful beliefs as well as changing common biased processes of information processing. Later work on the cognitive model has emphasised that possibility that change does not occur in such a liner manner, and that there may instead be multiple representations in memory that compete for activation. Beck's later work on modes also seems to make greater room for a more complex, pluralistic view in which there are multiple minds or selves that may 'come on line' depending upon a range of contextual factors. As Ottens and Hanna (1998) have noted, this notion of self-plurality can also be found in the works of the early existential analyst Binswanger (1963). Binswanger argued that an individual person can be seen to exist in a range of differing worlds and that the nature of the self-changed, depending upon the 'existential mode' characteristic of a particular relational context. The more complex updated cognitive model would also appear to emphasise the constructivist elements of CBT over the more traditional rationalist aspects that remain at the heart of its self-definition. From an existential perspective the question may be asked that, given the extent to which the model has become more constructivist in theory as well as practice, what would be lost as well as gained should this be more thoroughly emphasised it its self-definition?

Standard CBT, consistent with its traditional focus on the identification of cognitive processes and content implicated in the vulnerability to and maintenance of specific diagnostically identified 'disorders', conceptualises the work of therapists as one of 'treatment'. Existential psychologists may argue that there is nothing within the basic assumptions of the model however that require a belief in the existence of specific and separate psychological disorders and would prefer instead a focus on assisting clients with 'problems in living'. The much greater emphasis now being given to so called 'transdiagnostic' processes would also seem to be consistent with this. Existential concerns and universal aspects of existence would not themselves be seen as transdiagnostic concerns, but rather form the bedrock from which such transdiagnostic processes emerge. Again, from an existential perspective, the continuing emphasis on therapeutic work constituting a form of treatment for a diagnosed problem, would seem to limit the range and depth of dialogue that might otherwise emerge in therapeutic interactions.

Finally, potentially the most significant source of disagreement between existential and CBT therapists concern the significance given to the nature of the therapeutic relationship. This topic will be addressed in some depth in Chapter 11.

Schema Therapies—Existential Dimensions of Meaning

The evolution of a range of schema focussed therapies can be seen to substantially increase the potential for CBT therapists to address existential themes. A number of authors have noted the potential for existential psychology to inform schema focussed approaches. Ottens and Hanna (1998, p. 319) have argued that 'The 'cognitive core' of human experience is inherently existentially constituted'. The schemas identified by Young and others are seen by Ottens and Hanna (1998) as being ontological in nature, that is, they represent fundamental assumptions regarding identity, embodiment, and continuity of the self. 'They (schemas) deal with such issues as awareness, identity, being and nonbeing, isolation and belonging, and meaning and meaninglessness' (Ottens and Hanna 1998, p. 319). This represents a substantially widened agenda for therapeutic exploration. Therapy, within schema focussed approaches, can be seen as addressing a client's fundamental assumptions regarding the nature of existence.

Both schema therapy and emotional schema therapy advance important contributions regarding the status of emotion in cognitive behavioural therapy. In Young's model, drawing upon contemporary neuroscientific accounts, emotion appears as a distinct system, related to but not completely determined by cognition. Rational–logical strategies to work with cognition are seen as often helpful, but also insufficient on their own to work directly with more ingrained emotion-based processes. Leahy's model appears to elevate emotion to a given of existence and advocates a therapeutic stance that sees emotion as essentially valid, functional and essential as itself a form of meaning making and as inherently directed towards and related to a world.

Both schema models can be read as expressing something of a movement towards a more 'tragic' view of life as opposed to the supposedly more 'optimistic' and modernist perspective of traditional CBT. Young, whilst certainly presenting an ambitious aim of 'schema healing' also seems to acknowledge that once an individual has acquired a range of schema based negative emotional responses and potentialities, even when therapy is successful, which is often only after a long and arduous and never fully predictable process, there is always the possibility that these negative responses will be re-triggered.

In addition to the greatly enhanced depth and breadth of exploration advocated by schema-focussed approaches, it was also seen that these approaches have provided a greatly enhanced understanding of the centrality of the therapeutic relationship in promoting positive outcomes. Leahy's (2015) work on emotion schemas has highlighted the extent to which work on a client's beliefs about emotions is best undertaken within a relational context in which emotional expression is validated and accepted. Additionally, he has highlighted the extent to which the therapist's own emotional schemas and their emotional experiencing during work with clients may be implicated in what unfolds during and across sessions. In Young's schema therapy, the traditional CBT emphasis on the therapist as educator and collaborator is greatly expanded. In this model, the possibility of meeting the client's core emotional and relational needs directly (although to a limited degree) through the relationship with a therapist is promoted.

The emphasis on empathic confrontation and limited reparenting in Young's Schema Therapy, would likely be a key area of debate and dialogue between schema therapists and some existential therapists. The concept of empathic confrontation would sit quite comfortably with those existential psychotherapists such as van Deurzen-Smith (1997) who explicitly promote the notion of existential therapy allowing for a robust and passionate struggle with, and opening up, of the client's possibilities and limitations concerning their way of being in the world. As was noted earlier, the notion of limited reparenting is directly related to the schema therapy propositions regarding the existence of universal human needs. Existential perspectives may substantially enrich and extend this analysis by exploring the 'ground' for such needs: that is, what is it about human existence- its thrownness, openness and incompleteness—that is determinative of needs such as the need for attachment?

Young and Leahy, in their different ways, emphasise the often unavoidable and distressing or disturbing aspects of human existence as well as the possible limitations of what may be achieved within psychological therapy.

Constructivist and Post-rational CBT

Chapter 8 discussed a number of constructionists, constructivist and postmodern models and views and how they attempt to overcome, what is considered to be the limitations of a rationalist and objectivist perspective. These perspectives have promoted forms of post-rationalist CBT that emphasise the centrality of interpersonal relationships and self-other representations and 'possible selves', the central role of emotion and a more flexible and less structured approach to the conduct of therapy.

There are areas of agreement and lines of influence between various versions of constructivist thinking and existential phenomenology (Chiari & Nuzzo, 2010). Authors such as O'Conner (2015) and Rhodes (2014) draw upon both aspects of existential phenomenology and constructivist thought in their respective versions of narrative and constructionist CBT. At the same time, there are areas of tension, not least of which is the tendency of some postmodern authors to dismiss the notion of an embodied self as a centre of meaning making and action (however much of this must be understood from a more fundamental relationality) as well as dismissing existential philosophy and psychology as just one more example of a potentially oppressive meta-narrative.

According to Hoffman (2009), existential phenomenology and constructivism converge on taking seriously the philosophical and epistemological basis of therapy and psychological theory. Additionally, they can both be understood as challenges to the limits of modernism in psychological theory and practice and emphasise multiple 'ways of knowing' and the extent to which personal and cultural assumptions may condition and constrain knowing and action. Furthermore, both perspectives are sceptical of claims to knowledge of objective truth. Differences emerge however in the degree to which the domain of embodiment and affectivity is addressed with existential writers maintaining that the postmodern perspective tends to eclipse an understanding of lived embodied experience (although, as was discussed this claim is in turn disputed by the postmodernists). Additionally, according to Hoffman (2009) existential psychology remains more open to certain universal truths of existence such as death, freedom and the desire for meaning. Hoffman suggests that existential psychology can learn much from the postmodern discussion of issues such as diversity, oppression and culture which have been underdeveloped in existential psychology. At the same time, Hoffmann argues, the postmodern therapists could be 'grounded' by the existential emphasis on lived experience as their formulations have tended towards the highly and, somewhat ironically, abstract and rationalist.

As was discussed earlier, the claims that constructivist authors have made that it is possible to distinguish a post-rationalist form of CBT have been disputed. Indeed, Beck and others have at times emphasised and re-emphasised the more constructivist aspects of CBT and have disputed the claim that standard CBT is either rationalist or objectivist. The constructivist perspectives have also had limited impact on the field of CBT as a whole in large part because their critique has remained at the level of philosophy and critical psychology. This is perhaps understandable given standard CBTs commitment to quantification and experimentation as the basis for the furthering of knowledge. The challenge presented by constructivist and post rationalist CBT perspectives has largely been ignored, or quietly absorbed into the standard perspective. This is much less the case for the challenges presented by the range of third wave CBT approaches discussed in Chapter 9 as each of these models has largely maintained the emphasis on the centrality of experimentation and quantification.

Mindfulness, Acceptance and the Third Wave of CBT

It was seen in chapter nine that while a so called third wave of CBT can be identified, its boundaries are unclear and woolly. Some versions of CBT appear to situate themselves in a more traditional cognitivist and information processing perspective while others arise from a behavioural tradition that poses highly significant challenges to the cognitivist perspective. What can certainly be seen to draw these approaches together in a meaningful way is their emphasis on the value of assisting clients to 'be still' with their experience as an alternative to seeking to directly change the content of cognitions. In this, there is substantial resonance with the emphasis of existential phenomenological approaches that advocate therapeutic explorations as a descriptively focussed effort to attend to 'that which shows itself in the way that it shows itself'.

A second feature of these approaches has been an even greater emphasis on the centrality of the therapeutic relationship as a key vehicle for change. As CBT as a whole has advanced, it can be seen that therapists and writers across various models have emphasised the importance of the therapist paying attention to, challenging and considering the impact of their own presence and experience in the course of therapy. Within standard CBT for example there have evolved methods of 'self-reflection-self practice' (Bennett-Levy, 2019) that directly propose that, in order to provide good quality CBT, therapists need to be aware of their own beliefs, assumptions and emotions and how these are implicated in therapeutic dialogues with clients. Similarly, schema therapists and emotional schema therapists emphasise the importance of the therapist becoming aware of their own schematic vulnerabilities. This emphasis is further developed in third wave approaches such that mindfulness-based therapists are required to have developed and sustained a personal mindfulness practice and are also trained to embody mindfulness as a part of any mindfulness-based intervention. Compassion-focussed therapy too, emphasises that compassion, acceptance and mindfulness must be embodied in a real and direct fashion within therapy. Potentially the most consistently relational view has been advanced by proponents of functional analytic psychotherapy. In this model, the therapeutic relationship remains the primary focus of all interventions and the relationship is itself seen as the vehicle of change.

While there is much within the range of mindfulness and compassion focussed approaches that can be seen to be amenable to existential perspectives, possibly the most fruitful dialogues could occur with practitioners of Acceptance and Commitment Therapy. Indeed, it has been argued that ACT may rightly be considered to be a form of existentially attuned CBT in that it explicitly attends to questions of meaning and value to a degree and at a level far more general than that typically undertaken in a standard CBT analysis and treatment of cognitions related to defined diagnostic categories. ACT therapists are aware of the extent to which their model has dealt with themes and issues more traditionally at home in existential psychology. Hayes et al. (1999/2011) has, in particular, emphasised that ACT aims to do justice to the complexities of human existence and to create a behavioural science 'more adequate to the human condition'. However, in making inroads into the existential domain, ACT therapists have also emphasised that they do not come to the dialogue 'empty handed'. Indeed, Fletcher and Hayes (2009) argue that the existential phenomenological perspective has been made 'more scientifically understandable' through contemporary behavioural psychology. There is certainly room for a greater consideration of the possibilities and limitations of this contention. For example, within existential phenomenological approaches, the goal of therapeutic work has on occasion been framed in terms of working with clients to assist them in moving towards and sustaining a more 'authentic' existence. This notion has been a topic of considerable debate within existential therapy as some have seen the potential downside of any notion of authenticity suggesting the existence of a 'real' or 'true' self which may then lead to the therapist making value judgements of when a client is or is not moving towards authenticity (Cohn, 2002). Others such as van Deurzen-Smith (1997), however, have argued that authenticity can be understood in terms of a never final but always potential greater openness towards existence and a willingness to take leaps of faith in defining and taking responsibility for life goals and directions with passion and commitment.

It could be argued that the concept in ACT of 'psychological flexibility' comes very close to operationalising such a perspective on authenticity, as it includes such aspects as being willing to open up to direct lived experience, to defuse from the content of cognitions and to contact the present moment, experiencing the self as more like an open space rather than a fixed entity as well as capacities to choose and 'own' verbally undefended values for one's life direction as well as the capacity to persist in moving towards these directions despite the appearance of unwanted and unpredicted negative psychological phenomena. Indeed, it would seem that ACT as a model and the form of existential psychotherapy advocated by van Deurzen-Smith (1988, 1998) could be integrated in a highly productive fashion.

One of the most important critiques of behavioural psychology was provided by Woolfolk and Richardson (1984, 2018). In their critique, they argued that behaviour therapy can be seen to be based upon an 'ideology of modernity'. In describing their understanding of the ideology of modernity, they draw upon Nietzche's distinction between the 'Apollonian' and 'Dionisian' perspectives which can also be understood in terms of two poles of a continuum. The Apollonian end of the continuum emphasises values of restraint, order, reason and control. By contrast, the Dionysian pole emphasises intensity of emotional experience, spontaneity and passion. The ideology of modernity is seen as an extreme expression of an Apollonian sensibility further elaborated into a world view based upon 'technicism', 'rationality' and 'amorality'. Behaviour therapy, argue Woolfolk and Richardson (1984, 2018), embodies all of these, and in particular they see its 'amorality' in terms of it being unwilling or unable to address issues of value and meaning. In a recent revision and update of this article, Wolfolk and Richardson (2018) argue that while modern forms of behaviour therapy have included concepts of mindfulness and acceptance, in essence nothing at all has changed.

Arguably these authors have missed the extent to which the ACT emphasises on values, its emphasis on the importance of philosophy and clarity on philosophical assumptions and its explicit goals of attempting to work with clients in a manner that undermines unworkable attempts to control psychological experience, at least partially addresses some of the critiques they raise. Indeed, it could be argued that ACT represents a shift along the Apollonian–Dionysian continuum from the extreme end of the Apollonian polarity at least a few steps towards the Dionysian pole. It must be acknowledged, however, that this shift is possibly only a slight one. ACT and contextual behavioural science have been nothing but clear on the ultimate goal of their scientific work as being in the service of 'the prediction and influence of behaviour'. While 'control' has been softened to 'influence' the modernist commitment to a progressive behavioural science and a technology of behaviour change has been maintained and extended.

This clarity regarding goals is also helpful in that it allows the potential limitations to any rapprochement between existential psychology and ACT to be identified. Hayes (2016a) has been admirably clear that the experimental results of relational frame theory and the effectiveness research on ACT interventions do not in themselves provide any direct demonstration that the goals of 'prediction and influence' are correct, true or the only goals that could be taken. Hayes asserts these are value commitments which are owned as foundation but neither proven nor disproven by the results of scientific studies. Hayes (2016b) also writes of the extent to which the goals of prediction and influence provoke an unavoidable tension within the model. It was seen that functional contextualism and forms of descriptive contextualism share many foundational ideas including ideas of context and inter-relation as well as holism. One of the limitations of functional contextualism, according to Hayes, is that its scientific and technological procedures carry the risk of the researcher or therapist losing site of the more relational and contextual nature of human behaviour in a way that leads to a more mechanistic perspective. From an existential perspective this would certainly seem to be a key risk in the manner in which ACT is embodied as a highly active and at times process-directive and 'intrusive' intervention. There is the possibility that in the more frequent introduction of a range of (flexible and principles based) experiential strategies that instead what is produced is an intervention in which the client is being more obviously 'shaped' towards adopting what the therapist views as the more desirable and healthy form of psychological flexibility. The primary ACT textbook (Hayes et al., 1999/2011) contains multiple warnings and admonitions to the therapist to avoid 'canned' interventions and from attempting to directly educating the client towards adopting an ACT philosophy. Such attempts are likely to move the work into being a more directive and educative process in which the clients are encouraged to 'get it'. These warnings of course alert us to the possibility that such a risk exists.

Summary

If the range of CBT approaches are considered as a whole, with the possibility that practitioners may draw from different CBT approaches rather than seeking to locate themselves securely and exclusively in a single CBT model (such a choice of course exists too), then the following points of contact and dialogue emerge as pointers towards a more existentially attuned CBT:

Meaning

An existentially attuned CBT, like all of the forms of CBT reviewed in this book, places a central focus on the meanings people construct and find in their experience. While the specific forms of cognitive content and process identified by the various forms of 'disorder specific' CBT would be included in such an approach, meaning would also be seen to be a much broader and deeper concern and incorporate issues of value and purpose as has been identified in ACT and other approaches. Forms of existential meaning and existential issues or dilemmas would not be considered as 'transdiagnostic phenomena' as such but rather as levels of meaning and concern that are implicit and at times explicit in all forms of psychological difficulty presented to therapists.

Truth, Emotion and Change

Rather than adopting a rationalist perspective and a correspondence theory of truth as exemplified in standard CBT, an existentially attuned CBT will emphasise that meaning emerges through lived and embodied relational experience in a context or world. While cognitions will be seen as important, and frequently impactful on emotion and behaviour, the primacy of cognition would not be asserted in a manner that separates cognition from emotion and behaviour. Instead an emphasis on the inherently relational and embodied nature of human existence would lead to ways of working that are deeply contextual. Consistent with many constructivist versions of CBT, an existentially attuned CBT would be acutely aware that often significant psychological change is unpredictable and can, even when desired for by the client, lead to potentially destabilising and disturbing losses of meaning and coherence. An existentially attuned CBT, would be cognizant of the developments within standard CBT as well as a range of other CBT perspectives that attempt to describe experiences of multiple self-states and would de-emphasise any notions that psychological change can be understood as the correction or eliminations of cognitive errors or distortions.

Relationship

An existentially attuned CBT, such as functional analytic psychotherapy, ACT, constructivist and other CBT approaches, would regard the therapeutic relationship as one of the most significant vehicles of change. The FAP emphasis on exploring the way in which a client's reported difficulties are encountered in the therapeutic relationship and the way in which the therapist becomes for the client 'like others' but also 'not like others', will find substantial acknowledgment and further elaboration. Additionally, existentially attuned CBT will be able to drawn upon notions of Being-in-the-world and intersubjectivity in order to maintain and elaborate a more thoroughly relational understanding not only of the therapeutic relationship but also how all of a client's difficulties are best understood in terms of the manner in which the client attempts to structure and essentialise their relationally based experience of being in the world.

Values

The more one moves towards an existential view, the more challenges and dilemmas may be seen to arise from a CBT perspective. The existential psychologist will agree with Hayes and other ACT therapists, who assert the necessity of being clear about the goals of analysis. The tension between functional contextualists and descriptive contextualists arises due to differences in goals and purpose. As will be discussed further in Part 3 of this book, for existential psychology, as a form of human science, the principal goal and value is seen in terms of understanding rather than prediction and control. For ACT therapists understanding appears equivalent to the possibility of moving towards prediction and influence. For existential psychologists, understanding involves a widening of contexts and an opening up of phenomena as to their multiple possibilities of meaning. For the existential psychologist, the key dilemmas and conflicts that clients experience with aspects of existence itself are best clarified in a relational context that seeks to set aside any explicit attempts by the therapist at directed change. Thus, there may be limits to the extent to which CBT can move in an existential direction. There may be a range of possibilities for a productive, existentially attuned CBT as well as possible 'leaps of faith' that CBT therapists would choose *not* to take in a more existential direction. It is to these possibilities, challenges and limitations that we turn to in Part 3.

Part 3

Existential Challenges and Contributions

11

The Therapeutic Relationship

When running training sessions on the nature of the therapeutic relationship in CBT, I have often asked trainees to consider what they regard as the most important qualities that the therapist should attempt to embody and express, in order to facilitate the development and maintenance of a therapeutic relationship. To open this discussion up, I have also, on occasion, asked them to imagine that CBT is somehow magically fully embodied and 'made flesh', that is, what would CBT be like if they were an actual person? This exercise is often experienced as a highly engaging and provocative one and usually results in a long list of qualities such as:

- Organised
- Efficient
- Rational
- Collaborative
- Unemotional
- Optimistic
- Positive
- Obsessional
- Controlling
- Dull

These lists, which I noted to be remarkably consistent over many years of providing training, seemed to serve both to express what trainees found important and valuable in CBT and those aspects that they found

CBT and Existential Psychology: Philosophy, Psychology and Therapy,
First Edition. Michael Worrell.

limiting, or that they struggled with, or rebelled against in terms of how they themselves felt that they would most like to be in their relationships with clients. On occasion, particularly where the trainees experienced this exercise as a provocative one, I have asked them whether they had also visualised this 'CBT Person'. Most often this person was visualised as male, wearing glasses, and sporting a nerdish sort of 'tank top'. As I was often seen to be presented in just such a fashion, this was then a cue to move the discussion on to more serious concerns. In concluding these discussions about the relational aspects of CBT, trainees generally affirm that their answer to the question 'who are you being when you are being a CBT therapist?' includes such aspects as being a 'collaborator', 'guide', 'teacher of skills and strategies' and 'ally and client cheerleader'.

What are we referring to when we consider the notion of 'the therapeutic relationship'? Kazantzis et al. (2017, p. 17), writing from a standard CBT perspective, have suggested that, historically, CBT has lacked a clear definition of the therapeutic relationship and have offered the following:

> An exchange between therapist and client that develops for the purpose of sharing intimate thoughts, beliefs and emotions in an endeavour to facilitate change. This relationship is characterised by a safe, open, non-judgmental atmosphere that imbues trust and confidence.

These authors distinguish this broad definition of the therapeutic relationship with the more specific concept of 'the working alliance' which is described as:

> a coalition that is built on the therapeutic relationship and involves the congruence of strategies and exchanges that facilitate change. The alliance evolves from the therapeutic relationship and constitutes the therapist's knowledge and skill set, along with the provision of appropriate care. It combines the client's will and motivation with the therapist's passion to promote change. (Kazantzis et al. 2017, p. 17)

There is much within these suggested definitions that can support an ongoing debate regarding the nature and importance of relational factors in CBT. More broadly, the role accorded to the therapeutic relationship, and the qualities that therapists should bring to their relationships with clients, continues to be an area of significant disagreement and debate between practitioners of different forms of psychological therapy. Is the outcome of therapeutic interventions primarily a matter of the skilful application of techniques rather than the establishment and maintenance of a particular form of inter-personal relation? Is the therapeutic relationship to be understood primarily in terms of providing the necessary conditions for growth and development, a sort of soil or atmosphere that promotes psychic change? Frequently, therapists critical of CBT, assert that CBT therapists pay no attention to the therapeutic relationship or even, in particularly extreme forms of critique, assert that the relationships established by CBT therapists are expressive of efforts of control and power (House & Loewenthal, 2008). Leaving aside these more extreme forms of critique, that rely, for their, maintenance upon a principled avoidance of what CBT therapists have written regarding the therapeutic relationship, in what ways might an existential phenomenological perspective contribute to and challenge the range of CBT perspectives discussed in Part 1 of this book?

Is CBT A 'Non-relational' Form of Therapy?

As noted above, a not uncommon critique of CBT has been that it is somehow a non-relational form of therapy. The efforts to manualise therapy would seem to support this idea as is the effort to develop forms of artificial intelligence-assisted therapeutic interventions that are based on CBT principles but do not involve real time interaction with a therapist (Liu et al. 2022). Indeed, CBT therapists have historically downplayed the active role of the therapeutic relationship preferring instead to see the main driver of change as being the specific interventions employed by the therapist and enacted by the client, with the relational qualities at best seen as a necessary aspect of an overall therapeutic environment that makes compliance with therapeutic procedures more likely. In other words, questions of inter-relation have mostly been framed within CBT as being an issue of effectiveness and outcome, with relational factors contrasted with and compared to interventions or techniques. In one sense, it is as though relational aspects can be considered *as though* they were also technical aspects and considered primarily in terms of their instrumental value. Most contemporary CBT therapists, following the early work of Beck, regard both relational and technical factors as of importance. CBT interventions are to be delivered in the context of an overall positive therapeutic relationship. These relational qualities of the therapist in turn are regarded as forms of skill or competence. Arguably, CBT theorists and researchers have shown a tendency to somehow transform relational factors into technical intervention factors to make them measurable and manipulable.

Contemporary CBT discussions of the role of the therapeutic relationship cite a range of empirical research, *within* CBT, that asserts that there most often exists a positive correlation between the strength of the therapeutic relationship (particularly as this is experienced by and assessed by the client) and positive therapeutic outcome (Waddington, 2002). At the same time, much has been made of a number of studies that appear to indicate that a positive therapeutic relationship, as experienced and assessed by the client, is the *result* of competently applied technical interventions and consequent symptom reduction, rather than the therapeutic relationship itself being the driver of change (DeRubeis & Feeley, 1990).

Kazantzis et al. (2017), very much in the spirit of the instrumental view of the therapeutic relationship, have argued that not only do the relational qualities expressed by the therapist provide an environment in which specific CBT techniques are more likely to be effective, they also suggest that these relational qualities themselves may be strategically employed or tailored in the service of client belief change. That is, the relationship with the therapist can itself serve as a form of cognitive challenge as well as reinforcement towards new beliefs and behavioural possibilities particularly in the interpersonal realm. This perspective, as was seen earlier, is also consistent with the view of functional analytic therapy where client behaviours in the context of the therapeutic relationship are seen as a useful sample of the client's wider range of interpersonal behaviours and where therapist responses to these behaviours may reinforce client change in the direction of desired goals. The relational qualities that Kazantzis et al. (2017) refer to are understood in terms of generic elements of the therapeutic relationship and include such things as listening skills, empathy and appropriate expression of positive regard. In this, they echo Beck's suggestions that the relational qualities identified by Carl Rogers (1961) in his humanistic, person-centred therapy, namely congruence, unconditional positive regard and transparency, are necessary but not sufficient for the effective practice of CBT.

Discussions of the role of the therapeutic relationship in contemporary presentations of standard CBT, have stressed the notion of 'collaboration' or 'collaborative empiricism' (Kazantzis et al., 2017; Moorey & Lavender, 2018). In essence, the notion of collaborative empiricism describes the achievement of a form of working alliance in which the therapist and client work together in an attempt to both alleviate current difficulties as well as to teach and establish skills that will support relapse prevention and the maintenance of change over time. In one sense, where collaborative empiricism is in place, the therapeutic relationship at best becomes a background factor and a context for conducting the real work of therapy that is focused on problem resolution. As Judith Beck (2017, p. ix) states in her foreword to the recent text by Kazantis et al.:

> You also need to develop a strong therapeutic alliance so that clients can focus on the difficulties they will experience when they leave your office instead of spending undue time in session having automatic thoughts about you, about themselves in relation to you or about the process of therapy.

As Part 1 of this book has demonstrated however, as CBT has evolved and diversified, and as it has been applied to clients presenting with a range of more complex and long-term issues, the role and significance of the therapeutic relationship has also shifted. In Schema Therapy, an extension of standard CBT, the therapeutic relationship is understood as functioning to directly meet (to a limited degree) unmet relational needs. Similarly, interpersonal and constructivist versions of CBT place a far greater emphasis on the role of the therapeutic relationship as being a key driver of change and where the client's thoughts about the therapist, their relation to the therapist and the process of therapy are considered primary topics for exploration. Similarly, ACT, compassion focussed and mindfulness-based therapists have emphasised the extent to which mindfulness and compassion must be embodied and expressed directly in the therapeutic relationship for these interventions to have meaning and impact. Thus, just as there is no one unified form of CBT, there is no one agreed upon understanding of the role and function of the therapeutic relationship and what qualities the therapist might ideally embody and express within the therapeutic relationship.

Doing and Being in the Therapeutic Relationship

What the above serves to illustrate is the extent to which, in most forms of CBT and in particular in its more standard Beckian, and increasingly manualised and disorder specific forms, what is emphasised are the various 'doing skills' or qualities that therapist bring to their work with clients. Indeed, CBT has sometimes been characterised as a 'doing therapy' as opposed to a talking therapy and where there is an emphasis on therapist and client activity and behaviour change. Critics of CBT have tended to characterise this emphasis as one of 'the therapist doing something *to* the client' and with this there is the suggestion that this represents a mechanistic and objectifying view in which the therapist's authority as expert change agent is privileged over the client's own experience and autonomy. In contrast with this, CBT tends to emphasise a model in which *both* therapist and client are regarded as being experts, with the client as expert on their own experience and what has and has not been helpful, and the therapist as expert in general change methods and specific interventions that have been shown to be of help to other clients who have experienced similar difficulties (Moorey & Lavender, 2018).

The standard CBT perspective emphasises that it is the job of the therapist to attempt to engage the client in a collaborative relationship in which they work together as a team to achieve the resolution of difficulties presented by the client. Consistent with Judith Beck's perspective quoted above, the therapist's personal qualities and attempts to embody empathy, congruence and positive regard are seen as necessary but not sufficient conditions to achieve change. Indeed, the client's perceptions of these very qualities are seen as more likely to arise due to the therapist's competent employment of appropriate intervention strategies (Moorey & Lavender, 2018). Thus, the client's perceptions of the therapist's 'being qualities' here are seen as arising from their competent 'doing' skills.

Existential Views of the Therapeutic Relationship

> 'The primary concern is not about establishing a relationship but about experiencing relatedness as it presents itself to reflective experience' (Spinelli, 2014, p. 9).

Of all the potentially useful and enlightening contributions that existential phenomenology might make to CBT, its emphasis on the centrality of the therapeutic relationship, is potentially also the most challenging. In short, existential phenomenology would consider that the understanding of relational factors within CBT is not so much incorrect or unhelpful but rather that it is unnecessarily limiting. From an existential perspective, as should be clear from the earlier chapters in this book that have described the emphasis on 'inter-relation' as an ontological aspect of human being, there can be no such thing as a 'non-relational' form of therapy. All forms of therapy, including those in which the client is principally engaged with a manual or computer program, are inherently relational. There is, existentially speaking, no non-relational position that can be adopted. It is of course possible, to respond to the given of relatedness in a wide variety of ways, including possibility of closing oneself off and severely limiting exposure to the anxieties and uncertainties as well as possibilities of inter-relational existence (Cohn, 1997). The issue is thus not one of whether CBT, or any other therapy, is relational, but rather what possibilities of relationship are allowed, encouraged and discouraged by the assumptions and practices of CBT therapists.

Existential phenomenology is broadly in agreement with those models, contra standard CBT, that tend to emphasise the therapeutic relationship itself as being the primary site and vehicle for whatever beneficial changes a client may experience through their interactions with their therapist. Just what the qualities and aspects of a particular therapeutic relationship may be that prove to be crucial; however, is regarded as essentially an open and unresolved question. While there is increasing empirical evidence for qualities such as empathy as being key (Castonguay & Beutler, 2006), the question as to the essential, necessary and/or sufficient aspects of the therapeutic relationship, and the specific qualities brought by therapists in addition to the wide range of client characteristics and contextual factors, remains largely an open one. Thus, while existential phenomenological therapy is perhaps amongst the most relational in its emphases and practice, it does not purport to have demonstrated exactly what the essential relational qualities are nor how therapists should be trained or supervised to better embody these in any definitive manner. Rather the particular 'being qualities' that existential phenomenological therapy highlights as being crucial, are held to be so primarily in terms of what its stated goals are as well as its understanding of the nature of client problems in living and the process of change.

'Qualities of Being' and the Aims of Existential Therapy

It is widely accepted that the forms of relationship favoured by different therapists is at least in part an expression of the goals favoured by a therapeutic perspective as well as the tasks and methods best seen as leading to the achievement of these goals. In contrast to the explicitly problem solving and psychoeducational emphases of standard CBT, existential approaches tend to characterise therapy as being in many respects a form of co-constituted, qualitative enquiry. Thus, rather than explicitly highlighting educative or curative goals and consistent with its grounding in a human science model, existential phenomenological therapy emphasises goals such as 'clarification and challenge of the clients experience of living'. That is, existential phenomenological therapy is concerned with forms of interactive dialogue with clients, the purpose of which is to allow for the descriptive clarification of the client's experience of their dilemmas and anxieties of being. The particular problems issues and 'symptoms' that a client may bring to therapy are explored as openings into the client's wider experience of Being-in-the-world. Crucially, whatever emerges as instances of clarification or as possibilities of change, are viewed as the results of an interactive dialogue that is inherently uncertain and unpredictable and in no direct manner under the control of the therapist as expert change agent.

As was outlined in Part 1, the phenomenological method is embraced as a stance towards inter-relational experience that requires of therapists a willingness and an ability to, however temporarily and incompletely, identify their initial assumptions and biases (both theory-based and more personally based) in order to more adequately enter into and clarify the client's experience of inter-relational being. While this attempt places emphasis on what might be understood as the 'being qualities' of the therapist and client as they are expressed in the immediacy of the therapeutic conversation, there is also a sense in which these being qualities are expressed and embodied in what the therapist is attempting to 'do'. This 'doing' is at the same time not reducible to a technique or intervention. What is being attempted by the therapist is an act of entering into the client's experience or worldview in order to give back to the client their sense of what that world view contains, allows and disallows. This description overlaps in some ways with that of empathy as this has been described by Carl Rogers; however, rather than principally being understood in terms of 'this is my sense of what this is like for you' what is being attempted is a more thorough if incomplete and only ever more or less adequate 'this is my sense of what this experience is like when I attempt to experience this as though I were you' In one sense it could be argued that what is being attempted by the therapist is a form of behavioural experiment—that is, an attempt to experience the issues being presented and discussed by the client from within the client's cognitive, behavioural, emotional and relational world view. This attempt of course is then entirely dependent upon the client's willingness to disclose and explore their experience in as direct a fashion as they are able. Existential phenomenological therapy would argue that no direct challenging of the client's beliefs and wider world view is possible or desirable until the therapist has managed to engage and achieve some adequate degree of entry into and understanding of the client's experience in this way.

Thus, a crucial and demanding, and possibly (for me at least!) never completely achieved act of 'bracketing' involves the setting aside of any explicit or deliberate attempt to educate, cure or promote behaviour change in the client. The notion of setting aside the role of 'educator' 'teacher' and 'guide' might strike committed CBT therapists as being somehow perverse or at least an expression of abdication of clinical responsibility and care. However, rather than being an expression of some form of lax and irresponsible stance, for existential phenomenological therapy, this act of divesting oneself of much of the usual forms of therapist expertise and power is crucial in allowing the therapist a more adequate (if never complete and final) understanding of the client's world, as the client experiences this, rather than as refracted through the therapist's preferred theoretical constructions. Through this attempted 'entry into' the client's world, the therapist's descriptions and statements are more likely to be experienced by the client as respectful and open invitations to 're-search' taken for granted meanings, beliefs, values and ways of being.

A primary therapist being quality that might be evident in the above description is that of 'flexibility'. Similar to the descriptions in ACT of an 'open, aware, present and defused' (Hayes et al., 1999/2011) stance, the existential phenomenological stance requires of therapists an attempt to maintain a high degree of experiential openness towards their clients and to attempt to maintain this openness as much as possible in order to allow the client the reflective space, in an inter-relational context, that in turns allows the client the possibility of clarifying, confronting and challenging their beliefs and fixed positions.

While perspectives exist within the broad field of existential therapies that allow for the possibility of more directly educative or indeed even 'limited re-parenting' stances to be maintained, by far, a more fundamental and consistent stance is one that returns the meaning of 'therapy' to its original one of 'attending to' and 'being-with' clients, and emphasises the therapist's stance of 'not-knowing' or indeed as Spinelli (2015) has described 'un-knowing'. This stance is similar to the range of 'non expert' or 'one down' positions advocated by a range of constructivist and post-modern versions of CBT. The notion of un-knowing encourages therapists to adopt a stance that holds open the possibility that client statements and experiences, as well as their own responses and reactions, that perhaps initially seem clear or obvious or fixed in their meaning and significance, are at least potentially open to further revision and 're-search'. This possibility is maintained and supported by a primarily descriptive and exploratory stance that attempts to stay with the lived experience of the client as it is being disclosed within the context of the therapeutic relationship. As noted in Part 1, Spinelli (2015) has provocatively suggested that the benefits of this stance can be seen even more clearly if the therapist is willing to adopt the position of 'idiot' rather than one of expert. Rather than endorsing stupidity, the idea of 'therapist as idiot' serves to further emphasise this stance of holding open a space of uncertainty as to what the client's statements, concerns and difficulties might mean and contain to allow for a more adequate attempt at opening up these for further exploration and clarification.

In an important paper, CBT therapist Christine Padesky (1993) has advocated for a form of guided discovery in CBT that is characterised by open exploration rather than being explicitly or implicitly an attempt on the part of the therapist to 'change the clients mind'. This paper comes close to a phenomenological perspective in advocating for the benefits of the therapist being willing to be uncertain of where they are or where they are going to in their discussions with the client. This is contrasted with forms of guided discovery in which the therapist has pre-defined the end point of the discussion and where there is a correct, more rational belief that is explicitly or implicitly the target of the exploration. As Padesky (1993, p. 4) writes: 'In the best cognitive therapy, there is no answer. There are only good questions that guide discovery of a million different individual answers'.

To fully consider the implications of this, however, might also lead us to consider the use of the word 'guide'. In most circumstances, such as taking a trip, one would engage the services of a guide on the understanding that the guide does in fact know the terrain and the destination. Perhaps what is being offered is the possibility of engaging with a guide who has been on a number of 'trips' the destinations of which were also unknown at the start and as such has some lived experience of doing so but who has never before been on this particular trip. This form of guided discovery seems quite different from the type of more directed exploration that may occur in a manualised therapy where the key cognitions have been pre-identified at the start by the manual. The following example might serve to illustrate some of the admittedly rather vague and 'woolly' notions outlined above.

Sophia is a 30-year-old woman from a Greek background referred to me due to her experiencing several months of debilitating panic attacks. Consistent with many CBT discussions of the nature of panic attacks, Sophia described experiencing frequent 'rushes' of physiological arousal such as increased heart rate, sweating, dizziness and derealisation as well as a strong desire to get out of the situation where she was experiencing the panic, and to call a family member or friend for support and reassurance. These instances tended to last around 30–40 minutes and left her exhausted. Consistent with the cognitive model of panic attacks (Clark, 1988) it was possible to engage with Sophia in a form of guided discovery that included the so called 'downward arrow' that allows for the clarification of forms of 'catastrophic misinterpretation of bodily sensations' that are theorised as being the essential issue in maintaining the experience of panic, in addition to forms of 'safety behaviours' that prevent the disconfirmation of these same catastrophic beliefs. Following along standard CBT lines, the exploration with Sophia of her experience of panic went as follows:

M: Sophia can you describe a bit what this experience of panic is like for you? What is it that happens and how do you experience this?

S: Well, I can feel it coming on like a rush that starts in my stomach. I immediately start to get sweaty and shaky. I feel my hands are all clammy and I get pins and needles . . . then I start to feel as if I am somehow not really there. Everything feels distant and dream like. I absolutely hate it. My heart really starts to pound and my chest hurts. I feel I cannot breathe . . . I feel like I am gasping . . .

M: As you describe that now, how is that feeling? Do you have some sense of it now?

S: Yes, even as we talk, I can feel it a bit, it's not as bad as usual but somehow just talking about it I am more aware it could start at any moment. It does not feel so bad now as I'm here.

M: I wonder if you have any sense as to whether there might be anything about this current situation we are in that might mean that it is less bad, or whether there might be anything you are doing that, as far as you can see that somehow helps you to keep the anxiety at a lower level? (Noting inwardly the poor effort at guided discovery due to asking too many questions at once!)

S: I think I just feel safer, like if anything happens you will be able to do something. I do not know, maybe call a Dr. or something.

M: And when you are not here, when you are at work or at home its different, somehow it's more frightening?

S: Yes definitely, usually it's a situation in which I am alone even if briefly at work. Sometimes when I catch the train even if it's crowded it's not good.

M: And I wonder if you could describe a bit . . . when it's really not good . . . when all those feelings start, the heart racing, the breathing hard and the pins and needles and shaking and so forth.

S: I just really hate those feelings. It's so overwhelming and I cannot concentrate on anything at all. I just want it to stop, and it does not!

M: So, all of them together, those feelings, they are really overwhelming. And I'm wondering if there is a particular aspect of that, that somehow feels the worst?

S: Umm, well you know the worst aspect, and this maybe will just sound stupid to you, and I'm worried you will want to lock me up as I say it . . . I think it's the pins and needles and the shaking. It's that which frightens me the most!

M: Pretty sure I am not going to want to lock you up! But I wonder if you could tell me, when those feelings start or even before they start, what are you saying to yourself about what they might mean? Is there any idea or image or anything like that that crosses you mind?

S: Well, yes! I think it must mean that I *am* going crazy. A person who shakes and has neurological symptoms like that. Maybe I'm losing my mind! Its then that I start to feel not really there, and that just seems to prove it even more.

The dialogue described above is more or less consistent with a standard CBT model of panic attacks. There is, as hopefully can be seen, some limited sense in which I remain open to a variety of possible meanings. While the CBT model biases me in the direction of expecting the presence of catastrophic meanings, I remain sufficiently open to allow my client to state and describe the specific idiosyncratic meanings that she holds regarding shaking, pins and needles and so forth as indicating the possibility of a loss of sanity. There was of course much more to this dialogue and to an exploration of what she meant and understood by 'going insane' as well as an exploration of what she did in these moments to prevent this from occurring which principally involved calling a member of her family or, most often choosing to isolate herself in her room until the feelings pass and she feels she is able to interact with others again.

So far, so CBT. In subsequent sessions, Sophia and I also looked at a range of fairly standard CBT strategies such as 'interoceptive exposure' tasks designed to directly elicit her feelings of panic while also refraining from engaging in her numerous 'safety behaviours' to directly test out whether her catastrophic expectations came to pass. I was struck with her willingness and courage in doing so. Nevertheless, and despite her reports of the reduction in frequency of panic and corresponding improvements in her day-to-day ability to work and engage with others, she ended most sessions with the statement 'But this is all just so overwhelming, and I just feel this can't be me really. I don't understand'.

Taking these statements as both a significant expression of her actual lived experience as well as an indication that there must be important aspects of her experience that I have not been able to understand or have somehow not allowed to be given expression or 'voice' I subsequently encouraged Sophia to describe in more detail her sense of being 'overwhelmed' and 'not me'.

S: It's just that I feel so overwhelmed by this . . . and it shouldn't be happening. I mean I know what this is and that I am not actually losing my mind. But still, I cannot shake it. I know I am sort of better. But I am not better! I do not know!

M: You know, I am wondering. I know we have spent a lot of our time together really talking about these experiences of panic and what you have been worried they might mean. And you have been really courageous in confronting this. But I'm also wondering if it might be of some use to talk a bit more about what this whole experience has meant for you. I do not know if that makes sense . . . but what this has meant in terms of how you relate to others as well as yourself, since this anxiety showed up?

S: Well, I have been a lot more withdrawn . . . I tend to keep away from my family. My mother in particular. She has basically given me a free pass for the next few months as in 'ok you need to sort this out . . . this anxiety . . . you get better and then . . .'

M: And then?

S: Well for her it's like . . . well you get better . . . fix yourself as its time for you to get married and as soon as you're fixed we can get you married! That's all she talks about in fact that's all *they* talk about. I'm supposed to get married but now that I'm not well I am holding up the ship.

Through this discussion Sophia starts to describe her more general sense of being overwhelmed as well as her sense of 'not being me and not being who I am supposed to be in the eyes of my family'. Sophia also is able to 'own' the fact that as much as her experience of panic is overwhelming and frightening, at present it also allows the possibility of withdrawing and finding some space within a family that she experiences as intrusive and pressurising. At this point in my discussions with her, my attempt at experiencing her relationship with her family and in particular her mother, 'as though I were her' reveals a more general sense of being overwhelmed as well as a sense of pressure and 'emergency'. At the same time, I am aware of my own biases and tendency to encourage her expressions of anger in relation to this from the position of 'you are being pressured into getting married which is not what you want'. I feel myself very much aligned with her and somehow *against* her intrusive family. However, at this point Sophia takes the risk of clarifying further aspects of her concern that challenge me into a further step of unknowing and more adequate openness.

M: And so, it's just that you feel really angry, it's like they do not see all the things you have accomplished in your life. You can only be a 'good and dutiful daughter' if you follow the script and get married. And, you are saying that this is not what you want, that's not the future you imagine for yourself?

S: yes ... well ... no ... yes, I'm angry. But I do want to get married!

M: you do? (Confused now and struggling to remain flexible and open)

S: Yes! Just not now ... I do not see why it must be now ...

M: Ok ... so this also seems important. Can you tell me a bit more? You are saying that actually for you getting married is important, but not right now ... What is it then about this demand you experience from them ... to do this now ... that is really hard?

S: Well, it's like they just want to pass me over to a husband ... do their duty and be done with me!

M: And once they have 'done their duty with me?'

S: Then its finished. They can just accept that their responsibilities towards me are over and ... and somehow ... that's its now ok for them to die! I do not want that (sobbing and hiding her face). I just think . . . I do so much for them . . . how will they cope if I'm not there?

M: And . . . please tell me if you think this is off track . . . Is there also a sense of 'I'm not sure how I will be . . . or who and how I will be . . . if I am not with them'?

S: Yes! It's just so overwhelming!

This revelation turned out to be crucial for our subsequent work together as Sophia revealed that she had not until that point put this fear of her parent's death into words or connected it to her experience of panic in this way. Our work also subsequently explored her dilemma of 'who and how will I be if I am and if I am not the dutiful daughter' and her anger at her sense that her current relationship with her parents had placed her in a terrible bind . . . 'In order for me to be a good daughter I should do what my parents ask . . . but in order to do what my parents ask I must move away from my current experience of self-as-daughter and risk losing my relationship with my parents completely'. All these lived experiences were a challenge for me as therapist to attempt to stay with and explore. Crucial as well as challenging, were further explorations that revealed her sense of anxiety, that I too, like others in her family, was wanting to 'rush her forward' to 'do their duty and be done with me', as well as the ways in which, unlike others, I was willing to at least temporarily, set that aside in an effort to listen to her and to allow her the space to listen to herself. Perhaps the most significant experiential challenge provided in the therapeutic work was her sense that was I was at least willing to some extent put aside my strategies for 'overcoming panic' to attend to her experience more fully.

Acceptance in the Therapeutic Relationship

The above serves to also highlight another principal constituent of the therapeutic relationship according to existential phenomenological accounts, the attempt to embody and express 'acceptance' by the therapist. More than a simple willingness to be open to experience, the challenge for existentially oriented therapists to embody acceptance expresses a willingness to be open to and to stay with the lived experience of the client, without implying that the currently maintained stance of the client is in some way irrational, defective, inauthentic or based on faulty reasoning or learning. Rather, in their attempt to 'attend to' the client, the therapist informed by existential phenomenological principles attempts to stay with, experientially inhabit and 'open up' the client's way of being in order that it may be more fully clarified and explored (Spinelli, 2014). In my work with Sophia I believe, it was at least in part my willingness to attempt to remain open to the meanings associated with her experience of anxiety that allowed us to open up, clarify and subsequently challenge some of her implied stances in regard to self-as-daughter as well as the possibilities and challenges associated with her sense of what it may mean to become self-as-wife. In my view, examples such as this suggest that the CBT model of panic, and its associated practice recommendations, is not in any fundamental sense 'wrong' but rather that by biasing the therapist towards engaging in a dialogue with a pre-fixed destination, there is a risk that the resulting dialogue with clients becomes unnecessarily limited and limiting in regard to opening up the fuller implications of the client's experience and response to their dilemmas in living.

Summary

- Existential phenomenological principles highlight the therapeutic relationship itself as being the primary context and vehicle for therapeutic work, without proposing any specific necessary and sufficient conditions that in themselves are seen as the sole drivers of change.
- Consistent with its goals of exploration, clarification and challenge, existential phenomenology returns therapists to the position of 'attendant' rather than expert change agent and emphasises notions of un-knowing and 'being-with' clients.
- Therapists informed by existential phenomenology attempt to engage in open exploration of clients' experience from a position that emphasises their attempts to accept the experience and stances of clients as they are being expressed and explored in the context of the therapeutic relationship.

Experiential–reflective Practice: Challenging your 'Self-as-therapist' Concept

Alone or in a small experiential or peer group discuss your responses to the following: Consider an important aspect of your answer to the question: 'who and how are you being when you are being a CBT therapist?' Consider the commonly asserted aspects of 'teacher' 'educator', 'collaborator' and 'expert change agent'. What possibilities and anxieties might arise for you if you considered forming therapeutic relationships with clients in which those aspects are absent or significantly weakened but where you continue to assert that an exploration of clients' difficulties in terms of their implied or underlying beliefs, attitudes and values remains meaningful and possible? In what way would your practice of CBT become altered? What would be lost and what might be gained by this act of challenge?

Experiential–existential Practice: Phenomenological Listening and Clarifying

The exercises are best done in the context of an experiential training group. They are not intended as 'the right way to practice therapy' but are rather artificial experiments intended to assist the therapist in gaining a lived sense of what it is like to relate to a client from a phenomenological stance. In each exercise there are three roles: client, therapist, and observer. Ideally each person engages in each role and spends 15 minutes or so in each position.

1) Phenomenological listening and silence.
   In the first exercise the 'client' is invited to talk about an experience where they had some form of strong emotional response, be it positive or negative. The client is asked simply to describe what this was like, what came up for them in terms of thoughts, feelings, behaviours, memories, associations, etc.?

   The task of the therapist is: *Listen in silence*. Do not ask any questions or make any verbal comment. Nevertheless, attempt to try and 'enter into' the clients experience. Demonstrate by your non-verbal presence your willingness to do so. As you do so, pay attention to what you are experiencing as listener, what emotions, associations, thoughts, etc. arise as you listen to the other?

After the allotted time has ended, have each person present, client, therapist and observer describe what this experience was like for them, be it uncomfortable, interesting, boring, anxiety provoking, etc. There are no 'wrong' responses.

2) Phenomenological listening and descriptive clarification of embodied experience

As in the first exercise, the client is asked to describe an emotion-laden experience that occurred for them. The task of the therapist is primarily to listen and then to offer questions or comments whose sole purpose is to stay with the embodied experience of the client. What was this experience like for them at an embodied, emotional level? Try to avoid any questions that seek to identify and separate out cognitions or to offer comments or suggestions directed at problem solving or change. Try to 'stay with' and 'open up' the client's statements about their experience as this is being conveyed.

As before, after the allotted time, provide feedback and reflection on what this exercise was like from the position of client, therapist, and observer. In what way are these experiences, if at all, related to the discussion of the therapeutic relationship presented in this chapter?

12

Anxiety, Possibility, Uncertainty

> *Everything is without basis, without substance' and I never repeat it to myself without feeling something like happiness. Unfortunately, there are so many moments when I fail to repeat it to myself.*
>
> E. M. Cioran. *The Trouble with Being Born* (2013).

As we have seen throughout this book, existential phenomenological theory highlights anxiety as a central aspect of human existence. Its perspective on the nature of anxiety is in many respects radically different to that currently embraced within cognitive behavioural therapy (CBT). At the same time, arguably, it must be acknowledged that standard CBT has had its most significant success in developing a range of interventions for forms of the so-called anxiety disorders and it remains, for various agencies and lists of evidence-based treatments, the 'treatment of choice' for these. What, however, is the basic CBT understanding of the nature of anxiety and how might this understanding be potentially deepened and challenged through an encounter with existential phenomenological perspectives? This chapter describes in greater depth the existential phenomenological perspective on the nature of anxiety and how this influences the way in which psychological dilemmas, problems and symptoms are regarded as constituting attempted 'solutions' to existential anxiety, as much as they constitute debilitating and disturbing experiences that may lead people to seek therapy. This chapter argues that developing an attunement to the existential aspects of

CBT and Existential Psychology: Philosophy, Psychology and Therapy,
First Edition. Michael Worrell.

anxiety can assist CBT therapists in providing psychological therapy in a more collaborative, human, and dialogical fashion that allows them to also embrace and work from their own inevitable struggles with, and attempted, temporary and never fully complete, solutions to the 'given' of existential anxiety.

CBT Perspectives on the Nature of Anxiety

CBT perspectives emphasise that anxiety and fear can be regarded as natural and adaptive responses to the perception of danger or threat. While CBT is sometimes criticised as somehow aiming to rid a client of all anxiety or to 'take away' symptoms of anxiety, in fact CBT tends to stress that degrees of anxiety are inevitable in human experience and that it is often the desire to experience no anxiety at all, or the belief that any level of anxiety is unacceptable and a sign that something is very wrong, is itself irrational or dysfunctional. Instead, a basic, biological level of anxiety is assumed to be part of our evolutionary heritage without which human beings would not have continued as a species. In therapy, both CBT and existential, it is most often 'anxiety about anxiety' that is the focus rather than any attempt to eliminate anxiety once and for all. Anxiety about anxiety includes the experiential aspect, as encountered for instance in panic attacks in which the sufferer experiences severe bodily disturbance such as heart palpitations and fast breathing, as well as the behavioural and relational modifications an individual may attempt to avoid and evade anxiety, thereby 'shrinking their world'.

Issues of definition persist, particularly in relation to the difference between anxiety and fear. Barlow (2002, p. 104) defined fear as 'a primitive alarm in response to present danger, characterised by strong arousal and action tendencies.' Anxiety, on the other hand, was defined as:

> a future oriented emotion, characterised by perceptions of uncontrollability and unpredictability over potentially aversive events and a rapid shift in attention to the focus of potentially dangerous events or one's own affective response to these events. (Barlow, 2002, p. 104)

Highlighting a specifically cognitive understanding Clark and Beck (2010, p. 5) define fear as: 'a primitive automatic neurophysiological state of alarm involving the cognitive appraisal of imminent threat or danger to the safety and security of an individual', while anxiety is defined as:

> a complex cognitive, affective, physiological and behavioural response system (i.e., threat mode) that is activated when anticipated events or circumstances are deemed to be highly aversive because they are perceived to be unpredictable, uncontrollable events that could potentially threaten the vital interests of an individual. (Clark and Beck, 2010, p. 5)

Cognitive theory also emphasises the client's experience of vulnerability. Beck et al. (1985, pp. 67–68) defined vulnerability as:

> a person's perception of himself as subject to internal or external dangers over which his control is lacking or is insufficient to afford him a sense of safety. In clinical syndromes, the sense of vulnerability is magnified by certain dysfunctional cognitive processes.

The use of the term vulnerability is interesting as an existential interpretation of this term would emphasise the notion of 'being open towards'. To be vulnerable is to be open to the world and to others. As discussed earlier in this text, the key idea that problematic emotional and behavioural responses are expressive of distortions and biases in information processing, that can be corrected through therapeutic interventions, is expressed clearly in the CBT definitions of anxiety and fear quoted above. Where anxiety is experienced at a level that is regarded as disproportionate and as interfering in an individual's day-to-day life, it is assumed that such anxiety is expressive of: 'a false assumption involving an erroneous danger appraisal of a situation that is not confirmed by direct observation' (Clark & Beck, 2010, p. 6).

There are many situations that arise in therapeutic practice that seem to fit very well with the CBT emphasis on false assumptions and erroneous beliefs about the probability and aversiveness of negative events.

Sarah was referred to me due to a sever phobia of spiders. She had experienced this phobia for as long as she could remember but could not recall any specific traumatic event associated with spiders. Nevertheless, she described numerous instances when she had fled her house upon discovery of a spider, leaving doors and windows open, and the house abandoned, for several days before returning with the help of a relative, sworn to locate and kill all spiders in the house. Sarah maintained that she did not believe that the spiders would directly harm her. Instead, she experienced them as 'disgusting' and as 'having no right to exist' and that the spiders were somehow aware of her anxiety and so deliberately targeted her house. At the same time, she maintained that this could not possibly be true, she knew it to be 'irrational and silly'. She was also aware that others in her life regarded her anxiety as irrational, 'there are no dangerous spiders in England!' she has been informed repeatedly. When asked what she believed were to occur if she were to be confronted by a spider and be unable to escape, or where no help was forthcoming, she stated that she believed she would 'die from fright'.

In my view, there is much within CBT analyses of anxiety that would be informative for existential therapists. For example, Dugas and Robichaud (2007) described the extent to which 'intolerance of uncertainty' can be at the foundation of many difficulties with anxiety. Similarly Wells (2005) discuss how an individual experiencing generalised anxiety disorder can be seen to be experiencing the tension between two seemingly incompatible beliefs such as 'my anxiety and worry is uncontrollable and dangerous' and 'it is important to worry as worry ensures that I am always prepared'. Additionally, CBT analyses have pointed out the various ways in which people will engage in a range of safety behaviours that are felt to be essential to keep the individual safe but at the same time act to prevent the individual from experiencing something new about the trigger for their anxiety. However, these insights tend to be couched in the language of medical disorders as well as maintaining the objectivist and rationalist perspective. Additionally, these analyses tend to see the basic level of human anxiety as arising primarily from a biological given or invariant- anxiety as a physiological process essential for survival. Existential analyses would require the (at least initial) setting aside of the medicalised and rationalist view as well as the biological assumption, in order to address the question of what anxiety *is* as a distinctly human phenomenon.

Existential Perspectives on Anxiety

Existential writers are characteristically interested in the etymology of our commonly used words like anxiety. Cohn (2002) for example, explores the root meanings of the English word 'anxiety' and notes that it is related to the Latin 'angere' which means 'to squeeze, to strangle'. This is similar to the German term 'Angst' meaning narrow and tight and which is also related to the term 'anger'. Occasionally, Existential writers employ the word 'dread' as the English word anxiety seems much weaker than its intended meaning in existential philosophy (Langdridge, 2013). 'Existential dread' also serves to express the notion of this being a profound and general sense or background mood rather than a specific emotion in response to a specific trigger event or cognition.

Existential perspectives can embrace much of what is highlighted in CBT analyses in terms of the specific cognitive processes and behavioural strategies associated with anxiety. These analyses often clarify what is phenomenologically experienced by the client suffering from extreme forms of anxiety. Setting aside any notions that these experiences constitute forms of medical disorder would not, in my view, limit the impact of these analyses nor their therapeutic value as descriptions of frequently encountered forms of psychological distress. While existential phenomenological approaches characteristically approach the issue of anxiety from a philosophically attuned stance, nevertheless existential therapists have proposed that the particular, 'ontic', way in which a client experiences and responds to anxiety depends to a certain extent upon the life history and experiences of the individual. Cohn (2002, p. 70) for example, writes:

> The way in which we respond to existential 'givens' depends upon the experiential pattern we have developed throughout our life. For instance, early and continuing experiences of intense threat and insecurity will give an anxious 'tuning' to our way of experiencing the world. We may focus on catastrophic possibilities and live in constant anxious anticipation.

However, Existential phenomenological theory asserts that the nature of anxiety is not principally to be understood in terms of individual developmental experiences or conditioning or indeed in terms of specific catastrophic beliefs. Rather, existential anxiety is seen as an inherent aspect of existence itself. Anxiety, following Heidegger (1962), is understood as a fundamental form of attunement to existence and in itself is disclosive of the nature of human existence. Existentially speaking, we *are* anxiety. Drawing on Heidegger's philosophy, Cohn (2002, p. 70) outlines how anxiety is an inevitable aspect of human existence and reflects:

1) Our 'thrownness' into a world that we do not choose. For example, we are thrown into a particular culture, time, language and circumstances that we find ourselves in from the beginning. The common teenage taunt to parents 'well I didn't ask to be born!' betrays a degree of insightful, although annoying, existential awareness.
2) Freedom and choice: In as much as we do not choose our particular form of thrownness, we are nevertheless in a position of having to make choices, on the partial bases of choices already made, the outcomes of which are uncertain and unpredictable.
3) Our being-towards-death. Anxiety, for Heidegger is rooted in the awareness that our life, our being, is always moving towards our inevitable yet uncertain non-being. For Heidegger, 'authenticity' which implies being open to existence and awareness of possibility, is intimately related to our awareness of our inevitable movement towards death.

It can be a mistake to simply think of existential anxiety as being a psychological experience or emotion or feeling experience like any other. Its not the case that I have an episode of existential anxiety, perhaps experienced in terms of a panic attack, an obsessive worry, or a feeling of being socially anxious, and then recover, possibly through therapy and no longer experience existential anxiety. Existential anxiety is rather more like a background atmosphere that we exist in, we breathe existential anxiety. Therapeutically, as in life in general, the issue is more how we find ways of being with, accepting and being open to existential anxiety versus finding ways to cover up, avoid and escape existential anxiety. Existential anxiety is not therefore necessarily always negative. Indeed, many of our values and projects in the world can be described in terms of how they are responses to existential anxiety and express how we are open towards and 'responsive to' existential givens.

> James sought existential therapy, due to a long-standing sense of being 'stuck in his life' and being unable to move forward and to make commitments. He revealed that he long harboured a dream of becoming a writer and establishing himself as a well-known personality in the 'literary world'. Did he spend much time writing I asked? No, 'none at all', each time he sat down to write he was flooded with feelings of shame and anxiety. He could imagine all sorts of scenarios and characters for his novel when he was daydreaming but when it came to sitting down to write none of this seemed 'good enough'. James revealed that he also harboured the belief, that he knew also to be in some sense irrational, that he should simply be able to sit down and to write, the story should somehow come out fully formed and be delivered to the page with no correction or additions needed. 'And if it did so?' I asked; to which he responded: 'well then I would surely be discovered and recognised as a young talented writer with potential!' And if this indeed were to be the case? Then, he responded, 'I could retire fully from public view, It would somehow be the case that I had now finally established once and for all who I am and at the same time all possibilities would be open'. Over many sessions, James explored this interplay of his desire for both complete certainty and open and unfettered possibility and how this led to him being flooded with anxiety and shame whenever he attempted to 'risk himself' in any act of attempting to fulfil a particular embodied possibility.

Possibility and Choice

The existential understanding of anxiety is entwined with that of the notions of possibility and choice. The philosophy of Kierkegaard (1980) is of particular value and influence. Kierkegaard described anxiety as the 'dizziness of freedom'. This emphasises that anxiety discloses some form of 'possibility' which remains uncertain and inherently unpredictable. The American existential writer Rollo May (1983, p. 111) provided a particularly clear discussion of this notion:

> Anxiety occurs at the point where some emerging potentiality or possibility of fulfilling his existence faces the individual; but this very

possibility involves the destroying of present security, which thereupon gives rise to the tendency to deny the new potentiality.

As noted in Chapter 4, the existential emphasis on choice is often misunderstood to mean that we have a great deal of 'free will' to choose our circumstances and projects in life, and that any recourse to blaming circumstances is an inauthentic evasion. Quotes such as 'man is condemned to be free' from Sartre may be pointed to as evidence of this exaggerated position. It *is* the case, as asserted in the statement from Sartre, that the exercise of choice is viewed as a basic given of human experience. However, this must be seen alongside or indeed as located at the opposite side of a continuum at which is found 'facticity' or 'thrownness'. Thus, the existential perspective is not that we are free to choose the circumstances of our lives but rather that what choice does exist lies in our response to these circumstances. Even here, however, what choices may exist as psychological and behavioural responses may be significantly limited and conditioned by circumstances. Often the choice we face is one between accepting or 'owning' that which has arrived in our lives (such as a global pandemic) or choosing to attempt to deny, distort or evade this aspect of the given situation. Individual, groups and governments appear more than capable of such evasion. Existential philosophy reminds us, however, that whatever choice we make brings with it the cost of anxiety.

May (1983, p.112) discusses Kierkegaard's cryptic statement that 'Anxiety is the reality of freedom as a potentiality before this freedom has materialised'. This presents quite a different view of the nature of anxiety than analyses that might highlight the role of mistaken and exaggerated cognitions regarding the probability and cost of negative occurrences. For example:

> Stephen presents himself in therapy having diagnosed himself as experiencing 'social anxiety'. He is acutely aware of any upcoming social engagements. He is also a highly socially oriented positive individual with a great drive to connect with others. He describes himself as 'highly sensitive' and as somehow very physically reactive to these situations. Yet he denies experiencing any cognitions regarding the probability that others will perceive and respond negatively to him.

He believes that he will be seen as competent and friendly by most people, and he believes that sometimes that might not be the case but that he can cope with that. There is something though in his experience of the very possibility of engaging socially, in the possibility of being seen and understood by others and engaging with them. His anxiety expresses his stance of both being open to these possibilities as well as the possibility of avoiding them and closing-down.

Existential Guilt

The concept of existential guilt is closely related to that of existential anxiety (Hersch, 2015). It is easy to misread this as somehow expressing a moralistic stance where none is intended. In fact, existential guilt is only loosely related to the experience of guilt feelings and a distinction, although a somewhat confusing one, can be made between existential guilt and neurotic guilt in the same fashion as has been made between neurotic anxiety and existential anxiety. Existential guilt refers to the given of human experience that it is impossible for us to fulfil all our possibilities for being. That is, any choice we make necessitates the letting go of other choices and possibilities. In choosing the one, we also experience the death of many other unrealised possibilities. This is an inevitable and ever-present aspect of our existence. In choosing to read this book for instance, you are at the same moment letting go of other possibilities to, for example, read something else (perhaps something more evidence-based and scientific!) or to visit a friend or watch TV. In the same way as we evade existential anxiety, we may also struggle with and attempt to avoid existential guilt. We may behave, as did James in my example above, as if 'all possibilities remain open to me' or we may attempt to 'choose not to choose' as a way of delaying action. Existential anxiety and existential guilt go together hand in glove. Often, in discussing meaningful life choices with clients, it can be helpful to encourage description and reflection on what any particular choice appears to rule out and to say 'no' to, and what the client might experience if they were open to these various forms of 'loss' even where they face the possibility of a positive choice consistent with their values.

'Problems' as Attempted Solutions

Although contemporary versions of CBT do by and large attempt to contextualise a client's presenting issue in terms of their life story, beliefs about self, others and world, as well as their current and past environmental and social circumstances, there can still at times be the impression that whatever 'problem' is identified as the focus of therapy can be dealt with and improved in a manner in which the rest of the client's life and existence will be untouched and unaffected, other than perhaps a boost to the client's self-esteem. Thus, we can speak of attempts at 'overcoming anxiety attacks' in which the anxiety is seen as a specific problem, the outcome of faulty thinking, that can be corrected so that life can resume as it should, free of this difficulty. By contrast, existential phenomenological therapy views psychological difficulties as themselves constituting attempted 'solutions' to the given of existential anxiety. The notion of different forms of 'anxiety disorder' as 'attempted solutions' to the problem of anxiety, or as existential therapy would have it, the given of anxiety as an aspect of what it is to be human, also appears in the CBT perspective of Leahy (2007) who describes different anxiety disorders as constituting an individual's 'theory' of how best to deal with, respond to and minimise the effect of anxiety. For existential phenomenological therapy, the way these difficulties and disturbances constitute attempted solutions, furthermore, is viewed as always potentially expressive of the client's wider manner of being-in-the-world. Existential therapists therefore aim towards a more adequate understanding and description of the way in which the client's presenting issues are also attempted solutions in order that a clearer, although never complete or final, understanding is also possible of what the potential challenges and downsides of change might be.

Consistent with a range of constructivist and interpersonal CBT approaches, Existential phenomenological approaches view the client's beliefs and stances towards self, other and world as ways of structuring their ongoing process-like experience of being. That is, beliefs, assumptions, and expectations that a client might hold, in addition to being implicated in forms of psychological distress, also allow for the possibility of maintaining a needed sense of identify and predictability in the world. Any change in such structures, in as much as this may provide for the possibility of 'symptom relief' may also provoke unpredictable challenges in terms of greater degrees of uncertainty and anxiety,

> I am working with Dr. David who is a junior psychiatrist undertaking some CBT training as part of his training. He is very enthusiastic and intends to specialise in CBT as a Dr., as he is impressed by its scientific credentials and the short-term nature of its interventions. He is working with Samuel, a middle-aged man, a plumber with a large family, who has experienced panic attacks for the past 10 years. They work enthusiastically and positively together with a disorder-specific protocol for panic disorder. After nine sessions, the client reports that he no longer has panic attacks and Dr. David is extremely pleased and satisfied. In the 10th session however, Dr. David is completely flummoxed and confused. The client has returned reporting that he is now extremely angry. He is so angry that he has spent days pacing about and has shouted at his wife and family and has missed several days of work. Attempting to remain calm and collaborative Dr. David has asked the client what his anger is about: 'I just am so furious! I have spent 10 years with this problem, and you managed to help me in just 9 weeks! Think of all I have missed out on! All the trips I didn't take with my wife…I didn't need to just work in plumbing…why has this happened? What am I supposed to do now?'

The above example is in no way intended to suggest that attempting to assist a client to achieve positive change is unwise or doomed to failure. Nor does this imply that there are not a wide range of CBT consistent strategies that might assist the client above to better deal with his realisation regarding the limitations his experience of anxiety, and his previous way of coping with this, has placed upon his experience and possibilities in life. Rather, the existential perspective suggests that therapists maintain a necessary degree of caution and openness to what the consequences of change might be as these are inherently uncertain and unpredictable. On purely scientific grounds, it is the case that at our current level of understanding the nature and processes of human change is such that therapists are not able to predict with any degree of certainty exactly how a client will experience specific changes through therapy and how these will impact on their wider relations with self and other. Additionally, this is in no way an evasion of the fact that the client may be experiencing severe levels of disturbance and distress and be very genuinely motivated to finds ways of alleviating this. Instead, existential therapy, in a fashion that resonates with the proposals of third wave CBT, suggests that therapeutic possibilities are likely to emerge via the attempt to remain still with experience so that its meaning possibilities and implications can be clarified. The following case example might further clarify some of these ideas in a more direct and concrete fashion.

Is There an Equation for Life?

Adam is a 30-year-old economics PhD student. He has sought therapy initially stating that he needed to sort out some issues regarding his relationship with his girlfriend as he finds himself preoccupied by these to the extent that he is unable to focus on his studies. He describes mounting anxiety and rumination and feels desperate for some relief. His girlfriend of several years works in a bank and he describes their relationship in glowing positive terms. She is accepting and warm and able to put up with his 'various neuroses and general weird way of thinking'. The focus of his dilemma was a brief flirtation with another student at his university. Nothing came of this brief period of 'infidelity', yet he feels that he has somehow betrayed both himself, in terms of his own values, as well as his girlfriend. He wants desperately to know 'should I tell my girlfriend about this? Isn't that the right thing to do?' I am struck by the level of angst associated with this dilemma. He describes his girlfriend as warm and accepting and yet he believes at the same time that this 'indiscretion' could cost him the relationship. 'But what if I don't tell her? What if in years to come I just forget about it but somehow, she finds out- won't this reveal to her and to me that we have been living a lie? Everything could be lost!' I am very tempted to directly challenge the evidential basis to his beliefs regarding the apparent 'infidelity' and the discrepancy between his description of his girlfriend as warm and accepting and his fear that a disclosure, of what seems to be a very (to my mind) minor and inconsequential incident, will result in a catastrophic loss. I manage, however, briefly to set aside this challenge to understand what is at stake for him in this dilemma that is being experienced as an excruciating anxiety.

Adam lets me know that 12 months prior he was seen in a CBT group-based treatment service for anxiety, worry and low mood. He described having experienced several years of general anxiety, fears regarding his health and periods of low mood. He states that he found the treatment very helpful and can recall both the written formulation diagram as well as the various interventions that allowed him to step away from engaging in rumination and worry. But then with a degree of guilt he confesses:

A: 'But I think I have pulled the wool over their eyes really. . .I mean it definitely helped but I think I pulled back from it all in the end'.

M: 'In what way?'

A: 'well I think basically made a deal with myself. . .or the world. . .or god or something. Basically, I told myself, well. . .I probably can't be 100% sure that things are ok, that I am ok and that the future will be good. . .but as long as I have my relationship with my girlfriend, as long as that is secure then I can go on, I can tell myself its worth taking the risk'.

M: 'The risk?'

A: 'the risk that I'm wrong, that I can't rely on my sense of things, that Its all too uncertain and that my life then won't work out as it needs to'.

M: 'And so as long as I can be certain about this relationship. . .I can be certain about the future?'

A: 'yes exactly. . .I know that doesn't really make much sense!'

Adam then tells me that he has developed a very fixed sense of how his life should turn out. It is very important for him that he finish his studies and gain a good position in a company that allows him to secure his financial position in the world. To gain a good position he equates with 'it will be clear who I am. . .I am a respectable person. . .a person of substance'.

A: 'I don't know, it's like I am searching for the equation for life…'
M: 'an equation for life…'
A: 'I know there isn't…but it's almost as if I think there is…that I can find some way of knowing how to make things secure…make myself and the future secure…'
M: 'And if I discover the equation for life then…'
A: 'Then I can be certain that it will all work out…I will finish the studies and get the job. I will be in this relationship with my girlfriend, and it will be a good life'
M: 'But if the equation remains elusive. If it remains uncertain?'
A: 'I just don't know how to move forward'.

In our sessions, Adam continued to circle over the various arguments, all self-generated, about 'to tell or not to tell' his girlfriend. Soon however, what emerges are a range of other unintended consequences of his attempt to 'fix' his relationship with his girlfriend and to make it immune to any form of challenge or change. He states that, since the infidelity, he has been unable to have sexual relations with his girlfriend and that she has started to feel neglected and unseen by him. He also discloses that as well as attempting to resolve what he sees as the ethical issue of disclosure that he has been 'scanning' his mind and body for signs of sexual attraction to other people both male and female in an effort to discover the 'truth' of his sexual orientation and desire. Adam starts to see the similarity between the way he has approached his current and past concerns.

A: 'I guess it's the same as before, isn't it?'
M: 'In what ways?'
A: 'I'm trying to get to some certainty aren't I…and it doesn't work. But I still want an answer'.
M: 'I can really see how anxious this leaves you feeling…and how you are pushing yourself to find an answer. That there is the feeling that somehow there must be an answer. If I have understood at least some of what you have tried to describe however it seems to me that at a basic level there is this sense of "I have to make the future secure and certain. I need to know now that it will work out…that she and I will be together. That it's true and won't be somehow turned into a lie and be lost?'

A: 'yes I know its crazy to put so much on this relationship, but I do'
M: 'Because if its lost? What will I lose?'
A: 'So much possibility. . .I would lose. . . I would lose my future memories!'
M: 'I would lose my future memories. . .what's it like when you say that to yourself. . .how does that feel?'
A: 'I just feel really tense and heavy. . .and panicked. . .I know it sounds strange, future memories. . .like I already somehow want to know the future and what memories I will have'.
M: 'If I know already what my future memories will be. . .then?'
A: Long pause. . .'well I won't really experience it in the present will I. . .but at least I will be certain and not anxious. . .'

Adam struggled deeply with concerns regarding certainty, uncertainty, possibility and anxiety. There were many apparent opportunities during our conversations where I could have chosen to identify and then challenge what might be regarded as thought distortions or even 'unworkable' behaviours. For example, his thinking expressed a degree of thought-action fusion, the notion that having had thoughts of infidelity was equivalent to an act of infidelity. I refrained, as far as I was able, from doing this from position of therapist as expert, and instead, I attempted to work with Adam to listen to, and open up, what it was that he said to himself about his experience of himself, others, the world and the future. My therapeutic stance was an attempt of being receptive and accepting, as well as encouraging him to consider the un-reflected upon implications of his fixed stances regarding who he felt that he should be and should not be. This included his anxieties that in his relationship with me that he would somehow 'fail' to be the sort of client that he thought I might be expecting him to be. Key for Adam was the recognition that his engagement in repetitive thought about his infidelity and his attempts at scanning and controlling his reactions to others, resulted in him feeling less and less present to his actual relationship with his girlfriend, thereby bringing about the possibility of the very thing that he feared- the loss of the relationship. Additionally, his attempts at finding certainty through examining his thinking, his memories and his body reactions resulted in him experiencing greater rather than less uncertainty. Similarly, he started to become aware of those times that he was attempting to engage me in a process of providing him with reassurance in the hope that I could be the expert that informed him who and how he should be. Adam became more willing to experiment with letting go of attempting to come to a 'true and final decision' regarding his 'mistake' and becoming more present to his relationship with his girlfriend, which in turn provoked further challenges and anxiety. He was also able to state, guiltily "but perhaps I might also want her to end this relationship? And yet I don't want this also". Uncertainty, unpredictability, choice, and possibility are for Adam, painful and anxiety provoking aspects of existence. Adam desires to be 'a person of substance' yet often experiences himself and his relationships with others and the world as being insubstantial, as fragile and groundless. Therapy provided an uncertain yet reliable place where he could consider and reconsider his relationship with these aspects of existence, including the possibility that a life of substance includes risk and uncertainty.

Summary

- Existential phenomenological therapy potentially 'deepens' and 'widens' the CBT understanding of the nature of anxiety by clarifying how anxiety is an inevitable aspect of human existence.
- Existential anxiety arises from aspects of existence itself such as our being towards death, embodiment, temporality, being with others and the necessity of choice and inevitability of 'falling behind our possibilities'.
- Many forms of apparent 'psychopathology' can be understood as forms of 'attempted solution' and expressive of the way an individual attempts to evade and cope with existential anxiety. Both CBT and existential therapy highlight anxiety about anxiety as a key focus for therapy.

Existential Reflections

With a colleague or in a peer group consider the following reflective questions:

1) What impact, if any, would it have for your practice as a therapist to consider all forms of anxiety presented by a client in therapy as expressions of an attempts to deal with and reduce existential anxiety?
2) What impact on your way of practicing as a therapist would it have if you were to consider all forms of anxiety presented by clients as problematic and disturbing as also being expressive of the clients' attempted solutions?
3) Consider a clinical formulation you have constructed regarding the maintenance factors for a client's problematic anxiety. In what way do the processes and themes highlighted in this formulation also contain possible reference or resonance with existential givens such as freedom, choice, limitation, being-towards-death, being-with-others, temporality and embodiment? In what ways, if any, does this reflection on the existential aspects deepen or widen your formulation or understanding of the client's difficulties?

13

Dreaming and Describing

All that we see or seem is but a dream within a dream

Edgar Allan Poe

Working with dreams has been a central focus for many forms of psychological therapy. Sigmund Freud's 'The Interpretation of Dreams' (Freud, 1945), in which he suggested that dreams are the 'royal road' to the patient's unconscious, is an acknowledged classic in the psychological literature and most forms of dream work are derived in some respect from Freud's early work, even if their hypotheses about the nature of dreaming and the significance of dreams are vastly different from his. From an existential perspective, dreams have been regarded as less a royal road to the client's unconscious and more an 'opening' in the client's experience of being. This chapter proposes that CBT therapists can greatly benefit from incorporation of an existential perspective on the significance of dreaming into their work. Considering how dreams can be worked with phenomenologically, will also serve to illustrate the value of a descriptive approach, consistent with the 'understanding' (versus explanatory) aims of a human science perspective.

Dreams in CBT

Although recent work in CBT has highlighted the importance of mental images in various forms of psychopathology and has resulted in the creation of new methods for identifying, formulating and intervening to

CBT and Existential Psychology: Philosophy, Psychology and Therapy,
First Edition. Michael Worrell.

construct new, less distressing images (Hackmann et al., 2011); the same is not true for the status of dreams in CBT. However, the study of dreams, and consideration of how they might be used in therapy, features as part of the 'origin story' of Beckian CBT.

Introductory discussions of Beckian CBT often start with his early attempts to submit the psychoanalytic understanding of the significance of dreams to empirical analysis. In short, Beck's early research on the dreams of depressed patients were interpreted as initially supportive of the psychoanalytic notion that the manifest content of dreams (dreams as they appear to consciousness) revealed the presence of latent meanings (unconscious meanings and strivings, that are defended against and are admitted to dreaming consciousness only in disguise) such as 'the wish to suffer'. Subsequent reanalysis, however, was interpreted as providing support for the notion that the manifest content of the dreams of depressed patients did indeed reveal the presence of themes related to loss and defeat but that there was no direct support for the presence, or indeed the necessity to hypothesise the presence of, latent meanings (Beck & Hurvich, 1959; Beck & Ward, 1961). Subsequently, Beck proposed that there was a continuity between the themes and images of dreaming and the concerns and dilemmas of waking life, a position also adopted by Alfred Adler early in the history of psychoanalysis and contra Freud (and as will be seen below a position also taken by existential therapy).

Once the principles of cognitive therapy for depression had been established and elaborated, Beck (1971, p. 26), suggested that working with dreams could be incorporated into the approach as it was possible to: 'regard dream interpretation as a kind of *biopsy* of the patient's psychological processes'. He suggested that a patient's dominant schemas and core beliefs not only had the capacity to structure the content of waking experiences (automatic thoughts and images) but could also exert influence on dreams. As such the patient's cognitive distortions and schemas will often be brought into highlight by dream images and experiences. Beck (1967) also argued that changes in dream content over time in therapy can reflect and express progress and as such dreams remain worthy of consideration. Despite this, as Montangero (2009) has noted, dreams appear to have disappeared from serious consideration in CBT. In her historical work on the origin of CBT, Rosner (2018) has suggested that in part this was due to the need, in the early stages of the development of

CBT, to achieve some distance from psychoanalysis, especially as the behaviourists at that time had become interested in cognitive approaches but wished to maintain the emphasis on observable and measurable phenomena.

However, several mainstream CBT therapists have developed approaches to working with dreams from within a standard rationalist and objectivist perspective. These approaches broadly argue that the content of a client's dreams is open to the same types of cognitive restructuring of distortions and revision of beliefs, as might be used regarding a client's waking experiences (particularly the sort of images that appear related to various distressing beliefs and forms of psychopathology). Rosner et al. (2004, p. 7) have suggested that dreams are:

> messages from a part of our conscious selves that speak verbally, visually and metaphorically. Dreams are also connected to affective experiences, and so, we argue, cognitive therapists can appreciate dreams as the ultimate form of 'hot cognition', densely packed morsels of cognitive and affective experiences that bridge the patterns of meaning making from our earliest preverbal experienced in childhood with the current thoughts and concerns of daily life. They constitute a direct link—without the need of expert interpretation—to the clients' cognitive and affective schemata.

Key to the arguments of Rosner et al., as well as other mainstream CBT authors, is that dream images do not need to be regarded as 'symbolic'—as expressing something 'behind' or 'underneath' the dream image as it appears. This perspective is consistent with the existential view. Where the approaches diverge, as will be seen further below, is on the necessity to adopt a deliberately interventionist stance that emphasises the goals of 'restructuring' or 'psychoeducation'.

Doweiko (2004) has argued that CBT therapists can draw upon research on the neurobiology of dreaming to provide clients with psychoeducation about the nature of dreams and dreaming in order to help them adopt a less distressing understanding of the significance of a dream. For example, he gives descriptions for how to discuss the role of the amygdala in dreaming and how anxious and fearful aspects of a dream may be related to amygdala activation. Additionally, He points out that there is an important difference between the state of dreaming and the waking state in which a client is recalling and describing a dream to a therapist. Here, he suggests, a client will, of necessity, impose a structure onto the dream and that this imposed structure will also express the same cognitive distortions that the client uses in response to other waking experiences. Thus, the discussion of the role of the amygdala may counter a distortion that a dream, of being defeated by a work colleague in a dream job interview for example, is not expressive of a reality in which the client is inevitably incompetent and doomed to failure.

Similarly, Freeman and White (2004) suggest that clients can be socialised at the start of therapy to report and record their dreams for discussion. This, they argue, will facilitate a more in-depth understanding of the client's constellation of cognitive distortions and how these relate to the specific forms of psychopathology that they are experiencing. Furthermore, they argue that the thematic content of the dream is idiosyncratic to the dreamer and must be understood within the wider context of the client's life. Additionally, they regard the affective component of dreams as similar to the client's affective responses in waking life. Consistent with the objectivist and rationalist approach to CBT, they also suggest that the client can be taught to develop skills at restructuring negative or maladaptive dream imagery into more functional, less distressing imagery. Their approach as a whole appears to express both strategies to assist a client to remain open to, describe and 'stay with' the images and experiences of dreaming, as well as strategies intended to assist the client to gain mastery of, and to alter aspects of dreams, that are experienced as distressing as well as highlighting how dreams can provide a vivid and highly condensed picture of many of the client's central concerns, beliefs, assumptions and distortions.

Existential Perspectives on Working with Dreams

As was noted earlier, in many respects existential approaches to therapy have arisen in dialogue with, and reaction to, psychoanalysis. In approaching the question of dreaming, existential therapists have sought to distinguish the phenomenological approach to, and ways of engaging with, dreams, from the early Freudian one. Key to this is Freud's distinction between the 'manifest' and 'latent' content of dreams and the need for interpretation of dreams to illuminate the latent content. This is expressed clearly in the quotation below from Freud's 'New introductory lectures on Psychoanalysis':

> What has been called the dream, we shall describe as the text of the dream or the manifest dream, and what we are looking for, what we suspect, so to say, of lying behind the dream, we shall describe as the latent dream-thoughts. Having done this, we can express our two tasks as follows. We have to transform the manifest dream into the latent one, and to explain how, in the dreamer's mind, the latter has become the former (Freud, 1973, p. 38).

The distinction between manifest and latent content of dreams is one that existential therapists have, by and large, not accepted. In this, the existential approach and the CBT approaches discussed above are in agreement. Existential approaches emphasise the need to stay with the dream as it presents itself, in the way that it presents itself, to let its meaning unfold with reference to the dreamer's wider context (including the context of the therapeutic relationship). While the existential approach encourages us to remain with what reveals itself, in the way that it reveals itself, this is not the same as suggesting that the meaning of any particular dream element, or the dream as a whole, is obvious and straightforwardly present in a clear way. There is a sense in which the elements of a dream both mean what is apparent and that there are aspects of meaning that remain hidden from view and require exploration in order that further aspects of what they mean can be clarified. In existential therapy, 'descriptive interpretation' is used that allows both therapist and client to stay with, describe and 'unfold' what a dream might mean or what the experience of dreaming and recounting the dream may provoke for the client in terms of potential challenges and insights.

Medard Boss, drawing upon the philosophy of Heidegger, has also emphasised the way in which there is an essential continuity between our dreaming and waking existence. In this sense (like existential anxiety), dreams are not something we 'have' but rather: 'we are our dreaming state' (Boss, 1963, p. 261). As Existential therapist Hans Cohn has written, dreams 'are not puzzles to be solved but openings to be attended to' (Cohn, 1997, p. 84). To be fair, contemporary versions of Freudian Psychoanalysis have also emphasised the desirability of staying with the manifest content of dreams and the importance of not overwhelming the dream as it presents itself in therapy with heavily interpretative and transference–countertransference focussed statements. Schachter (2021) for example, points to the difference between 'listening for' versus 'listening to' in how dreams may be received by the analyst.

In working with dreams in therapy, existential approaches emphasise the following:

1) Dreams may provide a highly condensed, rich and affect laden picture of the clients current 'existential situation'. This is highly similar to Beck's notion of the dream as providing a form of 'Biopsy'. A client's way of being is expressed as much in their dreaming state as it is in their waking state. An existential approach regards dreaming as a mode of being or an essential way of being human and as such worthy of description and clarification. Our waking state and our dreaming state may each 'throw light', as well as shadow, upon the other.
2) This 'existential picture' (or as Freud has it, 'text') can be read as expressing both aspects of the client's currently maintained world view as well as aspects of their experience of living that are not sufficiently attended to in waking life and as such may potentially challenge their world view. A dream may provide new experiential possibilities for a client to consider, reflect upon and explore in a therapeutic context. Their creative and expressive nature may support exploration in a therapeutic dialogue.
3) The phenomena encountered in dreams are not regarded as symbolic—as stand ins for something else. So, for example, a white dog encountered in a dream would not immediately be understood in terms of 'repressed sexuality or aggression' or 'depression' (although it may of course also express aspects of these). The phenomena of 'white dog' can instead be unfolded for the many different meanings this may have for the dreamer/client as they are disclosed and elaborated. The point is that, from an existential perspective, the therapist is not in a position of having access to a more accurate or privileged position in which the meaning of a dream can be deciphered with reference to a theory (this includes existential theory).

4) Disclosing a dream in therapy, due to its potentially highly revealing nature, can be an intimate as well as an anxiety provoking experience for the client. Thus, a cautious, collaborative and exploratory approach is favoured in which the client is encouraged to stay with their recounting of the dream to the extent that they feel themselves able and willing to be. There is no true and final meaning to any particular dream that must be arrived at. Thus, a dream, or a dream series, can be revisited many times and may provide an overall metaphor for an entire therapy. Alternatively, working with dreams may be relatively brief and occur as a thread within an ongoing dialogue and where there is no specific point at which working on the dream begins and ends in any pre-planned, overly structured way.

There is thus no manual for dream work in existential approaches to therapy. There are however guidelines and suggestions that can be used, that allow a phenomenologically derived approach to working with dream that are, in my view, highly consistent with CBT practice. The central difference is that there is no attempt on the part of the therapist to encourage a more rational, functional revision of the dream. It is not that the sorts of restructuring interventions have no value, especially when a client reports experiencing dreams in a traumatic, repetitive fashion. Rather, consistent with a human science approach, the phenomenological method can be used to encourage the client and therapist to stay with and slowly reveal more of the potential meanings and challenges contained in a dream. From a CBT perspective, some of these could be understood as forms of exposure which have been demonstrated to be helpful regarding particularly anxiety laden aspects of a dream.

Below I have outlined a series of steps, based on the work of Spinelli (2015) and others, for working with a dream. The assumption would be that the therapist has created a therapeutic relationship in which discussion of dreams is as welcome and as relevant as any other discussion of experience. There is no requirement or explicit recommendation to report on dreams, rather the therapist remains open to all aspects of the client's experience of living as it is disclosed. Consistent with the perspective outlined in chapter eleven on the therapeutic relationship, the disclosures regarding dreams in the therapy session may at times contain resonance and challenges to the therapist as much as they do to the client.

A Dream of 'the boxing ring'

Brian is a 50-year-old man White British man who has lived in London his whole life. He was referred to me specifically for depression and anxiety because of ongoing workplace harassment from a manager. He often presented in a somewhat overcontrolled manner, trying hard to remain 'rational and positive'. He spoke of how shocked he has been by the treatment he had received from this manager whom he had for some time believed to be his friend. They had disclosed personal information about each other's lives and families. Unbeknown to Brian, the manager had been using this information to wage a war of rumours against him in an effort, it seemed, to have him fired and replaced. Brian presented as a highly moral, and somewhat inflexible man. He prided himself on being 'a good man' and felt that this manager's behaviour had violated all he knew to be true about how to treat others in the workplace. After about six sessions, Brian stated that he had the night before the session experienced a distressing dream that was still very much with him, he felt panicky when he recalled and recounted the dream and stated that the dream led to him experiencing a severe headache.

Brian dreamt that he was in a boxing ring and that there was a large crowd of people in the audience that were cheering and shouting. In the opposite corner of the ring, he saw the manager and previous 'friend'. They were both wearing old fashioned boxing gloves. In between them was a referee in white. To his horror, Brian saw the manager place a horseshoe in his boxing glove. The crowd started to roar out their disapproval of this and to point at the manager, however, the referee seemed not to notice or care. The match commenced and Brian was knocked to the floor several times by punches from the manager with the horseshoe glove. Each time he got up from the floor and the crowd both roared their support for him as well as shouted at the referee to intervene. The referee just looked on impassively and motioned for the next round to commence. In the dream, Brian thought to himself that if he were knocked down again, he may not be able to get up.

Below are a series of steps that can help structure an exploratory process with dreams such as the above. It is important to keep in mind that the therapist, during this process, adopts an inviting and receptive stance and refrains from imposing their own interpretations upon the dream. At the same time, the therapist strives to remain open and receptive to the images, thoughts memories, etc. that arise for them as they listen to the client. The therapist's attention also 'stays with' the client's dream as remembered and opened for reflection within the context of the therapeutic relationship. As such the reporting and exploration of the dream may also, at times, throw light upon how the client experiences the current relationship with the therapist.

1) *Give the client space and time to describe the dream in any way they choose.* This could be briefly in passing or the client may describe in detail their dream and how they felt during or after it. Ideally the therapist remains receptive and quiet and notes whatever the client says just after the dream is described as this also may reveal potential lines of meaning and exploration even if these initially seem vague or irrational. In the case here, Brian simply states 'I had a dream I was fighting! So strange. I awoke with a headache and feel so tired and heavy today' saying this he looks at me with a weary smile. After this it can be of help to invite the client to explore the dream more fully, if they wish. A brief piece of psychoeducation may be appropriate as in 'well sometimes it can be useful for us to explore a dream together, if it seems relevant to you, we could slow it down a bit and look at what it may contain and refer to. Would you like to do that today?'
2) *Ask the client to again describe the dream, this time in the present tense, so that they, in a sense, re-enter the 'dream world', and note what additional details, elements, people, scenes, emotions, etc. appear.* Note also how the client experiences this process. Is it distressing, anxiety provoking, or is there also a sense of interest and curiosity present? It can also be helpful at this point for the therapist to give back to the client the story of the dream as they heard it, again placing themselves 'in' the dream as they do this. The client is then invited to say how they experienced the process of listening to the dream being recounted by the therapist. In the dream above, Brian, surprisingly for me, started to smile even more. 'This just seems like a cartoon or like a Charlie Chaplin movie!' he hooted! I wondered whether he was, at this point,

distancing himself a bit as it also appeared to me that he felt distressed, or at least I did as I attempted to enter this dream. In the dream, it seemed that 'I as Brian' felt exposed, vulnerable and yet also defiant. And my thoughts to his Charlie Chaplin association led to notions of the 'comic hero'.

3) *Ask the client to offer any additional thoughts that they have about the dream, what they feel it may relate to, whether there may have been something that occurred for them recently, or historically that comes to mind.* Often direct questioning is not needed, as the process of entering the dream will itself lead the client to make such links and to offer these. This was the case with Brian, who immediately after listening to my attempt at retelling the dream to him from the position of 'I as Brian' stated 'Just as you said all of this I immediately thought back to when I was a kid. . .my father used to make my older brother and I do these boxing matches in the street whenever we had a disagreement. . .every single time! Even if we were just arguing over a colouring-in book, it was 'right, let's get the gloves on and solve this properly' as if that ever solved things as I always lost as he was bigger!' Brian was clearly moved by this memory as it also led him to talk of his grief as losing his father and how his father had provided for him in many ways a clear role model of how to be and how important the notion of 'justice and fairness' was, despite the seemingly contradictory stance that was expressed in this memory.
4) *Invite the client to explore and describe the various elements in the remembered dream, noting the relations that emerge between the dreamer and each element, as well as the potential relationships between each element.* For Brian the main elements that he felt of relevance were: The boxing ring, the gloves, the horseshoe, his opponent-friend, the referee, the onlookers. Again, although the preceding can sound highly detailed and structured, this exploration can be conducted in an open, dialogical fashion where it is the client who decides the level of detail of what invitations to pick up and respond to.

   This contextual descriptive exploration can include (but is not limited to) the following:

   a) *Emotional attunement: what was the prevailing emotional state during the dream?* Both dreamer him/herself but also of the other people in the dream, as well as the overall affective atmosphere? For Brian as dreamer, he described his primary emotional state as one of anxiety, hopelessness, and defeat but also, at the same moment, defiance and determination. Brian immediately referred to his waking world experience with his work situation and manager and the experience of the investigation. He continued to feel anxious and yet defiant in both the dream world and waking world. He described next his opponent's apparent state of aggression, hatred and a triumphant sense of 'I can get away with anything!'. Additionally, he described the crowd's expressions of 'disbelief, outrage and protest' contrasted with the referee's expression of 'indifference and at times seeming amusement and dispassionate curiosity'.

b) *Temporality and spatiality*: Existential temporality highlights the 'multidimensionality of lived time', the present moment contains aspects of the past carried forward and projected into a future. Dreams can be described in terms of the sense of temporality, action occurring swiftly or slowed down, as somehow occurring in the client's past, the present or future. In this dream, Brian felt that he was in the present and yet time slowed at the point of him falling to the canvas and contemplating what the future will hold should he get up again, and yet he also knew that he was about to get up as no other possibility seemed present for him. Brian experienced the space of the boxing ring as cramped and enclosed 'there is no way out- I couldn't just climb over those ropes and escape', by contrast the watching crowd seemed to him to be a sea of people with no end in sight, no boundary, a dark swirling mass of people.
c) *Embodiment: What was the dreamers embodied sense of being within the dream?* This could include everything about what the dreamer noticed that they were wearing, the look and feel of these as well as embodied gestures and actions in the dream. For Brian, the action of him holding up his hands, to form a guard or defence seemed particularly important and stood out.
d) *Contextual aspects of the dream world: what objects and features of the dream world stand out, are they clear or blurred and indistinct?* Brian's descriptions seemed to centre on the action of his opponent-friend placing the horseshoe in his boxing glove. The horseshoe was large and silver while the boxing glove was an old-fashioned brown leather. The horseshoe seemed to shine brightly, 'how can the referee miss it? How is it he can't hear the crowd complaining and protesting?'

5) *Once the various elements have been more vividly and adequately described, the client can be invited to again repeat the dream, ideally in the present tense.* If significant behavioural elements stood out, the client can also be invited to enact these (in whatever way that is feasible and appropriate) as the dream is re-narrated.

   Brian repeated the dream, this time with greater emotional connection, he held up his hands in a 'guard position' and stated 'I have no choice but to get up and fight, this is just so unjust and unfair! How is it the referee would not stop this fight? He seems not to care at all that this will mean I am knocked out! The crowd do not seem to want this and yet I still must get up. I know I am going to be knocked out, but I have to get up!'

6) *Explore whether this, richer repetition of the dream provokes and further thoughts, images, emotions, or memories.* Often, no direct questioning is required as the client's fuller engagement with the remembered dream world will often open a path of exploration. This was the case with Brian who stated 'But this is exactly the situation I am in really, this whole situation with my manager who I thought was a friend. I feel I am being told that I must stand up to him and make a complaint that I know will fail. He cheats and lies and is devious, the people at work can see it, they just want me to be the fall guy, to see if I will be successful'. This discussion also led to him to describe more fully his relationship with his father and older brother, where he felt that he was instilled with a sense of 'the importance of justice and being a moral person, of sticking to moral precepts. If I am moral and conduct myself well then surely, I should be seen and recognised for this!' At the same time, he recognised that in the 'boxing matches' with his brother there was an element of injustice—he always lost as his brother was older and bigger and yet he was encouraged and rewarded for 'fighting on'. This led to the clarification of a key fixed belief 'I must always act rightly and with moral correctness, If I do then others should see and respect that, I will be valued for this'.

7) *Ask the client to sum up the dream in a single sentence. Notice what theme is emphasised in this and then explore what has emerged from the descriptive exploration of the dream with reference to the presenting issue the client has brought to therapy and specifically the extent to which the dream both supports the client's world view and also challenges this.*

Brian felt that this dream threw a great deal of light on his situation. The dream also allowed us to speak more directly about the emotional aspects of his situation in a way that did not seem as readily available when he was describing his waking experience. In his waking life, as it was expressed in therapy, he often presented himself as 'coping and attempting to do the right thing'. He would often assert that he was progressing as he felt that this was what a good client would do in therapy. Brian, in describing his experience of his friend-opponent in the dream was also able to stay with, express, and explore his feelings of anger and outrage towards this man and his desire to 'knock him down!' which challenged some of his beliefs about how he should be in relationships with others. Together we were able to explore his sense of 'no way out' and that he lacked choice about whether he should 'fight on or find an exit to the ring'. I wondered to myself at times whether the 'referee who doesn't see his distress or seemingly care' could express an aspect of his relation to me: had I in some way failed to gain a good enough sense of his distress and what was at stake? This also led to an exploration of his experience of grief at the loss of his father and how loyalty to his father's beliefs system was a key feature of his psychological life.

As is often the case, the exploration of Brian's dream took up considerable time in the session and yet it served as an overall metaphor for both his existential situation and his engagement in therapy. It also allowed Brian to speak about his dilemmas and concerns in a much more experientially direct and engaged manner as compared to how he spoke about his difficulties with 'depression'. He often referred to the dream when considering the possible range of choices available to him regarding fighting on or exiting, as well in discussions about his sense of justice and the extent to which his difficulties with depressed mood and headaches were related to the fact that his experience with his manager had challenged so many of his fundamental 'rules for living'.

Dreams in Supervision

Occasionally, dreams may also be reported in the context of supervision. This could include reports of a client's dream, reports of a therapist's dream regarding a client as well as supervisee's dream regarding supervision or indeed a supervisor's dream! Depending upon the contextual constraints and time available in supervision, exploration of such dreams can also throw light on central concerns and dilemmas in an experientially rich and impactful fashion. As noted above, due to their intimate and revealing nature, the supervisor is encouraged to approach this work with a high degree of respect, collaboration, acceptance and caution. Below is a brief case presentation of a dream occurring in supervision.

I have been working as supervisor with Stephen, an experienced clinical psychologist completing a CBT training and with a prior background in a range of constructivist approaches. He is a highly intelligent, very ethical, and focused therapist who seems to me always to be striving to do the best he can for his clients as well as ensuring that he understands fully the essential principles in whatever he is doing with his clients. Stephen has been describing his work with a female client, Alice who presents, having been diagnosed with generalised anxiety disorder. She shows a great intolerance of uncertainty and struggles to make decisions in her life. This has been explored and challenged in the work with Stephen. A particular incident that occurred for Alice, in which she had bought a pot-plant with the intention of painting it, had become metaphorical for Stephen and Alice. Alice was unable to decide on the colour and was also unable to let go of the project of painting the pot-plant. Alice had become 'The lady with the pot-plant' in our supervision sessions, a shorthand for their mutual sense of stuckness. At the beginning of one supervision session, Stephen exclaimed, 'I had a dream! I dreamt that I was in supervision with you, describing the work with Alice. Instead of your usual good-natured acceptance and tolerance for my confusions about what to do, you suddenly became very strident and critical, you said 'well don't you think you should just hand over this client to me so that I can do it properly? I mean if you are not going to listen to me and do what I say then you really should do that. If not, I really don't want to hear about any of this again!'. Using an abbreviated process of the steps outlined earlier, we were able to explore this dream together to a limited degree that was appropriate to supervision. Central issues that became clarified included:

1) A sense of relief and possibility that could arise should Stephen drop some of his perfectionistic standards for providing perfect therapy as well as anxiety about what that could mean.
2) Some sense of anger and frustration with his client for remaining stuck, and himself for also being stuck.
3) A sense that perhaps our supervisory relationship was at times 'too cosy', was there room for me to be more openly critical of him? or even more challenging, was their room for him to be more openly critical and challenging of me?
4) A challenge for me to reflect on my 'imaginary relationship with the client'—as the dream seemed to indicate, I really did find the work with Alice very interesting, it seemed rich and full of existential themes, and I imagined how I might work with her to explore and challenge these.

Through this, admittedly brief and incomplete exploration, that he was then encouraged to continue on his own, Stephen and I were supported in our mutual project of exploring and challenging his (our) dilemmas and anxieties about what it means to 'be a good therapist'.

Summary

1) Dreams and dreaming, from an existential perspective, are aspects of our experience of being, we do not 'have dreams' as much as 'we are our dreaming state'.
2) Dreams may serve to highlight and dramatize the clients 'existential situation'. There is a continuity between the dreaming state and the waking world.
3) As well as continuity, aspects of the dream may be read as offering potential challenges and alternatives to the client's currently maintained beliefs about self, other and the world.
4) Working on dreams descriptively, can offer to client and therapist alike, a highly experientially direct and intimate means of addressing core issues and dilemmas.

Existential Reflections

With a colleague or in a small peer group, take turns working with a dream, either your own or a client's reported dream. Use the steps outlined above either in full or to any extent that seems to throw light upon the dream. Attempt to make your explorations as descriptive as possible and avoid attempts at transforming the dream images, events, and characters into something else, into symbols.

Consider the following:

1) What was the experience like of disclosing a dream and exploring this with another? What emotions were present, did you find yourself drawing back, avoiding or instead did you find this exploration freeing and enjoyable?
2) How, if at all, do you think working with dreams in this descriptive fashion may enrich or potentially challenge your current way of working with dreams?
3) If you have not considered working with dreams, what does this possibility seem to offer you and what might the limitations of this be?

14

Towards an Existentially Attuned CBT

> *The claim that the ultimate concerns never arise in therapy is entirely a function of a therapist's selective inattention: a listener tuned into the proper channel finds explicit and abundant material*
>
> Irving Yalom (1980, p.13)

This final chapter of Part 3, draws together the key themes explored in this book so far. Following Spinelli's (2015) suggestion, it has been argued that the relationship between CBT and existential phenomenology can be explored at two levels. At the first level, a range of themes identified by existential philosophy and therapy such as death, meaning and meaninglessness, embodiment, etc., can be explored by CBT therapists using a range of CBT perspectives including first, second and third wave varieties. These themes and dimensions, it has been clarified, do not sit alongside other clinical problems or processes as new clinical entities, so to speak; rather, they are dimensions that underlie lived experience. While they can be thought of as 'transdiagnostic' they in fact 'transcend' any form of diagnosis as they are equally present in our lived experience when this is not considered a form of psychological problem. Neither do the existential dimensions cause the expression of psychopathology in any linear determined fashion. In that sense a client presenting with a fear of coffins, for example, is in no way presenting with a more existential issue than a client presenting with anxiety regarding a transition from secondary school to university. The themes of temporality, anxiety, possibility, identity, embodiment, etc. underlying both presentations.

CBT and Existential Psychology: Philosophy, Psychology and Therapy,
First Edition. Michael Worrell.

Developing specific interventions to overcome a fear of coffins therefore, understood as a fear of death (which a fear of coffins may or may not directly express) should not be mistaken as somehow uniquely an existential approach. Nevertheless, different forms of problems in living can be seen to express the individual's stance (and their overall world view) towards, and struggles with, various aspects of existence.

The exploration of such existential themes may therefore extend, and to some degree challenge, the CBT perspective being used. However, at this level, the underlying world view of the therapeutic model remains largely in place. At the second level, the underlying world view of existential therapy is entered into and considered as to its implications and possibilities, a form of existential behavioural experiment, and this can challenge the therapist to consider the anxieties and uncertainties that may arise when embracing a 'non-expert' position. Both levels of engagement between CBT and existential phenomenology are potentially productive, challenging and enlightening. This chapter further explores then, what this encounter between CBT and existential therapy may lead to at these different levels. Working at either level, however, requires that the therapist develop and maintain an existentially attuned ear.

Tuning an Existential Ear

What makes an existential attunement of the therapist possible? Such a receptivity to existential concerns is more likely where the therapist has themselves become aware of, has confronted, and wrestled with, existential tensions and dilemmas in their own life. Many therapists may in fact be drawn to the field due to their engagement with such issues and dilemmas. Having space to engage with and reflect upon such issues within training would therefore also seem useful in developing an existentially attuned therapeutic ear. Training sessions that link the history of CBT to existential therapy are useful in this regard, as are experiential training exercises that allow trainees to consider the possibilities of phenomenologically derived ways of listening and describing. Just as Leahy (2015) has recommended that CBT therapists become acquainted with their own schematic vulnerabilities in relation to emotion, it could be argued that some awareness of their own 'existential schemas' and vulnerabilities is relevant and necessary.

As Ottens and Hanna (1998) have argued, schemas are at a fundamental level about existential concerns. Therefore, this may be more about tuning into and clarifying the existential aspects of schemas that are also about emotions, relationships, embodiment, etc. While it may be possible to produce an existential schema questionnaire, from an existential perspective this would be somewhat beside the point, as existential concerns underlying all schemas.

While existential concerns can be understood as implicit in most problems in living, such dimensions are more likely to be clarified and become a focus for dialogue in therapeutic engagements that are characterised by a greater degree of therapist receptivity and flexibility as compared to highly manualised and therapist-led interventions, that principally focus upon psychoeducation. Allowing existential themes to emerge, requires therapist presence, and space for listening. A therapist stance that embodies openness and acceptance and an ability to 'stay with' experience, as well as tolerating uncertainty, rather than one that rushes in to identify cognitive distortions, or behavioural avoidance, or seeks to immediately find possibilities of problem solving, is more suitable to exploration of such dimensions. Allowing existential dimensions to be clarified and explored is not equivalent to identifying cognitive distortions as it does not require a theory led, or therapist led 'narrowing down'. Such dimensions of existence are more likely to emerge within a dialogical process of 'widening the context for understanding' (Cohn, 2002). As encountering these aspects of living brings the therapist into contact with their own stance towards these dimensions, and their own conflicts and anxieties, an ability to remain with an uncertain, non-expert stance (however briefly) will be more effective in encouraging a client to also stay with and explore such concerns.

Being present as another human being, rather than, an expert change agent, one who encounters and struggles with the same dimensions of human existence as the client, is more likely to allow for the possibility of the client experiencing their own struggles as valid and meaningful. Therapeutic explorations of this type offer the possibility of a form of 'existential validation' of the client's struggles. This has little to do with the particular therapeutic model being used, and more to do with the therapist's ability and willingness to hold that model lightly and to emphasise a human and humane dialogue with the client, rather than conceiving what is being done as a form of medical or technical intervention. The embodiment of such an existential attunement may then allow for, but by no means makes certain, the possibility for existential themes to emerge and become clarified. In tuning an existential ear, what is *not* being suggested is that the therapist should attempt to interpret, assess, formulate or isolate any particular existential theme. While such an approach is of course possible, if the existential dimensions are just that, dimensions of existence, then they require no specific technique in order for them to be revealed. Rather, creating a relationship in which it is possible for clients to reflect upon their lived experience will often allow such dimensions to be clarified, by the client. Existential therapy advocates for a descriptively focussed approach as the most suitable when the goal of understanding is embraced. In most circumstances, a philosophical discussion, or educating clients about existential issues, is not required; these themes are instead encountered, clarified to the degree possible and lived. As Heidegger (2001), in his Zollikon Seminars, reminded therapists, therapeutic work is best focused upon the ontic dimensions (our lived experience of existence), a fear of coffins or worries about university, distressed relationships, etc., rather than a direct attempt to teach the client about ontology.

Existence Themes and Ultimate Concerns

Existential concerns and themes can be seen to arise naturally in therapeutic work with a wide variety of people and presentations. Individuals who have experienced significant loss, or who are facing the prospect of such loss, can often present with a heightened and distressing existential awareness. Much group based, existentially informed work, has been conducted with people experiencing terminal cancer, for example (Vos et al., 2014). People who have experienced forms of trauma are often facing the task of rebuilding a meaningful sense of existence and their place in the world. Even where therapy is being conducted via a manualised approach for a specific presentation, existential issues may arise. Smucker and Dancu (2005), for example, in their manualised CBT treatment for adult survivors of childhood trauma, recommend that the therapist explicitly address larger existential themes in relation to building a more coherent sense of meaning in life. These authors even recommend that clients are asked to read Frankl's (1984) '*Man's search for meaning*' as a homework assignment, as a way of supporting such reflection. Individuals who have moved countries and changed languages, or who face relationship separations or significant life transitions, can also be found to bring 'existential questions' to their therapist. Below are a range of 'clinical examples' intended to illustrate the emergence of such themes within a therapeutic process that is guided by principles and frameworks from a range of CBT perspectives. This approach to CBT practice, includes such aspects as shared formulations, co-created between session tasks and behavioural experiments, but from within an existentially attuned stance. The therapeutic process is more open and less subject to a highly structured, agenda-led process that characterises some current standard CBT disorder-specific approaches. It can be seen below that while a particular example is chosen (constructed) to illustrate a particular theme, that in fact all the themes are present in all the examples at greater or lesser degrees of clarity. Again, it depends upon how the ear and eye are attuned.

Temporality and Being Towards Death

This is perhaps the most readily accessible of the various existential themes and tensions to be identified. As discussed in Chapter 3, it is also the theme that has been subject to the most empirical investigation. Consistent with existential thinking, these studies have, on the whole, supported the notion that we construct various forms of defence or avoidances in the face of 'death salience' and that these defences, depending upon their rigidity and pervasiveness, can also be associated with various forms of problems in living. In supervision and training of CBT therapists, it can be productive of reflection and discussion simply to ask in what way 'anxiety about death' may reveal itself in various forms of clinical problem. While initial suggestions may focus on obvious areas such as panic attacks and health anxiety, it is not long before the general conclusion is reached that it appears relevant in all forms of clinical presentation, even if only implicitly.

As was also noted earlier, various efforts at working with death anxiety directly and explicitly have already been undertaken within CBT (Menzies et al., 2018). These may hold promise in furthering the effort of developing transdiagnostic interventions as well as increasing the effectiveness of currently existing models. Further empirical research will no doubt throw light upon this possibility. Alongside this work, Acceptance and Commitment Therapy has presented itself as potentially the most clearly existentially attuned version of CBT yet devised. Within ACT, the existential challenge of death awareness is explicitly addressed in a range of ways. This has included asking clients to write their own eulogy or to imagine their own funeral and to use this challenging and potentially anxiety provoking scene as a way of clarifying 'what is most important in life'. Yalom (1980) recommended that when working with clients who present with clear and distressing 'death anxiety', that the therapist look also at the other end of the polarity—'life anxiety'—and explore the extent to which the client has so far avoided actualising various possibilities of being that appear to them as important and meaningful. The contention is that the greater the sense of 'falling behind one's possibilities' (Existential guilt) the greater the likelihood there will be of significant anxiety about death. Working with the client to clarify and risk moving in the direction of values is central to the existential approach. This finds a direct parallel in ACT, where clients are challenged to identify important values and risk-taking steps in their direction while remaining open to the distressing psychological phenomena that may arise as they do so.

Working with issues surrounding 'anxiety about death' is always at the same time an investigation into the issue of temporality. As was noted earlier, the existential view of time is that of 'the multidimensionality of time' where the present moment always includes the past, as it is remembered now, and directed towards the future. Various forms of clinical problems have been explored in reference to how these are associated with, and reveal modifications in, the client's experiences of 'lived time'. For example, in depression the client may describe a sense of 'the loss of the future' of time having slowed and become 'stuck'. In manic presentations there may be a sense of time having sped up and existence as offering unlimited possibilities if only these can be grasped. In anxiety, there may also be a sense of lived time as 'rushing headlong' towards a dreaded terminal point. The investigation of the experience of time and its modifications in different forms of psychological distress, has been a major topic within the field of phenomenological psychopathology (see Fuchs, 2019).

Clinical Example

Anne has sought therapy due to a range of problems including obsessions and compulsions, worry, general anxiety and anger. She experiences anxiety that she may be attacked and killed when out in public and enacts obsessive rituals to protect her boyfriend from being killed or dying from an illness. She presents as angry, frustrated and very tense. She dates the onset of her difficulties to a series of financial investments that she made several years earlier. She is plagued by the fact that in her last investment, she 'cashed in' too early. While she made a profit, she made much less profit than she would have had she 'done nothing' and waited. Since then, she has been plagued by indecision and uncertainty. 'How can I trust myself to make any good decisions now? I should have known better, and I should have achieved more'. She describes increasing low mood since that time and an inability to engage meaningfully with others. She feels that her life has lost a sense of meaning. 'I should have done something better with my life and I am running out of time!' When asked what that might be? She draws a blank but then says, 'I think I should be an actress- but its only meaningful if I can be a top actress. An A lister'. Anne then says that she feels that she could and should be such an actress but then says 'I can see that I can't . . . I have already run out of time . . . there are things I can't now do, like be a lawyer or a surgeon . . . I mean maybe I could . . . no . . . I know I can't'. The sense of 'possibilities lost' feels unbearable for Anne. Work with Anne has included a range of standard CBT strategies, including formulation, exposure and response prevention for obsession rituals, behavioural activation for low mood and behavioural experiments regarding her prediction that 'small levels of meaningful behaviour are ultimately without meaning. There is no point!'. Slowly her mood improves as does her willingness to consider the question of 'values' as well as challenging her 'self-limitation strategies' (Leahy, 2015) that both function to protect her and rob her of a sense of meaning. At the end of one session, she looks me straight in the eye and states with some dry humour 'I can't believe the cure is to live my life!'

Meaning and Meaninglessness

That existence is ultimately absurd and without meaning is in fact only one end of a polarity at the other end of which is 'meaningfulness'. While perspectives differ between philosophers regarding the ultimate meaninglessness of existence, there is a general agreement that a seeming invariant of human existence is that we attempt to either impose, construct or find a sense of meaning in the face of apparent meaninglessness. Phenomena and experiences that seem meaningless can provoke unease and anxiety and as such we attempt to find some meaning in them even where this meaning may also be restrictive and anxiety provoking. Current CBT perspectives on psychosis, for example, highlight that the sufferer may have experienced a period of 'anomalous experience' upon which is imposed some form of rigid and distressing meaning, that nevertheless serves to stabilise experience (Garety et al., 2001). The clearest point at which CBT and existential approaches meet is on this question of meaning. Again, the ACT emphasis on values can be read as an existentially focussed way of addressing the larger questions of 'meaning in life'. For existential approaches however, meaning is always understood with reference to its polar opposite, meaninglessness. Thus, existential therapy tends to take a much more cautious approach to changes and shifts in meaning. The argument is that any attempt at making a meaning system more open and flexible, such as the change in an individual's rules for living and schemas, in as much as these might provide the possibility for new behaviours and a lessening of distress, may also contain the potential to provoke unpredictable experiences, as a shift in meaning may include a shift towards an awareness of greater meaninglessness. The question of meaning, in existential approaches, tends to be addressed via the principles of inter-relation, uncertainty and anxiety. Thus, the Beckian Triangle of self-world-future would be read as inherently relational. Any meaning or belief associated with one point of the triangle, implicates the others.

Clinical Example

Suzanne has come for therapy due to her experience of social anxiety and panic attacks. These have had a profound impact on her life and she has become increasingly withdrawn, unable to attend her work as a solicitor or to meet new people. In therapy, she is able to speak openly about the extent to which she fears that she will come across to others as 'weak, foolish, as red as a beetroot and as absurd as a clown'. She responds well to work that explores self-focus of attention. And shows considerable bravery in engaging in video-assisted exposure work to test out the necessity of her various safety behaviours as well as her predictions that she will come across in a manner that others judge as weak and foolish. Her panic attacks also respond well to work to help her identify catastrophic beliefs and safety behaviours. After about 12 sessions it becomes clear that Suzanne maintains a core belief of herself as 'weak and vulnerable' and others as 'rejecting and demanding' and the world as 'hostile and precarious'. After making considerable progress, Suzanne decides to take a big step and invites some colleagues over for a dinner party including one who she has always found to be critical and distant. To her surprise she experienced little in the way of social anxiety at this event and no panic. In the next session, she begins happily by reporting her progress, and then, to the astonishment of her therapist reports 'But . . . this will sound odd, I just feel somehow that I don't know who I am anymore. I'm sorry I know I should just be feeling good'.

Isolation and Being-with-Others

One of the most fundamental existential polarities or tensions is that between the desire to individuate, to become a separate individual with a clear and unique identity, on the one hand, and the desire to become one with a group or another, to merge and to 'belong'. Both individuals and cultures can be seen to differ in terms of favoured orientation to this polarity, with some cultures, particularly western ones, favouring a highly individualised view of separateness and other cultures valuing a greater sense of group belonging. This polarity can be seen expressed in Yalom's descriptions of the two defences against death anxiety, the ultimate rescuer—that expresses the desire to merge with a powerful other or ideology and thereby to be protected or alternatively the defence of 'specialness'—the desire to 'stand out' and be different in a way that will mean death does not approach one as it does to all the others. This polarity may also show itself in couple work, where one partner expresses a drive for individual achievement in the world and expects the relationship to support that, while the other longs for connection and togetherness and experiences significant time alone as a challenge to this. From an existential perspective, being-with-others is a given, it is fundamental to being human, it is not just an aspect of our way of being, it *is* our way of being. Existential isolation may be experienced as a sense of uniqueness and individuality, and as such welcomed, embraced and even celebrated or alternatively as an unwanted sense of aloneness and vulnerability. The lived experience of isolation can be strongly associated with different forms of psychological distress.

Clinical Example

Ian is a 50-year-old English man who has come to see me in a primary care surgery. He is significantly overweight, drinks too much and experiences agoraphobia. He seldom goes out of his house and can only attend sessions if he brings along his pet dog, who is the one being in his world with whom he has any form of meaningful trusting relationship. He lost both his parents when he was in his teenage years, never married and has no children. He used to work in a biscuit factory in his early 20s but lost this job due to automation and somehow found he was unable to take advantage of any offers of retraining. He has often been depressed and has taken antidepressants for years, seldom having the dosage reviewed. In therapy, he has responded well to graded exposure and basic strategies to counter catastrophic thinking. He is often 'chatty' in therapy and acknowledges the therapeutic relationship as one of the few experiences where he has felt that he has permission to speak openly about his experience in a manner that he does not feel will be judged and rejected. He reveals a long-standing interest in music and states that he has over 1000 Vinyl albums of all form of music. Intrigued, I asked him more about this and whether he often listens to his collection, and whether he has favourites. 'Oh no' he states. 'I can't possibly listen to the records . . . I can listen to the radio. I feel that if I listen to a record, it's quite possible that at that point in time, I am the only living person on the planet listening to this particular piece of music, this thought, no, it's not a thought! it's like a crushing sense of isolation and being incredibly small and insignificant . . . I can't stand that feeling, it could drive me crazy'.

Freedom, Choice and Facticity

Early behavioural models presented a picture of the human being as determined by organism-environment contingencies. A sense was given that freedom and choice were illusory. One consequence of the shift to a cognitively based model is a softening of this stance so that the possibilities of reflection and choice arise even if this is within a context of learned behaviour, contingencies and limitations. This view is highly consistent with the existential one that sees freedom and choice as always already situated within a context. As Heidegger has it, we are 'thrown' into the world and largely have little choice in relation to the range of situations and challenges with which we are faced. At the same time, we are inevitably confronted with the necessity of making choices in unpredictable and changeable circumstances. Often, in therapy, clients will speak of circumstances and issues that appear to them to be uncontrollable, and their choices as limited or non-existent. Both CBT in its various forms, and existential approaches, highlight the value of helping clients to become aware of the choices that they have and continue to make, even where these choices may be limited to that between the choice to acknowledge and remain open to that which present itself in their experience, versus the choice to disown this awareness and to seek to live 'as if' the situation can or should be altered.

Clinical Example

James is a young man of 25 who is seeing me for issues related to depressed mood and a 'lack of direction' in life. He sits in his chair, dressed in black, smelling of cigarette smoke. He is often disengaged and highly negative about the prospects of therapy being of assistance to him. James has struggled to engage either with further education or with any vocational training or temporary work. Slowly, and with considerable reluctance and at times open hostility, James engages in behavioural activation as well as work identifying his values and possible direction for his life. He engages in small behavioural experiments to test out his predictions that any deliberate action to gain a sense of pleasure, mastery or meaning will be futile. In one session he suddenly announces that he has come upon a possible direction that he believes will be meaningful to him: he wants to study martial arts! He then spends three sessions agonising over which martial art he should chose. What is the best one? Which one will be the best for his body type, is there a superior one that will 'work' in all circumstances? He cannot seem to decide and then despairs that in fact in his local area there are only three possibilities and each of these seems not to be the 'ultimate most effective art'. Will he take a risk that he could make a wrong choice and study a martial art that is not the best and most effective but that could nevertheless be meaningful? For the moment he is only able to partly acknowledge that he is 'choosing not to choose' in the hope that the best way forward, or a choice that is not available suddenly, magically, becomes so.

In all the examples discussed earlier, existential themes and concerns arose within a therapeutic process that also included work from a CBT orientation. The existential aspects of the work, once they were clarified, acted to deepen the therapeutic engagement and to increase the sense that what was being discussed in therapy, including the technical interventions, were vitally related to the client's experience of life. This offered a form of existential validation in a therapeutic encounter that contained a sense of engagement and mutual dialogue. What might the implications then be, of more fully entering into and engaging with the underlying world view of existential therapy?

Existential Challenges—A Human Science Approach to CBT?

A more thoroughgoing encounter with existential phenomenological thinking brings with it a range of significant challenges. We have seen that existential therapy can be considered a form of human science, where the goals of the endeavour are principally aligned with that of 'understanding'. This is contrasted with natural science approaches, such as CBT, where the goal is to develop causal-explanatory models or indeed as ACT continues to assert, to pursue the possibilities of 'prediction and control of behaviour'. We also saw, however, that while at a theoretical and conceptual level, CBT presents itself as primarily a form of explanatory science, at the level of practice it clearly draws upon, and indeed necessarily employs, a human science perspective on understanding. That is, CBT as a practice is not sufficiently accounted for or described by a natural science framework. What might arise if the human science aspects are more fully embraced?

The Question of Therapist Expertise

We have seen that one of the central challenges of an existential approach, principally arising from phenomenology, is the desirability of taking up a 'non expert' stance in relation to the client. This is expressed in terms such as 'not- knowing' or 'un-knowing' or even, most provocative of all, 'therapist as idiot'. This stance arises directly from the phenomenological approach, that requires the setting aside of as many preconceptions and hypotheses as can be identified in order to, temporarily and only ever more or less adequately, adopt a degree of openness to what is encountered. For the CBT therapist, schooled in a variety of technical intervention skills, this can potentially seem an unwelcome and even irresponsible position to take. However, the adoption of a non-expert stance in fact requires its own form of expertise. It can be a challenging stance to maintain as it is both cognitively and emotionally demanding. The principal quality of being that existentially oriented therapists' attempts to embody is one of a willingness to accept the client's experience of the world as it is being expressed in the way that it is being expressed. The therapist's expertise consists in their willingness and the degree of flexibility that they can maintain in order to attempt some degree of understanding of how the client experiences themselves and themselves in relation to others and the world, including their relation to the therapist.

At times, this stance of the therapist is likely to expose them directly to client worlds that appear so different and full of anxiety and distress that the encounter becomes disorienting and difficult to sustain. The therapist may become defended, drawn back and subtly or not so subtly express forms of non-acceptance of the client's experience, at times expressed via 'helpful' suggestions of what the client can potentially 'think or do better'. Alternatively, the therapist may come across client worlds that are in many respects highly similar to their own, and their attempt to enter into, open up and challenge these worlds, 'from the inside' so to speak, exposes them to potential challenges of their own world view that they have not previously considered. Roberts Leahy's (2001) work on possible forms of schema match and mismatch between therapist and client, seems to pick up these possibilities in an insightful and helpful way.

Learning to listen and describe phenomenologically can also be understood as a form of skill, although one that needs to be embodied and lived rather than employed or implemented from a manual (see Ihde, 1986). Clinical supervision becomes the principle means for doing so. Most often, such supervision will focus upon a challenging exploration of what it is about the encounter with the client that the therapist finds difficult to stay with and accept. In existential work the being of the therapist is always implicated in what arises.

The Questions of Objectivity and Formulation

We have also seen that existential thought challenges the notion that therapists are able to take a privileged, objective stance, towards the client's difficulties. This phenomenologically derived stance makes it difficult to talk usefully of client's distorted thinking as there is no position in which the therapist can be seen to have a more rational or more objective view on the nature of external reality. Both CBT and phenomenology agree that human perception is characterised by significant biases and limitations. However, once the idea that it is possible to directly identify and change distorted thinking by virtue of the therapist having access to an objective view is challenged, therapeutic practice by necessity becomes more consistent with the exploratory, tentative and open process that a variety of constructivist, third-wave CBT, and existential therapies favour.

This perspective also has implications for the place of clinical formulations as well as how the therapist approaches the issue of structuring sessions. In standard CBT practice, formulations are ideally co-constructed in a highly collaborative fashion that the client experiences as a useful redescription of the nature of their presenting problems. At the same time, from a natural science perspective the sense is given that the formulation is undertaken as an initial step to ensure that there is a correct view of the nature of a static existing problem before the appropriate intervention is then implemented. From a human science perspective, the formulation emerges from the process of dialogue itself. In this sense, the formulation *is* the intervention, it is not an initial preliminary step of ensuring an objective view of the actual situation is taken. The act of description and staying still, paradoxically may lead to movement and change.

Therapy as Dialogue

In the training of CBT therapists currently, much focus is initially given to the issue of 'structuring sessions'. Therapists are instructed in strategies to ensure that each session is planned carefully, with discrete periods of time allocated for specific tasks and topics. This can lead to therapy sessions that appear more like a business meeting, with a set agenda that favours an intellectual and limited form of engagement. Edwards (1990) has argued that existentially focussed therapists may be too quick to dismiss the potential effectiveness of the direct cognitive change strategies used within CBT, especially when delivered within a highly collaborative therapeutic engagement. Nevertheless, he argues that there is a tendency within CBT for the potential of the therapist's 'presence' to be more technical and efficiency focussed which may in turn limit the potential impact of therapeutic exploration. He states:

> For cognitive therapists, well versed in strategies for change of proven effectiveness, the phenomenological perspective offers a challenge to cultivate a depth of human presence to complement technical skills. Trained to access surface meanings and to move rapidly into the restructuring phase, their attempts to structure the session, teach skills, help plan homework projects and otherwise control the content of therapy sessions can result in the relationship becoming business like in quality and therapists' empathy becoming rather shallow (Edwards, 1990, p. 115).

The idea of structuring sessions arose in Beck et al. (1979) work with depressed clients. The task of providing structure and focus was intended to provide some degree of initial engagement and hope to very demoralised individuals. That is, adopting a structured approach expressed: 'this session with me can be meaningful and focused, it will address central concerns that you have ... it will also be time limited'. Such a stance can, in other words, be highly functional in a situation where the client finds it very difficult to focus their attention, to remember what is discussed or to experience any hope that what is discussed will be useful. Unfortunately, this stance appears over time to have been generalised to situations where it becomes less necessary and seems more to express the therapist's anxiety about needing to maintain control over the session.

The existential perspective favours the notion of dialogue or conversation. Therapy as dialogue asserts that therapeutic conversations are more likely to occur to the extent that the therapist sets aside any attempt to control the content or focus of the session. A true dialogue is not something that the therapist can pre-plan, control or bring about on their own. It requires a degree of mutuality and openness on both participants for it to emerge. It can be challenging and unpredictable for both participants.

Therapy as Education

Contemporary CBT explicitly aims at helping clients to become their own therapists. There are some challenging and useful implications of this stance. At one level such a stance aims, as the old behavioural perspective has it, to 'give therapy away'. This is in contrast to therapeutic approaches, and there are many of these, that present the therapist as knowledgeable expert and where this knowledge is necessarily too complicated and arcane to be directly shared with the client in a transparent way. CBT aims to attain a degree of transparency with clients and to assist them in testing out directly, whether the skills and knowledge of the therapist is useful to them and something that they wish to take forward. Existential approaches, on the other hand, challenge the idea that the therapist can be in a position to directly educate the client or determine, in a controlled pre-planned way, what the client will take from therapeutic sessions as meaningful and helpful. It is not that education and learning will not occur, but rather that this is not in the therapist's gift to control and delimit. Existential therapists, in adopting a human science aligned phenomenological approach, are just as likely to provide clients with a setting and a relationship that promotes learning. Indeed, it is highly likely that in existential work the therapist models directly a human science approach to the exploration of problems in living that the client may well then experiment with, without this having been presented as the correct rational or logical approach that must be taken.

For existential therapists, the human science and phenomenological stance is one that is ultimately lived and embodied. It is not graspable as a technical strategy and is resistant to manualization. Experienced CBT therapists also embody the CBT model in a flexible way that is an expression of their way of being with themselves and others. Ongoing dialogue between CBT and Existential Therapy continues to be, a worthwhile although challenging and uncertain enterprise. In the final section of this book, we turn to two such attempts at dialogue, the first between three CBT therapists who have a shared interest in existential perspectives and the second with an existential therapist.

Summary

- Existential themes and concerns arise naturally during therapy.
- Becoming aware of these requires that the therapist tune an 'existential ear'.
- Therapy conducted along a less structured, more open, receptive and flexible manner is more likely to facilitate an existential attunement.
- Working with existential themes often confronts the therapist with their own anxieties, uncertainties and evasions of the existential dimension of their experience of living.
- Working from a human science perspective that draws upon phenomenology, requires the adoption of a non-expert stance.
- Therapy that includes the existential dimension is best conducted as a form of conversation or dialogue rather than a technical intervention.

Existential Reflections

In a small group of peers, or alone, consider the following:

- In what ways, if any, does the discussion of the existential dimensions of human existence open new avenues in your current way of working with clients?
- What do you consider to be the possibilities and limitations of a 'non-expert' stance to your current way of practicing as a therapist?
- Discuss an experience you have had in your therapeutic work with a client where you found it difficult to stay with and accept that client's way of being. What was revealed for you through this experience?

Part 4

Dialogues on CBT and Existential Psychology

15

Thomas Heidenreich and Alexander Noyon

What was missing was the soul, the heart

Michael: Tell me a little about your engagement with existential ideas and existential therapies.

Alexander: My contact with existential thinking was more or less 'by accident'. It was at the end of my psychology studies at Saarbrücken University, in 1994. To be honest, I was a bit disappointed by my clinical studies so far. I really got into contact just with cognitive behaviour therapy and with psychoanalysis, and back then both didn't suit me, especially because of different degrees of reductionism. I strongly felt that something was missing here—psychoanalysis was way too pathology oriented to me, and CBT seemed to be pretty mechanic, technical, and partly inhuman (I still remember that I was disgusted when our CBT lecturer back then told us in one seminar, that it was usual practice in the inpatient treatment of patients with eating disorders, that when they didn't gain weight they were punished by being forbidden to visit the toilet and that instead they were given a bedpan that they had to take care of themselves).

In retrospect, I must state that I clearly didn't make the best of my time during my studies, because my point of view was pretty limited, and I really was far from having an even superficial knowledge about the different paradigms of clinical psychology. Then, in that mood of disappointment and slight disgust, I was gifted a book by Viktor Frankl

CBT and Existential Psychology: Philosophy, Psychology and Therapy,
First Edition. Michael Worrell.

(in my opinion his best book, the 'Ärztliche Seelsorge'), and that really was something new! I immediately felt at home and considered his anti-reductionistic approach really refreshing. I began a four-year-training in logotherapy and existential analysis, and more or less parallel to the beginning of that course I took up my first post as a psychologist. I worked in a clinic treating paraplegia and clients with neurological issues (intracranial injuries and such). Of course, with this job came the obligation to begin psychotherapy training in an approved method.

Back then, in Germany, that was just CBT, depth psychology and psychoanalysis. I chose CBT, the training in which thereby I started half a year later than my training in logotherapy/existential analysis. At first, I really was sailing under a 'false flag'. During the selection interview for the CBT training, I didn't tell anybody about my existential training, and my thinking was something like 'I have to do the CBT training, even if I don't want to, but I need the paper, so what else could I do?'. But from month to month or half year to half year I realized more and more, that in fact CBT and existential ideas are perfectly complementary to one another. I pretty early realized, that—at least to my estimation—CBT was really very strong in the technique section. They had an idea, a specific method, for every thinkable problem. But what was missing was the soul, the heart, a real anthropology, a conception of man. In logotherapy, it was exactly the other way around: the philosophy, the humanism, the ideas about life as a whole were all there, but from a methodological standpoint it was almost hopeless. But since I had the combination, it wasn't a problem to me. The longer both trainings took, the more I was able to integrate the CTB-techniques with the anthropology of logotherapy. Up until today I would say that the way in which I encounter people (not just patients, but also people in the world outside my practice), the way how I try to grasp what life is about, the basic ideas about that interesting / weird / often sad / often joyful / confusing / enlightening / exhausting / refreshing / . . . / journey that our life is to my experience, is strongly based in the 'existential branch' of my psychotherapy training, while the methods I use, the specifics of what I really do with my patients, is strongly based in my CBT perspective. To me this really is the basic condition making the job of a psychotherapist possible in the first place—there is no contradiction between the often complex and confusing existential perspective on life and the totally hands-on- and practical CBT-approach on a specific problem.

Thomas: It's hard to pinpoint the start of my engagement with existential ideas. In fact, I would say that (as is often the case with engagements!) my first encounters with existential ideas in a broad sense were 'flirts': I am not sure if my first flirt with existential ideas lay in the liturgy of the catholic church that I encountered most Sundays during my childhood and teenage years or whether it was reading 'The Brothers Lionheart' by Astrid Lindgren around age 12 (and some years later experiencing the death by cancer of the friend who had lent me this book)? In any case, the fact of death and the fragility of life had deeply touched me at an early age, and I struggled to come to terms with this. Some years later I was deeply impressed by the novels of Fjodor Dostojevski, first and foremost his 'Brothers Karamasov' that asked a number of fascinating questions that I would later learn to label 'existential' (such as Iwan Karamasov's 'if god is dead, everything is allowed'). Probably the first existential writer in a narrower sense that really got to me was Albert Camus: when all the schoolmates that learned French in a very intense way were reading 'La Peste' and admiring Dr. Rieux and his brave deeds in the face of death, I was struck by 'Le Mythe de Sisyphe' and Camus' idea of the absurd. And Simone de Beauvoir's 'Tous les hommes sont mortels' was a novel that cured me from the idea that living forever would be a good idea in and of itself.

When I had started to study psychology (which, as seems to be true all over the world by now, at the University of Konstanz was understood as a branch of natural science rather than a 'Geisteswissenschaft') all these ideas were still quite active in my mind but actually they never really made 'connection' with what I learned during the first years of my studies—I enjoyed getting into empirical psychology and into sophisticated methodology (and philosophy of science) but yet I kept on reading novels and more 'existential writers' (in private) and was lucky to meet Rita Vörg (my first boss as a student) who was very open towards the more philosophical roots of psychology and a voracious reader—I remember discussing a lot of ideas (some in the area of the history of psychology), some of them quite existential from my current point of view. After my studies, I started working in the Clinical Psychology department of Frankfurt and simultaneously started my CBT training and in the early years of the internet on a listserve-based psychotherapy discussion group came to know a colleague from California (Dr. Lothar Graudins) who called himself an 'existential psychotherapist'. As the saying goes 'opposites attract each other' and so a young and unexperienced PhD candidate and CBT-therapist-in-training and a quite experienced existential psychotherapist got to discuss a lot of existential and other things in personal mails. Not all of these discussions were easy, of course: I was furious at his narrow 'rat-conditioning' understanding of behaviour therapy (which was obviously rooted in his personal experience of early behaviour therapy) while my attempts to lobby for empirical studies of psychotherapy did not impress him much. Fortunately, we had the chance for a personal encounter in his house in Los Angeles in March 2015 where we spent an evening and a long night discussing, drinking Moose drool beer, playing Doom (of all games) and discussing some more until dawn. . . And of course, during the next months and years I read whatever books of Irvin Yalom I could lay my hands on (and, again, with the feeling that even this highly respected colleague has a somewhat outdated view of CBT, at least in his book on 'Existential Psychotherapy').

Reflecting on Alexander's experience of 'disappointment and slight disgust' with his early CBT experience I realize that my personal experiences were more favourable: while the psychiatric ward at the local psychiatric clinic (Reichenau) during my time of studies has been famous for introducing token economy systems, I never felt disgust (even though these systems met quite heavy criticism). I was surprised to see some ideas Lothar had understood as typically (and solely) existential (having written his PhD thesis in 1975 on 'Value issues in substance abuse rehabilitation') in the CBT standard text 'Self-management Therapy' by Kanfer, Reinecker and Schmelzer. However, I shared the feeling that 'something is missing in CBT' and what I felt was missing is quite close to what Alexander described as 'the soul, the heart, a real anthropology, a conception of man'. For me, this included the realization that being deeply affected by the fact of mortality and other 'existential ideas' is nothing to get rid of by cognitive restructuring or similar techniques, but rather something to be faced openly with fellow mortals that we label 'patients' in some contexts. I never undertook formal training in an existentialist tradition such as logotherapy but was very fortunate to meet Alexander in 1997 when we soon discovered our overlapping interests in existential ideas.

Alexander: Even during the four years of logotherapy training I realized that logotherapy to me was in fact extremely important, but more like an eye-opener and an invitation to that whole body of existential approaches. Because pretty soon I noticed that religion plays a very important role in logotherapy (at least in Frankl's logotherapy). Logotherapy is all about values and meaning of life, and to Frankl the foundation of his ideas of what is valuable and what is meaningful is God. Back then, I was in my 'agnostic' stage—my personal belief was that we just cannot know if there is a god or if there is not, and that thereby the need of a God as a basis for a system is a big problem.

During my studies, I one day stumbled upon Irvin Yalom, and again I had that 'eye-opening'-experience. Where Frankl's work is completely centred around the meaning of life, Yalom's thinking is—at least to my opinion—much broader. There are four topics in the centre of his perspective—meaninglessness, freedom, isolation, and death—with a clear favourite—death and dying. And in relation to Frankl a very important different wording: meaninglessness vs. meaning. Yalom is atheistic, in his following the French existential philosophy. While reading Yalom I didn't immediately 'convert' to atheism—I kept my agnostic position, but Yalom's constructivist thinking (instead of Frankl's 'meaning and values really ARE out there, you just have to find them!') reduced one boundary and enabled to also work with clients who were not religious.

Thomas: And this is probably where Alexander's and my reading experiences converged for the first time (even though we were to meet a bit more than two years later): Lothar sent me a book by Irvin Yalom ('Love's executioner and other stories') for Christmas 1994 (about 3 months into the start of my CBT training) and I found this incredibly fascinating. Part of this fascination may have been due to his psychodynamic approach (Which, in spite of all my empirical psychology experience has continued to fascinate me) as well as the more existential themes in his works.

Soon after Alexander and I met in 1997 started discussing existential ideas on a regular basis, very often in a restaurant near Frankfurt University and we developed a long and deep friendship that encompasses both personal and professional areas and, fortunately, lasts to this day. Looking back, it is fascinating to see the similarities and differences in our encounter with existential ideas: while I had read some of Frankl's works, they did not impress me as much as the works by Yalom and I had trouble grasping some of Frankl's concepts while Yalom somehow seemed to flow smoothly with what I felt was relevant. Having read

Camus quite early the idea of 'constructing meaning in life' rather than 'finding meaning in life' did come as no surprise to me (although, getting older, I sometimes think that the idea of 'constructing' one's meaning in life is hubris) and my relationship to Frankl's works was not close enough to be disappointed by his focus on 'finding meaning outside'.

Alexander: In fact, it was until really just 2 or 3 years ago that I changed my perspective to 'atheist', but I would say a 'relaxed atheist'. I try to integrate humour and irony (at best: self-irony) as deep as possible into my therapies and into my life. Because I think humour is the by far best answer to all the difficulties and absurdities that life throws at us. And I try to help my clients to adopt that position, as much as possible.

Michael: You both seem to see great potential for dialogue between CBT and existential thinking, where do you both see points of contact as well as points of difference between CBT and existential thinking?—However again I think it is more interesting to read about how this exists at a personal level rather than feeling it must all be worked out rationally and conceptually in a way that there is no apparent tensions between the two.

Thomas: For me, the main difference between CBT and existential thinking with regard to conducting psychotherapy lies in the epistemology both are based on: while CBT has an impressive set of approaches both regarding assessment and treatment, the main focus is on a 'third person perspective': emotions and thoughts as well as physiological reactions and behaviour are described in a very clear way but always as phenomena that are observed from an outside perspective. This stance can be traced back to behaviourism's refutation of 'introspective psychology' and the resulting scepticism regarding 'insights'. Existential approaches in contrast highlight the subjective 'first person account' of what is going on in the subject that is in focus and thus are closely related to phenomenology. On a more practical level, the stance therapists take towards their clients and patients is quite different: in standard CBT in these days, a problem or a symptom is translated into a syndrome which in turn is translated (if applicable) to a (ICD or DSM based) diagnosis for which a set of therapeutic techniques are available. However, this emphasis on diagnoses (and following these, manualised treatment approaches) have not always been the hallmark of CBT (and behaviour therapy): earlier approaches stressed a detailed behaviour analysis (or in cognitive traditions case conceptualisation) and analysed behaviour (and cognitions) with regard to operant conditioning. Existential approaches on the other hand allow a much more personal approach to the therapeutic relationship where meeting a client or patient is not merely a professional encounter but also a quite human one. Also, the focus of existential approaches are on phenomena like death, responsibility, freedom and meaning—an impressive set of ideas for 'analysis of existence' in Frankl's words. . . Having said this, I wonder whether this distinction really reflects what is going on the therapeutic relationship: some early research into the amount of empathy therapists of different school show come to my mind and I wonder whether (at least some) 'hard-nosed' CBT therapists have shown a quite phenomenological stance for decades.

Michael: I wonder for both of you—how has your interest in existential ideas affected your sense of 'CBT therapist as Expert'?

Thomas: thank you very much for these highly interesting questions—I will get to them at one day but at the moment I feel that we—and this means the world and humankind in general—are in a very existential moment—when I wrote in this Dialogue for the last time some weeks ago most things seemed 'normal' more or less, of course with information on a thing called Corona Virus in china, now, in late March the world has changed dramatically—thousands of people have died, many countries are in a state of lockdown and 'social distancing' is the current imperative. I remember that I wrote about my youthful fascination with Albert Camus and that many of my schoolmates had read (or had to read) 'The Plague'. So one issue we might explore here is: what does existential thinking have to offer in the current situation, can there be any support from this side. Having re-read 'The Plague' a short time ago, I was struck by Dr. Rieux' stance in pest-infected Oran: there nothing much that he can do as a physician at this point, yet he can work for the suffering people of Oran—so I think that this stance (what is called 'Haltung') in German is important. Another issue of course is that existential thinking (like many religions all over the world) has always posited that we as humans are frail and that it takes some humbleness to live in this world.

Some months ago, in a conversation with my friend and colleague Johannes Michalak I learned the old phrase 'Conditio Jacobaea'—similar to the Muslim ‘Insh’Allah’ this means that even the best plans we make are nothing but plans that may succeed—or not, like so many in this time. As Robert Burns stated ‘The best-laid plans of mice and men gang aft agley’). Which brings me to another thought in this conversation: Alex has explained his changes in religious/spiritual attitudes from agnostic to atheist. One thing I observe is that many Christian traditions (Matthäus passion by Bach, the psalms as rendered in the ‘German Requiem’) deeply resonate with me because they express this human situation perfectly. Yesterday in the news, I saw a film about a 41-year-old man in northern Italy infected with COVID-19. He was carried of to a hospital and paramedics ask his young children ‘did you say goodbye to your dad’—implying that death is likely or at least possible and that visits are no longer possible. This is really heart-wrenching and brings to my mind a song from the German requiem: ‘Herr, lehre doch mich dass ein Ende mit mir haben muss und mein Leben ein Ziel hat und ich davon muss’). While I write this my eyes are filled with tears but somehow this music helps me to face these situations. I don’t think it’s ‘opium for the people’ but rather the clear knowledge that this fate is something we are not immune to. Small wonder that the football fan song ‘You’ll never walk alone’ is one of the most-played songs in these times of social distancing.

Continuing the dialogue-virtually. . .

Thomas: I will go back to Michael’s last ‘Pre-Corona-question’ (‘So my question to you both—what has your encounter with existential ideas led to in terms of your stance of “therapist as expert”?’.). Thinking about this question I realised that this might probably best be answered by my patients rather than by myself and a patient I hadn’t thought of in years popped into my mind: I treated her for the first time during my time at Frankfurt University Clinic, probably in the late 90s for a severe depressive episode (that brought her to the clinic) and several anxiety disorders. The combined pharmacological and CBT treatment was quite effective—after inpatient treatment, I saw her for some outpatient sessions, and she had recovered remarkably). Looking back, I would characterize my therapeutic style as ‘CBT-beginner-playing-expert’ and that seems to have worked well: I used the appropriate treatment manuals for depression and anxiety, the patient recovered, and all was well. . . The same patient contacted me again several years later (probably 2005, as I was working at the psychological institute of Frankfurt again, now together with Alex)—as is often the case, she had experienced a recurrence of her depression and had found out my new position. We agreed to do a limited number of therapy sessions and, again, she recovered. What probably brought her—of all the patients I treated these years—back to my mind was a number of comments she made on how I (or my therapeutic role) had changed between these two treatments: after one of the first sessions she commented 'you have changed a lot' and when I asked her to describe this in more detail she didn't answer verbally but made a gesture of opening her arms widely adding the comment 'when you treated me first you were like this (arms quite close to each other), now you are (arms wider apart)'. Relating this experience triggers a bit of professional shame (oh, come on, this is just one patient, you have grown older by about 5 to 6 years between these two treatments of the same patient) and there are lots of other potentially confounding variables such as the setting (psychiatric institute vs. psychological institute), having become more experienced in conducting psychotherapy etc. but I still think (or hope) that this also reflects my encounter with existential ideas: while posing as a 'therapist as expert' was important for me during my training and early professional years, I probably was more of an expert but did not appear as such, at least for this patient.

Alex: One of my patients, yesterday, she sent me a link; a video from 2008, Leonard Cohen, where he produced a video, and the opening line of the video and what he sang there was '*There is a crack in everything, and that is where the light gets in. that's how the light gets in*'. it was new for me and this is really a good description of it—the cracks are everywhere, really everywhere, in this dog behind me (19 year old Ally lying behind Alex), in this open window up there and everywhere and our stance, probably, especially integrating humour in it is this trying to get the light in, wherever we can. . . and that's how we are dealing with each other, with others, that's how we are dealing with patients, and with the whole experience of living

Thomas: I'm really glad that you cited Leonard Cohen, because he's one of my favourite artists for a very long time, and there are really very many songs where I think that he grasped deeply existential issues, so while the latest. . . I think Leonard Cohen always has the reputation of being depressed—which he was in fact, so he had one or the other depressive episode, but I think his ability to really tap into basic existential things is very fascinating. And that's one thing I would like to add or stress—well, in some way it's reassuring to see 'Oh look, somebody in the psalms or whatever has experienced similar things that you do in the moment, and some of it is really great stuff'.

Michael: I wonder to what extent can we include in training and supervision, reflections or perspectives from existential phenomenology? Recently, a client re-contacted me for a virtual session, after nine years! I thought it was very interesting that it was this client that contacted me, because I've talked about the work with this client in teaching since those nine years. She was, when I saw her first, having panic attacks. She was experiencing them on the Underground station on the way to work, and I did what probably would be regarded as a fairly protocol-driven, on-model piece of work, using David Clark's model of panic, and it 'worked' in the sense that the panic attacks stopped within six sessions. At the same time, I was aware that there were a whole range of issues and concerns that she had and had discussed briefly but that were not more fully addressed. However, as soon as she experienced some relief from the panic attacks, she basically announced 'Right, I'm off now to travel the world'. And I thought 'Well, this is too soon, you've got all these other issues to deal with, we need to address these – you'll be back', and of course, she wasn't back, she went travelling. And in my teaching, where I'm often teaching counsellors about CBT, I have often discussed this case in terms of questioning our assumptions of what the client 'needs' and what's helpful and the rest of it. But she's come back and she said to me: Well, during these nine years, I did struggle with anxiety, but I continued to use some of the basic strategies that we learned, and she said 'Those six sessions really did change my life; I've been able to do things that I didn't think I was going to be able to do, and in the meantime I've had two children, got married and started a business'. But she's come back, in this situation of the pandemic where she's isolated, and experiencing quite severe health anxiety, but the anxiety is really focused on her children, and 'What would it mean if something happened to me, what would happen for them in their future?', and it really seemed to me that she was talking about some quite basic existential concerns that certainly show up with parenthood, and she was looking at me, and at one point, said to me: '*So tell me what to do*!' [all laughing]. '*Nine years ago,* *you told me what to do – can you do that now?'* And that really put me on the spot, because we started to talk about the overall situation, and basic existential concerns, and that this theme of *'your anxiety and your children and your future'* is a basic anxiety that must be lived with.

Alex: This reminds me of a distinction that I'm making, and I'm not sure if I ever talked to Thomas about it, so it's going to be interesting if he agrees or not, and I'm not absolutely sure how it is in Great Britain or England or however you would call yourself right now. . . In Germany we have a distinction between psychotherapy and psychoeducation. Do you have this, too?

Michael: Yes, we do.

Alex: Ok, and I would say that everything like classic CBT, like what you did nine years ago with her, telling her how to overcome simple anxieties, to me, this is not really psychotherapy, but it's psychoeducation. You can teach those things, and teaching those things is only possible because you know how to do it, and she doesn't, and then you tell her, and if she agrees then the knot will dissolve. It's not as easy as I'm putting it right now, but I think you get the message. And psychotherapy is a whole different story, it's not simply educating somebody about several issues, but it's really going into the deep waters where nothing is really clear and. . . like Yalom and the red couch, and one of his favourite statements is that there are very many similarities between patients and therapists, especially when it comes to existential issues, and the main similarity is that neither patient nor therapist know where they are heading, where they are going, and the main difference between the two of them is that the therapist is less anxious. If I have to differentiate between what you experienced nine years ago and what you are experiencing right now is that as a psycho-educationalist you have to know, and you have to teach, and as a psychotherapist you have to be pretty fearless in heading toward the existential things and issues without knowing anything that takes all the pain away and that gives a clear landmark or whatever. For me, that is the most important distinction.

Thomas: I always get some trouble with dichotomies, so I think we could say it's psychoeducational versus psychotherapy, so I don't object to this basic terminology, but I think what you just outlined is a very broad definition of psychoeducation, because I worked with David Clark for quite a long time on Social Anxiety Disorder and my experience of this kind of therapy is that it's very experiential, so I would not say that it's something that you teach like 'Look, this is a safety behaviour, this is attention', but rather you try to bring the patient into a position to have a personal experience and that's a very important principle, so I guess if I would use this a continuum, much of CBT would be farther from just simple psychoeducation, but I agree that there's a certain limit to that, and one thing that we might discuss is the dimension of things that can be fixed, and things that can't be fixed, or, in one way, that can be confronted, that can be lived with, but that will stay there, and that's why I like your patient example, Michael, because of course, there are CBT techniques to treat health anxiety, even health anxiety related to 'What happens to the kids after I died from COVID or so?', but in some way I often feel that this misses the real point that people ask me, so I think that psychotherapy at its best really grasps and embraces the whole person, and I think what we need to discuss in how far classic CBT is able to do this or where it fails, probably, but my personal opinion is that existential issues, the whole background of it, is not limited to Existential psychotherapy or Existential philosophy, but to this whole background that enables us to say 'Yes, that's the position we are in, and I'm not different from what you are'.

Michael: So how can we include that sort of existential attunement in CBT?

Thomas: This is also a question that I've been thinking about for some time, that of course both Beck and Albert Ellis have come from psychodynamic training backgrounds, and I think one school of thought says 'Ah, look, they were trained, but then they saw the light of Cognitive Therapy and they ran away from it', but I don't really believe that's the case, but as you just said, being able to do psychotherapy means being able to see a person in a broad way, not necessarily psychodynamic, and then being able to see symptoms and other things in the bigger picture. In fact, I think that probably the influence of existential issues on CBT, at least in Germany, has been a lot earlier than it is usually assumed, and one very important book for me was Fred Kanfer's self-management therapy, I think it came out in German first because Fred Kanfer came to Germany lots of times to run workshops, and he published it with Hans Reinecker and Dieter Schmelzer, and what was it, Alex, the Seventies, probably, the first edition?, they didn't really check it out and what they outlined, there was a seven-step proposal on how psychotherapy would work from the first impression until maintenance of treatment, and I learned that early on in my psychotherapy training and the most interesting thing that we could discuss now is that doing interventions like disorder-specific interventions comes at a very late point, like in phase five or so, and before, we have things like values clarification and setting therapy goals based on the values of patients, and that always struck me as existential in some ways because it's close to Yalom and of course Frankl, and I never really figured out how this came into it, but I would assume that it was via Person-Centred Psychotherapy, so for me much of what we discuss as existential now was present in some branches of CBT early on, although probably not the whole thing of it.

Michael: With Acceptance and Commitment Therapy, existential issues seem very present with the work on values and committed action, and the notion that suffering is basic to the human condition. But what I find interesting in the ACT model is this emphasis on getting to the basics of language and cognition, but if you look at the basic model, Relational Frame Theory, that it's about the search for 'prediction and control'. And this just leaves me wondering how well these two things sit together, an existential sensibility, and the idea, the value, of prediction and control.

Alex: In Germany the whole 'Third Wave' is *the* thing. In Germany, if you want to be a CBT therapist, and if you want to be ok, you must be Third Wave. So, this is what German CBT looks like. They are not focusing on technical issues; they are more and more focusing on emotional activation, acceptance, and ambivalence. You pointed out the prediction-and-control aspect of Relational Frame Theory, and existential thinking points out 'You do not control things', and ambivalence is what, to my opinion, is one of the key aspects of Existential Therapy, and the tension that we must hold as therapists, and that we shouldn't try to get off the table only to focus on one of these points. I think that modern Third-Wave approaches are capable in doing this.

Michael: Yes, and to be fair, in practicing ACT the theme really is 'control is the problem not the solution'! That it's fine as a scientific goal for theory building but doesn't 'work' well in relating to your own experience of living.

Thomas: Although Steve Hayes always points out that the philosophical background is Functional Contextualism, it is still pretty Skinnerian in what he said about prediction and control, and even though being a CBT therapist from training on, I was very reluctant with Skinner because I somehow didn't like his mechanistic approach. Some years ago, I took a look into Skinner's 'Beyond Freedom and Dignity', I found it interesting to read; it's just another meta-level to bring into it, because each and every action an organism is doing is regarded from the position of 'Is it reinforced?' somehow, I found it's an interesting position, but it's one that really clashes with existential views,

Alex: Maybe I can add one more aspect. Why is the UK so motivated towards guidelines? Maybe we have another dimension here, because having guidelines and having simple solutions gives the illusion of control, it's a certain aspect of professionalism; you are only a professional when you are in control, and when you really have causal relationships between the elements of your profession. And the existential perspective deviates from that. We don't really agree with that picture of the world; it might be a very soothing position in terms of letting yourself feel good and powerful and 'the force is with me' and so on, but in fact, probably, Thomas and I, we would agree, and you too, Michael, as I understand it, we would agree that our 'special power' is to acknowledge our weakness, and the lack in our knowledge, and that our professionalism is especially to keep eye contact with the client while saying 'I don't know – I don't have a clue!'

Thomas: Art is very important for me, and one thing that really brings this thing together for me is a quote from Rainer Maria Rilke, Duineser Elegien, the part of this poem is 'Wir ordnens. Es zerfällt. Wir ordnens wieder und zerfallen selbst', so if you translate it, it means 'We sort it. It falls apart. We sort it again and fall apart ourselves'.

Michael: What an excellent existential moment on which to close! Thank you both!

16

Ernesto Spinelli

The theory is there to infuse the therapist's embodied way of being with the client

Michael: So firstly, thank you for agreeing to this attempt at dialogue regarding the possible relationship between CBT and existential Therapy. After all, the idea for such a project was yours although that was now over 10 years ago! I'm really interested to hear what you feel may be points of possible contact as well as tension between the two schools of thought and practice. Do you see much value in such an enterprise? Is there anything in this that may be of interest to Existential therapists as much as CBT Therapists?

Ernesto: Thanks, Michael. I'm really pleased to see that you've pursued this idea we had all those years ago. I'm all for dialogue and I would find it difficult to believe that practitioners from both CBT and Existential Therapy (ET) wouldn't be intrigued to explore what might be shared by them as well as what might be key areas of divergence. More than that, though, I'd hope that both approaches would not only be open to, but welcome, challenges to their beliefs and assumptions so that these might be more adequately clarified and either upheld or amended. We seem to have become a challenge-averse society, such that we increasingly retreat into groupings that share our views and either avoid considering those voices that challenge our perspective or else demonise them to protect the 'purity' of our stance. I see it as a sad, divisive, state of affairs and

CBT and Existential Psychology: Philosophy, Psychology and Therapy, First Edition. Michael Worrell.

would hope that therapists from any model and approach would promote an alternate, dialogical, stance.

Having said all that, CBT and ET do seem to have a long history of misunderstanding one another and possibly emphasising critiques of each other that 'score points' but also miss the point. Which is not to say that there aren't significant disagreements between the two approaches. But if I can employ an analogy from couple counselling—and from Sartre—there is a way of viewing the conflicting positions between them that, while by no means removing that conflict, nonetheless reveals a willingness to attempt to take on the other's perspective and significantly enter into it as far as one can. In this, previously unnoticed and unacknowledged points of agreement may emerge, thereby bringing to the relationship a clearer awareness that their conflict contains both disagreement and agreement.

Michael: Perhaps the first step it to acknowledge that both CBT and Existential therapy are similar in the sense that they are in no way unified schools of thought or practice. Just as there currently exist quite a few different versions of CBT (and the number of these continues to expand) there exist a wide range of approaches that have identified themselves as existential. This makes any simple and clear comparison difficult.

Ernesto: If I follow on from your point, it seems that both ET and CBT have multiple identities. In part, I guess that this is because neither has a founding figure agreed upon by all practitioners who identify with the model. This can be seen as both a strength and a weakness. However, I want to focus on two other aspects of this dis-unity—or multiplicity—as applied to ET that I think might be unique to it. First, there is the significant and ongoing debate as to whether ET should be considered a model or approach in its own right. Irvin Yalom, who is probably the most well-known living existential therapist, nonetheless has argued strongly that a model or approach calling itself ET is somewhat absurd. Instead, he argues that there are various 'existential themes' (such as death, isolation, meaning, etc) that should be addressed directly in whatever model of therapy is being applied because they would enhance the focus and depth of that model's therapeutic enquiry. I imagine that many CBT practitioners would agree with this and be more willing to explore ET from this perspective.

In contrast, others, like myself, have argued that ET *is* a distinctive model or approach and that it is not these themes—and many others—in themselves that provide it with this distinctiveness. Rather, it is the 'existential lens' through which these themes are understood and addressed that distinguishes ET from other models and approaches. In my view, this 'existential lens' rests upon three key principles—relatedness, uncertainty and anxiety. But, of course, that's just my view. So that's the first point of contention within ET. The second source of dis-unity that I think may be unique to ET—and which, to me, is far more significant—is the ongoing debate as to how ET understands the very idea of 'therapy'. The great majority of therapists—including, it has to be said, many existential therapists—have adopted a view of therapy that is centred upon a quasi-medical perspective concerned with the amelioration or removal of distress and disorder. This is broadly a change-focused, generally educative, approach. But another view of ET—of which, again, I am an advocate—takes the idea of therapy back to its etymological roots, *therapeia*. Namely: the idea that therapy is understood as the attempt to stand beside the other. Now what this somewhat obscure and poetic attempt suggests (to me, at least) is that this view of therapy is much more focused on the attempt at 'staying with the other who is present' and exploring as deeply and accurately as possible how it is to be that being in the moment of encounter with this other being who is the therapist. In this sense, ET is much more about attaining stillness rather than providing directive means to change.

More deeply, it seems to me, its message to the client is that the therapist is attempting to accept and be with the person who *is* rather than demand, however subtly, that the person becomes someone else. In brief, this attempt at acceptance on the part of the therapist who is 'the other' to the client is likely to be a pretty unusual, if not unique, experience for the client and, more often than not, leads to the client's stance towards themselves to shift toward attempting a greater acceptance of oneself as they are being rather than as who they should be, once were, or might become. Which—surprise! surprise—can, in itself, provoke significant therapeutic change.

To me, it is this stance toward the whole idea of what therapy means that really makes ET stand out as a unique and distinct model and approach. As I see it, it is also a way of understanding ET that is very much keeping to its phenomenological roots and principles of investigation as is possible. *But* it's not an easy enterprise to maintain, not least when the dominant zeitgeist of therapy is that which promotes it as a predominantly curative enterprise. So . . . Regarding any exploratory links between CBT and ET, it seems to me that at least some of the Third Wave approaches in CBT have a good deal of sympathy with the 'stillness' view of ET that I've mentioned above. My only concern is that, again as I have understood these CBT approaches, they are still 'hedging their bets' in their willingness to remain with, and try to adhere to, the full implications of this approach. What this requires, as I understand it, is the willingness to attempt to set aside any implicit/explicit assumptions, demands, or directions regarding curative change. From an ET standpoint, you can't mix the two strategies together. As I understand it, CBT seems to think otherwise.

Michael: I think it's certainly the case, as I have attempted to show in this book, that various CBT therapists have become interested in existential themes such as anxiety about death, intolerance for uncertainty and broader questions of meaning and values in the way that you have suggested. There are now attempts, for instance, to evaluate the efficacy of interventions that directly target death anxiety as a potential 'transdiagnostic' phenomenon. Elsewhere I believe you have referred to these sorts of efforts, which show up across different forms of therapy as 'Existentially Attuned Therapy' or EAT (excellent acronym I think!).

Ernesto: I would just want to say that I don't wish to suggest that EAT approaches are somehow wrong or less worthy pursuits to take up. I guess that what I'm pointing to is that if we seriously want to take an ET route to therapy then there is a price to pay for that in terms of what might be seen to be 'evidence-based' beneficial impact. I do think that ET is very much *for* a scientist-practitioner ethos. That's not the problem. The problem lies in the somewhat restricted assumptions as to what it means to be both a 'scientist' and a 'practitioner'. An ET scientist-practitioner focus is very much—if not exclusively—rooted in what Dilthey referred to as the 'understanding' (as opposed to 'explanatory') focus of science. Each has its aims and structures, but they reveal different pursuits that cannot really be combined. Nonetheless, while separate and distinct, each focus can be of great value to the other insofar as it can assist in the clarification of any number of factors in both one's own as well as the other's overall aims and pursuits and, thereby, potentially increase the adequacy of views, assumptions, and conclusions being held by both. I don't think that the understanding focus advocated by ET is a threat to the explanatory focus advocated by CBT, or vice-versa. But many seem to experience it as such and, like the couple in therapy whom I alluded to earlier, each in its own ways seeks to argue that its focus-view is superior, or worse, that it is the *only* view to take.

Michael: Perhaps the most obvious meeting point is the emphasis that both CBT and existential therapy place upon 'meaning'. Both approaches stress that human beings have an active, interactive, or inter-relational, role regarding the construction of meaning in response to lived experience. Potentially, one way in which they may enrich and inform each other is through the fact that CBT has tended to focus on the clarification of forms of meaning that are highly specific to forms of common human suffering such as depression, panic attacks and obsessions and compulsions. Additionally, while CBT has stressed the typical forms of such interpretational processes, as a practice it has emphasised the need to be very specific about the client's particular way of making sense of their experience. So, in this sense there are both explanatory and 'understanding' aspects to the approach. CBT does indeed seem to attempt a mix of these. One way in which existential approaches may contribute to CBT is via its focus on broader forms of meaning—issues around values and 'Meaning in life'—which has also become a focus for ACT therapists.

Ernesto: Yes, I agree. The issue of meaning is one where both ET and CBT have something interesting and important to say and, as well, dialogue between them on this might well be of significant value to both approaches. ET, as I understand it, takes a relationally-attuned view to the meanings each of us constructs, lives by, and, as you rightly point out, might well suffer from. In this sense, each individual expresses and represents a broader, world-derived, sphere of meaning and meaning-making. In other words, meaning-making is never an exclusively individualistic enterprise. Every individual's worldview is ultimately unique, but its uniqueness rests upon a relationally-derived grounding. For ET, many of the dilemmas associated with individuals' meaning and meaning-making arise when the existing meaning has become too rigidified, or 'sedimented', such that no re-interpretative possibility is evident. In this sense, ET's concerns are more around the interplay between meaning and meaninglessness (as in, the degree of re-interpretative possibility existing in any currently maintained meaning—including any radical re-interpretation of that meaning). In brief, ET concerns itself with clarifying my openness or closedness to the possibility that the current meaning given to any and every one of my meanings might be altered, perhaps subtly, perhaps significantly.

But, before going any further, I should say that when ET talks about meaning, it is including within that term one's beliefs, values, assumptions, expectations, demands, feelings about, and behaviours toward, any and every aspect of self, other/s and the world. When meanings are challenged, re-viewed, and re-interpreted they impact upon all of these aspects of one's worldview. It is this broad sense of meaning that forms an important exploratory aspect of ET. I suspect that something similar is there in CBT as well. But here's some possible points for CBT to consider (if it has not done so as yet). Because of ET's key principle of relatedness it argues that a) the diverse meanings that constitute one's sense of being need not be coherent or harmonious. Indeed, the opposite is the case most of the time. We are not only complex, we are also deeply contradictory and it is how these contradictory aspects of the total meaning hold that being together, so to speak, that demands close investigation. Why? Because, once again, from its lens of relatedness ET argues that b) any change in one aspect of meaning, will impact upon all aspects of meaning. Or, more generally, change experienced in any part will affect the whole. How or to what extent the whole will be affected remains entirely unpredictable. It might be dramatic or subtle. The point is to be aware that any part cannot be isolated from the whole and, as such, we can't know in advance if any seemingly 'beneficial' improvement to the part that is achieved through therapeutic intervention may actually generate significant disturbance—perhaps even greater disturbance than that which was 'fixed'—to any or all other parts of the whole.

Which leads to yet another ET insight: c) every presenting problem is also an attempted solution. Removal of the problem without sufficient understanding of what that problem may be maintaining which is experienced as a solution (i.e.: is desirable or something that the client does not wish to lose) is, at best, naive and at worst dangerously arrogant on the part of the 'fixer' (therapist). In part, this cautious stance advocated by ET keeps its enterprise very much within a descriptive, rather than prescriptive, mode. And, actually, I think that, in doing so, it reaches a similar conclusion to much of therapy's overall understanding regarding what makes the enterprise beneficial or is experienced as worthwhile by the majority of clients. It is this: most therapeutic success is not frequently about the removal of disturbing thoughts or behaviours. Rather, its successes are usually about clients' *altering their relationship* to those thoughts and behaviours such that their disturbing qualities are muted and such that previously unforeseen possibilities of psychic movement (or openness) within those qualities become available. Broadly, ET would consider this shift as being one from dissociation from—or dis-ownership of—the disturbing thoughts and behaviours to one of ownership or re-incorporation of such within the meaningful whole rather than as alien attacks upon it. I don't think that CBT would strongly disagree with this conclusion, would it?

Michael: I don't think most CBT therapists would disagree strongly with this. In mindfulness-based approaches and ACT this notion of a changed relationship with thoughts rather than the editing and deletion of thoughts is explicitly embraced and promoted. In fact, I think it's a misrepresentation of CBT to suggest that it somehow aims at the removal or deletion of thoughts and beliefs. Both the possibility of greater ownership of beliefs and stances as well as openness to disturbing thoughts and experience is present within CBT practice. I think some contemporary versions of CBT, based on contemporary cognitive science accounts and research, are also open to the possibility of a much greater degree of complexity in terms of beliefs, schemas and indeed 'modes of mind' existing in parallel, as complex and competing and not necessarily at all in a linear or consistent fashion. Indeed, current notions of change seem to emphasise more the possibility of new ways of thinking, feeling and behaviour in some sense competing with older ways, as existing alongside as possibilities for experiencing that can hopefully be strengthened when these are felt to be more hopeful and less rigid.

Ernesto: This is important information, Michael. And it's also really great to hear that these views are being embraced. What I would add from an ET perspective is that, in being so relationally-attuned, ET seeks to remind its practitioners that the same complexity and inconsistency exists for the therapist as it does for the client. As such, if the therapist takes this on board, then a good deal of the security and certainty that might have been there in terms of knowing how to be and what to do goes out the window. In this sense, the presence of the existential therapist is one that in various ways parallels that of the client in that they are both uncertain, uneasy, beings experiencing the difficulties and possibilities of both 'meeting' and 'missing' one another.

One of my great heroes of therapy is the relational analyst, Leslie Farber[1]. Among the many wonderfully wacky views he maintained was that, for him, therapy really starts to become effective when the client begins to feel pity for the therapist. As I understand it, what Farber is getting at is highlighting that point when the client *humanises* the therapist. Which is to say, the client sees the therapist as this imperfect being who is trying so hard to meet and engage with the other who is the client and who keeps failing in those attempts. The client's reaching out to the other who is the therapist also provokes the client's reaching out to themselves as well. Feeling pity also contains an important element of care, affection, and acceptance. And, as we both seem to be pointing out, it's that shift perhaps more than anything else which provokes the beneficial outcomes of therapy.

Michael: I think this notion of the client experiencing 'pity' for the therapist's attempts at understanding is both highly challenging and very clarifying. I recall one very vivid example of working with a client. This was many years ago but the experience of this remains with me. This young woman client came to see me due to a whole host of difficulties and disturbances. She also came with a narrative of her family situation as highly chaotic and disturbing. What I found though, was that any effort on my part to provide some sort of descriptive statement or clarification (what in CBT might be seen as a 'capsule summary') was met with 'no . . . that's not right . . . you don't understand'. This continued for many sessions, each of my attempts at summarising or reflecting back what she had said was met with a definitive 'no! that's not right'. This schedule of non-reinforcement and punishment led to a definite reduction in my willingness to say anything at all . . . yet I persisted. Eventually, after one particularly difficult session that left me feeling like a total dunce (and I of course tried many alternative strategies such as 'well perhaps there might be something difficult or frightening about the possibility of me understanding something?' . . . No! . . . "Perhaps you are letting me know something about how things are for you . . . that others just don't seem

1 Farber, L. (2000). *The Ways of the Will: Selected Essays*. Basic Books.

willing or able to understand?". No! etc etc). Then finally, she seemed to momentarily become calmer and more open and said something like 'well . . . I don't know . . . It feels like you don't get it but I can see that you are really trying . . . maybe there is something in what I am saying that I need to think about more . . . ' This really was the turning point in that therapy, although I remained someone who like almost everyone in her life didn't and couldn't understand but at the same time someone who did try and perhaps to a limited extent did understand something, and this was novel.

There was much within this client's past and current relationships that could have been drawn upon to make hypotheses about why she experienced the possibility of being understood as threatening, disturbing or remote. Certainly, her early childhood history could have been drawn upon with this aim in mind.

Ernesto: I think that Farber would have loved reading your account. What strikes me most about it is that although you might have felt like a dunce some of the time, you didn't make any attempt to make your client feel like a dunce by in some way or other insisting that you were right and that she, therefore, had to be wrong. In brief, you stayed with her stance rather than insist that she adopt a new one that was more in line with yours. And yes, it must have been difficult and frustrating at times, not least because you were doing your best to offer her something that might assist her. But, as I see it, in staying with your frustration, you provided the possibility for her to experience a novel sort of encounter with an other. Namely, one where the other (i.e. you, the therapist) didn't assert the sort of power that imposed itself upon her worldview and forced it to change. Maybe, from what you write about her background issues, her expectation was that, like the others in her life, you, too, would insist upon her adopting your preferred worldview. Except, what she discovered was that you weren't like the others in her life as far as the exertion of power was concerned. And, in realising this, she saw your efforts in a different light. And, at least as importantly, saw that her worldview wasn't under threat and that she could begin to explore it non-defensively.

Michael: One area of further resonance between CBT and ET may be that both approaches seem to stress a focus on the clients consciously lived present experience rather than adopt an emphasis that seeks to explore the client's childhood history as the possible cause of current disturbance. I would also argue that CBT attempts to embody values in relation to transparency and collaboration. Rather than hold onto elaborate theories about the client that are not shared, CBT attempts to place whatever theoretical construction is considered useful literally on the table between client and therapist.

Ernesto: Once again, I think there is much here that is shared and shareable between CBT and ET. Past and future are crucial components of our temporal experience, but both are given expression (or fail to be expressed) by the currently present being. What I remember about my past, and how I remember, or give meaning to, my past is shaped by the meanings that maintain my present way of being. That's why, it's hardly a surprising phenomenon that when the current being undergoes some form of experienced change, they might remember totally new or previously forgotten memories or, alternatively, that the memories in question will suddenly be full of novel (re-)interpretative possibilities. As to your point about CBT's putting one's theory on the table, I would argue that the theory is there to infuse the therapist's embodied way of being with the client. As with CBT, my understanding is that it's not my task as an existential therapist to educate my clients with existential theory or to convince them of its correctness. The theory is invaluable—but it is so for me, the therapist, such that my way of engaging with the client expresses how I embody the theory. Going back to an earlier point in our discussion, this might explain the diversity within ET, and possibly CBT. Each practitioner/exponent of the approach is a living, breathing exemplar of it (as it is understood by that particular therapist). As such, we might conclude that there are as many models of ET—and possibly CBT—as there are practitioners.

Michael: Let me throw a deliberately provocative question to you: why not a manual for existential therapy?

Ernesto: The challenge I want to throw back at you, and at CBT I guess, is this: *What's so great about Manuals*? What are their avowed benefits? I'll open that up a bit: Somewhere or other, I recall reading a recent report that suggested that the beneficial impact and effectiveness of therapy as a whole (including CBT, of course) has declined substantially over the years. For some reason or other, therapy's therapeutic potential is weakening. This may be for all sorts of reasons that we can think of, but I want to propose one possibility: Can you guess what that might be? Yes, exactly: therapy's growing reliance upon the manualization of therapeutic encounters. Why would I say this? Because, as I see it, the increasing reliance upon manuals reduces the therapist's sense of ownership and embodiment of being a therapist and doing therapy.

Reliance upon the manual reduces—if not removes—commitment, uniqueness, maybe even care for oneself and for the client. After all, if I'm just the one who implements what is stated in a manual, this 'I' who does so, could be anybody. It's ultimately the manual that provides the therapy, not the therapist and the client working together. I know I'm being somewhat extreme here, but I do see it as an increasing limitation upon the creative possibilities of therapy as a whole. And there is more: Just what sort of message does the manual-following therapist give to the client? Does my reliance upon the manual somehow 'manualize' both the therapist's and the client's way of being, such that it might empty it of so much that is valuable and, dare I say, meaningful to them?

Let me 're-frame' my comment. Way back in the early days of phenomenology, there was a group that went by the name of gestalt psychologists. They were very interested in studies of perception and were among the first to develop and make use of so-called ambiguous figures in order to clarify their findings and hypotheses. One thing they found was that with ambiguous figures, such as the (in)famous 'Young woman turning her head/Crone', a lot of people wouldn't initially perceive any ambiguity. They would perceive one of the figures but be surprised to hear that an alternate figure could be perceived as well. So, how could these people learn to perceive both? Basically, there were two strategies that the gestalt psychologists employed. The first was a directive, focused, step-by-step approach. So, say that the person could only perceive the young woman but not the crone. Then the psychologist would say things like 'see this as the crone's nose' or 'here is the crone's mouth' and trace the part of the image under discussion. As a second alternative however, the psychologist would avoid any direct/directive focusing and instead tell stories or make broad allusions while the person stared at the image. Both strategies worked in that most people would eventually perceive both ambiguous figures. But . . . with the second, indirect, strategy, the perceptual awareness of the ambiguity tended to come on suddenly and unpredictably and, most significantly, in a way that was experienced as being exceedingly powerful not least because the person felt much more connected to the process in all sorts of different ways. Now this second strategy was much more uncertain, unpredictable, 'messy', and surprising to both the perceiver and the psychologist. Equally, each psychologist who applied this strategy applied it in their own particular, unique, way. There was, of course, a generally shared, and broad, structure to their way of working, but there also was, just as importantly, a uniqueness in how that broad structure was given expression and worked with. The first way could be seen as being definitely open to manualization (i.e. first trace the outline of the crone's nose or the pearls around the neck of the young woman, then move to the crone's mouth or the young woman's hair, etc). The second approach highlighted the broad features of the associative strategy being applied, but it couldn't provide much beyond that because each psychologist was able to apply that broad structure in ways that make sense to them, or, perhaps, which served to express who/how they were.

I think you can guess the point I'm making: CBT seems dedicated to the first strategy while ET emphasises the possibilities that arise when the therapist attempts to apply the second. Both are valid and effective. *And* I would argue that there are additional benefits to the second that should be considered—not least, that the second's dependence on the practitioner's unique ways of engaging with the client provide a sense of 'not just going through the motions' that makes things like 'burn-out' far less likely to happen. I suspect that the most effective CBT therapists are actually much more reliant upon the second way once the office door is shut. And, in the same way, I suspect that the most effective ET therapists are the ones who are least likely to ask themselves 'What would Heidegger/Sartre/Merleau-Ponty/etc say?' in the course of their encounter with clients. Anyway, it's yet another area of more detailed discussion to be had between representatives of the approaches.

Michael: What's so great about manuals? That's a good question. I think I should confess that I am at the ambivalent end of the spectrum when it comes to therapy manuals. There is a long tradition within behaviour therapy (I was originally trained in Applied Behaviour Analysis rather than cognitive therapy) that emphasises the intensive study of the specific individual in a specific environment and in which manuals do not feature. What is valued is highly idiosyncratic formulation of the clients' difficulties rather than adherence to a manual. I recall working in a service for severely cognitively and physically impaired people when I was newly qualified. I really struggled in this role as I found it hard to understand what was happening for the people who exhibited very challenging and sometimes violent behaviours. What I discovered however was there were psychologists there, all committed behaviourists, who showed an extraordinary capacity to gain some understanding of what the experiential world might be like of the non-verbal clients we were attempting to work with, and to come up with formulations of these that in some way made sense of apparently bizarre, as well as distressing behaviour. This seemed to really help the other team members even when there was little that could be done to change these behaviours. None of this, of course, appeared in any manuals.

More recently I have been involved with CBT approaches to couple therapy. This has been very rewarding for a host of reasons. One aspect is that the approach is explicit in its rejection of the possibility that the therapy can be manualised. Again, I was asked 'well why not?' by another senior member of an accrediting and validating body. It becomes quickly apparent that couple-based sessions require a great deal of flexibility and moment by moment responsiveness and openness to what the couple bring. If a therapist were to routinely plan sessions with a strict agenda and hope to be able to stick to this it is likely that they would soon choose another focus for their work.

However, as I understand it, one of the empirical challenges has been that it has not proven possible to demonstrate that the manual driven therapies are inferior to the individualised treatments. Additionally, there has been a stream of work that has shown that CBT therapists, will often avoid using some of the more experientially challenging strategies such as exposure-based interventions due to their own anxiety and beliefs about possibly distressing clients. There has been the argument that the avoidance of these more directive and challenging interventions results in less effective therapy (therapist drift) and that adherence to manuals will somehow correct this.

Ernesto: Michael, while considering your comments, my mind came up this ridiculous thought: If we caricature CBT therapists as walking-talking Manuals, then we can also caricature ET therapists as walking-talking Manuels (as in Manuel the waiter from that old sitcom *Fawlty Towers*). Manuel's catch phrase was 'I know nothing! I know nothing!'

And, in a way, this is the starting point that ET takes when it first approaches the novel and the unknown—such as a client. If Manuals' aims are to make us appear to be wise and full of expertise, Manuels act to assist the ET therapist in initially taking on the role of 'the idiot' who 'knows nothing' in terms of not having a clue as to what clients mean or are experiencing when presenting the issues or problems that have brought them to therapy. Just to be clear, it takes a lot of expertise to adopt—and retain—the stance of an idiot. But, in brief, I think that stance resonates quite closely with what you've described above regarding the approach taken by Applied Behaviour Analysis as well as current CBT approaches to couple therapy. In a way, all these 'expert as idiot' perspectives are returning the idea of diagnosis to its origins—where it was the patient, not the medic, who initially diagnosed. From an ET sense, when the client comes in and says things like 'I'm anxious' or 'I'm depressed', the ET idiot therapist tries to move that abstract statement into one that is more concrete, specific to the client's experience (and hence unique to the client), and that might eventually become 'owned' by the client rather than be experienced as some alien intruder. As to the evidence for the effectiveness of Manual-Driven approaches, I'm wondering whether this evidence might be pointing to something that is more about the CBT therapist's identification with and belief in the Manual, rather than the effectiveness of the Manual itself.

Michael: I want to ask more about practice! Often existential therapists seem to be to be very close to many of the assumptions of psychoanalysis in the way that they practice. The notion of going for a walk with the client, for instance, could be the subject of a week-long existential conference. CBT therapist will on the other hand go for a walk, or take a lift, or go to the zoo or go to the client's home, where this is seen as relevant and useful as there is nothing within CBT theory that asserts there should be 50-minute sessions in a therapist's office. Despite there being nothing in existential theory either that would assert this, existential therapists seem mostly to adhere to the frame conditions adopted by psychoanalytic theory. I am of course being provocative; however, the serious point might be the possibility of CBT offering ways of practicing that could be of value to existential therapy as much as the reverse?

Ernesto: I agree with you entirely on this point. I guess that some existential therapists would argue that the original approaches to

ET—Binswanger's existential analysis, Boss's daseinsanalysis, and Frankl's logotherapy—were all directly influenced by psychoanalysis. And, with each, although they developed alternate theories, they stuck with the psychoanalytic structure for therapy. Like you, I see no reason why contemporary ET needs to keep doing so and, indeed, whether it is questionable or even contra-theoretical to keep doing so. I guess that many fear that to not do so would be unprofessional in some sort of way. And, I sympathize. Sadly (to my way of thinking at least) many of the professional bodies for psychotherapy and counselling increasingly promote a model of 'doing therapy' that is deeply influenced by psychoanalytic assumptions. So yes, ET could learn a lot from CBT about frame flexibility. Actually, if there is anything remotely positive for existential therapists that has come out of the past two years of living with COVID-19, it is that, out of necessity, they have begun to look at the frame in much more open, and creative ways. Some are walking in open spaces with their clients, some are reconsidering their session times so that they may be shorter than the magical fifty minutes, some are playing with the frequency of meetings, and some are even using VR technology in order to meet with clients in a virtual space in which both or all also appear as avatars.

Michael: As you have noted in several of your publications, the major difference in the way that meaning is approached arises from the fact that standard CBT adopts a far more rationalist and objectivist stance such that becomes possible to speak of 'distortions' and 'dysfunctional beliefs'. Additionally, from this perspective, the role of the therapist becomes one of assisting the client to become aware of these distortions and to 'correct' these by aligning their thinking with reality. As I tried to show in this book, this is by no means the complete story within even standard CBT as it has always included substantial constructivist components. I think this has arisen from therapeutic experience where it really doesn't work to challenge the evidential basis of forms of belief which really are more questions of value. When working at the level of 'rules for living' seldom is it ever sufficient to explore these simply in terms of how well they align with 'reality'. It becomes much more a question of costs and advantages to holding particular perspectives on 'how I must and must not be' with the acknowledgement that change in these beliefs, even where change is desirable, will also be associated with trade-offs and unforeseen consequences.

Ernesto: I'm glad and relieved to read that this may be happening within CBT approaches. Perhaps one of the most important challenges that ET can offer to CBT is that of limiting reliance and judgment upon distortions and dysfunctions. As was briefly discussed earlier, 'a problem is not only a problem, it is also an attempted solution'. And yes, if the client is able to explore not only what might be gained but also what would be lost to them if the distortion or dysfunction were to be removed, they might well come to the decision that this would be too great a loss for them in terms of effects upon their values or meanings or whatever. But of course, even in arriving at that decision to retain the distortion or dysfunction, the *way* it would be retained would not be the same as before, not least because it would be an active choice on their part to do so rather than feeling themselves to be victims to, or enslaved by, some solely problematic agency.

Michael: It seems to me that CBT also takes a more optimistic stance which suggests that while there may be trade-offs it will be on balance in the client's interest to shift on beliefs that are implicated in the maintenance of psychological difficulties. So there is this mix of objectivist and rationalist stances alongside more constructivist ones and even in more recent elaborations of the CBT model you find this—an emphasis on greater constructivist elements and some softening of a rationalist stance and yet at the same time an assertion of the central CBT principle of 'the primacy of cognition' and the notion that therapy is still in its essence a process in which the therapist assist the client to clarify and explore these in the service of then aligning these more closely (although not ever fully) with reality.

Ernesto: Again, there is much here that both CBT and ET might well agree upon. Not least, the focus on exploration and clarification. If there is a point of disagreement, I guess that it rests upon the notion of 'reality'. Whose 'reality' are we talking about here? And, actually, are we even really and truly talking about 'reality' or are we, more accurately, addressing dominant ways of being that are accepted and valued by any number of powers-that-be? Maybe I'm being unfair here, but . . . It has seemed to me that CBT has tended to be much more willing to adopt and implement views of reality that reflect the current zeitgeist rather than question and challenge them. I know that politicians and medical bodies and insurance companies go on about how their preference is for CBT treatments because CBT is so evidence based. But could it be ever so slightly possible that what they really and truly like about it is that it doesn't rock their boats too much in terms of challenges to currently dominant values and expectations surrounding thought and behaviour that maintains the status quo surrounding notions of 'reality'? Therapy, as a whole, used to much more challenging of society's views and assumptions. Increasingly, it has become more and more an advocate or representative of them. This is therapy as a whole, I'm speaking of, not just CBT. Maybe, going back to an earlier point, this may be an important factor in its becoming less effective? Maybe ET, because it is in so many ways on the periphery of therapeutic acceptance and social acceptance, can act as a stimulus to CBT to rekindle its more revolutionary possibilities?

Michael: I would tend to see the interest in and support of CBT by insurance companies and government as primarily reflecting issues of cost, both cost of training and cost of provision. Additionally, the longstanding interest of CBT in evaluation, from a quantitative standpoint, definitely fits within the current zeitgeist. In these senses CBT can be seen as supporting currently dominant views. A number of highly critical papers have been written by various authors that essentially see CBT as fitting within and acting to maintain a neo-liberal orthodoxy. I think the best paper I have read on this is that by Woolfolk and Richardson (1984) that analysed behaviour therapy as expressing 'an ideology of modernity'. This was written prior to the rise to dominance of CBT however they have recently revised this paper to account for this, where the punch line seems to be 'well nothing much has changed there'. Of course, things are not so black and white. I guess a deeper question is the extent to which you consider the expansion of psychological therapies a 'good thing'. While the improving Access to Psychological Therapies Programme (IAPT) in England has been criticised strongly for its over reliance on CBT and for its original suggestion that one of the primary benefits to arise will be that people successfully treated will return to work and reduce the burden on the state for financial aid associated with incapacity due to mental illness. At the same time the result has been that many more people have received psychological therapy who might otherwise have received only medication or nothing at all. And as you seem to be suggesting, CBT also contains within it the possibility to be critical of socially based beliefs and assumptions that are implicated in the development of psychological distress such as the highly individualised, atomised and competitive view currently in ascendence. But isn't the key critical thrust of ET likely to be towards those approaches that privilege a notion of an isolated individual—a subject with strong boundaries aware of its market value and able and motivated to go out and meet its 'needs' in relationships of exchange? This critique would seem to apply to a whole range of therapies.

Ernesto: I wouldn't want readers to think that I was suggesting that CBT therapists were all promoters of some neo-liberal agenda. I'm sure that the range of political views and affiliations is as wide among CBT therapists as it is among therapists of any other model or approach—including ET, of course. The focus I wanted to highlight was more along the lines of how key principles within a model veer it *as an approach* toward or away from dominant socio-political-economic attitudes and assumptions. CBT has very deep—but not exclusive—North American and, more broadly, Anglo-Saxon roots and it would be surprising if it did not have an in-built bias toward more individualistic and capitalistic assumptions. ET's origins are in European Continental philosophy and as such it has it more inter-relational roots which can carry it to more socio-politically extreme positions, be they more socialist/communistic or fascist. Because of this more extremist influence, ET is less likely to reflect dominant social perspectives regarding any number of therapeutically-focused concerns. I'm aware that I'm making huge generalisations here, but . . . the point I'm making is that *as models* one (CBT) is more likely to be welcomed by those agencies that represent and want to maintain the status quo. The questionable success of CBT-dominated IAPT would suggest that there is something about the way 'evidence-based' is understood. Again, the ET challenge here might be: How are we defining 'evidence'? And again, implicit in that question is that 'evidence' has come to be equated solely with explanatory-focused science (which deals with correlation and causality). 'Evidence' from an understanding science perspective doesn't seem to be getting any sort of look-in. Personally speaking, the only thing that continually irritates me when I engage with CBT practitioners is that they seem to promote explanatory science as the *only* form of scientific enquiry. They know better than that. And their own movement within Third Wave approaches makes it evident that they know. But they seem reticent to inform treatment providers who wouldn't necessarily be expected to know.

Michael: I think the next area to look at would be the therapeutic relationship. As I again tried to show in this text that CBT has come a long way since its earlier days, more associated with behaviourism, where the relationship was seen as at best a helpful facilitating factor and by no means the main driver of change or the focus of the work itself. In my view, from an existential perspective, the issue is not so much that CBT doesn't take note of the therapeutic relationship but rather that its view of the relationship and the forms of practice it promotes, lead to a very limited perspective and also to a limited range of what might show up in the therapeutic relationship. This seems to me though to be a consequence of the aims of the approach and what it is that CBT therapists believe themselves to be doing and being when they are engaged with clients. That is, the approach remains to an important extent within a medical model of treatment even where it is not so much that the therapist does something to the client to fix or cure them but instead to directly teach them strategies for managing or changing their behaviour and thinking.

So, it's a mix really of educational and skills-based interventions within a perspective that emphasises focussing upon tightly defined (and sometimes explicitly diagnosed) disorders. By contrast existential therapy, by aligning itself with a 'human science' perspective sees therapy principals in terms of an investigative and clarificatory enterprise. This is one that encourages therapist to attempt to set aside any agenda of Educating or teaching a client skills but instead attempts a form of relationship the principal aim of which is to clarify, open up and challenge the clients world view. This seems to me to be the source of the greatest differences and potential tension between the two approaches. I think this plays out in a clear embodied way in how therapists from these two orientations would approach each session. On the CBT side we have the explicit attempt to set and adhere to a clear agenda from the beginning of the session. A session should be planned in advance (albeit flexibly and collaboratively) and at the end of the session it becomes possible to review the extent to which the session achieved what was set at the beginning as the explicit goals for problem solving. Existential therapy by contrast emphasis the notion of dialogue which requires the therapist to a large extent to set aside any notions of being able to direct or plan or control the way a session unfolds. This doesn't however mean the session lacks structure or focus but rather that this focus and structure seems to clarify itself as the dialogue unfolds.

Ernesto: I think that you've summarised the points in question really well. And maybe there is significant space for a non-defensive dialogue between the approaches with regard to their differences. For me, the crux of the matter boils down to a point I raised earlier. Namely: what definition/understanding of therapy are we adhering to? I accept that I am in a minority here—both within therapy as a whole and probably within ET as well—in that I seek to limit the immediate associations made between therapy and notions of 'cure', 'education', 'treatment', 'directing change', 'helping', and so forth. Namely, all those views that, in the nicest way possible (at least most of the time) communicate to the client: 'You are wrong to be the way that you are being and I, the therapist, have the authority, know-how, and arrogance to make it my task to turn your way of being into the right way to be.' I know that many clients come to therapy because they have convinced themselves that their way of being is wrong in some way or other and they are looking for an expert who will set them right. But what if the most foundational 'wrong' about their 'wrong way of being' is actually the belief that it is in some way 'wrong'? Then any attempt—even a successful one—to 'righten to presenting wrong' would actually be maintaining, if not strengthening the 'foundational wrong' belief such that its benefits in the long run would be limited, perhaps minimal, and might potentially worsen the client's overall relation with their way of being. Whatever, this is a huge debate. And I'm not here to suggest that one side of the debate is entirely correct or that the other is entirely wrong. All I'm hoping for is that, through books like yours, practitioners will recognize that there is something to debate here rather than just dismiss, or worse, not even be aware of the existence of one view or the other.

Michael: I'm particularly interested in the 'existential mantra' that you have suggested" 'The client is always right'. This seems initially very simple. Recently, however, I have experimented with keeping this mantra in mind both in therapy sessions as well as in supervision sessions. I can confirm that it can at times be very challenging to maintain. Supervisees have reported that they have found it very helpful particularly when they are experiencing a sense of stuckness with their clients. It seems to promote a greater willingness to stay with the client's experienced reality. At one level it seems the very opposite of a CBT perspective in which what the therapist is on the lookout for, in a manner promoted by the theoretical perspective, are the ways in which the client's beliefs are distorted or irrational. However at the same time, within CBT more broadly there has always been the perspective that promotes a 'functional' view—that even the most apparently irrational belief or behaviour serves some function, it is purposeful and works in some fashion. The job of the therapist becomes understanding how things are working functionally. So in this sense exploring the ways in which the client's beliefs and statements are right also seems present as a possibility.

Ernesto: Thank you for treating the mantra as having some possible value and for even passing it on to your supervisees. The mantra follows on directly from the points being discussed above, and I guess throughout our discussion, concerning what we understand 'therapy' to mean and how we then work with that. I think that it also clarifies something in the example you provided earlier of the client who kept disagreeing with and dismissing all of your attempts at clarification. The stance that you took with her, it seems to me, is one that is in tune with the mantra. It drove you crazy, but you stuck with her in her insistence that very thing you said had to be met with 'no!'. And, in doing so, something shifted for her. Maybe no one—herself included—had ever allowed her to be right and experience herself in that way. Perhaps I should add a little sub-clause to the mantra: 'And the therapist, at least initially, has no idea as to what the client is right about'.

Michael: We have covered a great deal of ground and hopefully this has opened up for consideration and reflection a wide range of points of contact and difference, tension and disagreement as well as agreement between CBT and ET. All good dialogues of course are in a sense never final, although they are inevitably interrupted and incomplete. Ernesto thank you!

References

Ainsworth, M. D. S., & Bowlby, J. (1991). An ethological approach to personality development. *American Psychologist*, *46*, 331–341.

Alford, B. A., & Beck, A. T. (1997). *The integrative power of cognitive therapy*. Guilford Press.

Anderson, H., & Goolishan, H. (1992). The client is the expert: A not-knowing approach to therapy. In S. McNamee & K. J. Gergen (Eds.), *Therapy as social construction*. Sage.

Anderson, R., & Cissna, K. N. (1997). *The Martin Buber-Carl Rogers Dialogue: A new transcript with commentary*. State University of New York Press.

Bacon, T., Farhall, J., & Fossey, E. (2014). The active therapeutic processes of acceptance and commitment therapy for persistent symptoms of psychosis: Clients' perspectives. *Behavioural and Cognitive Psychotherapy*, *42*(4), 402–420.

Baer, R. A. (2014). *Mindfulness-based treatment approaches*. Academic Press.

Bakhtin, M. (1973). *Problems of Dostoevsky's poetics*. Ardis.

Bamelis, L., Bloo, J., Bernstein, D., & Arntz, A. (2015). Effectiveness studies. In M. van Vreeswijk, J. Broersen, & M. Nadort (Eds.), *The Wiley Blackwell handbook of schema therapy: Theory, research, and practice*. Wiley-Blackwell.

Barlow, D. H. (2002). *Anxiety and its disorders: The nature and treatment of anxiety and panic* (2nd ed.). Guilford press.

Bazzano, M. (2019). *Nietzsche and psychotherapy*. Routledge.

CBT and Existential Psychology: Philosophy, Psychology and Therapy, First Edition. Michael Worrell.

Bazzano, M. (Ed.) (2021). *Revisioning existential therapy: Counter-traditional perspectives*. Routledge.

Beck, A. T. (1967). *Depression: Clinical, experimental, and theoretical aspects*. Hoeber.

Beck, A. T. (1971). Cognitive patterns in dreams and daydreams. In J. H. Masserman (Ed.), *Dream dynamics: Science and psychoanalysis* (Vol. 19). Grune & Stratton.

Beck, A. T. (1996). Beyond belief: A theory of modes, personality, and psychopathology. In P. Salkovskis (Ed.), *Frontiers of cognitive therapy*. Guilford.

Beck, A. T., Emery, G., & Greenberg, R. L. (1985). *Anxiety disorders and phobias: A cognitive perspective*. Basic Books.

Beck, A. T., & Freeman, A. M. (1990). *Cognitive therapy of personality disorders*. Guilford Press.

Beck, A. T., & Haigh, E. A. P. (2014). Advances in cognitive theory and therapy: The generic cognitive model. *Annual Review of Clinical Psychology*, *10*, 1–24.

Beck, A. T., & Hollon, S. (1993). Controversies in cognitive therapy: A dialogue with Aaron T Beck and Steve Hollon. *Journal of Cognitive Psychotherapy: An International Quarterly*, *7*(2), 79–93.

Beck, A. T., & Hurvich, M. S. (1959). Psychological correlates of depression 1: Frequency of "masochistic" dream content in a private psychiatric sample. *Psychosomatic Medicine*, *2*(1), 50–55.

Beck, A. T., Rush, J. A., Shaw, B. F., & Emery, G. (1979). *Cognitive therapy of depression*. Guilford Press.

Beck, A. T., & Ward, C. H. (1961). Dreams of depressed patients: Characteristic themes in manifest content. *Archives of General Psychiatry*, *5*, 462–467.

Beck, A. T., Wright, F. D., Newman, C. F., & Liese, B. S. (1993). *Cognitive therapy of substance abuse*. Guilford Press.

Beck, C. J. (1993). *Everyday Zen: Love and work*. Harper.

Beck, J. (2017). Forward. In N. Kazantzis, F. M. Dattilio, & K. S. Dobson (Eds.), *The therapeutic relationship in cognitive-behavioral therapy: A clinician's guide*. Guilford Press.

Beck, R., & Perkins, T. S. (2001). Cognitive content-specificity for anxiety and depression: A meta-analysis. *Cognitive Therapy and Research*, *25*(6), 651–663.

Becker, E. (1973). *The Denial of Death*. Souvenir Press.

Bennett-Levy, J. (2019). Why therapists should walk the talk: The theoretical and empirical case for personal practice in therapist training and professional development. *Journal of Behavior Therapy and Experimental Psychiatry, 62*, 133–145.

Bennett-Levy, J., Butler, G., Fennell, M., Hackmann, A., Mueller, M., & Westbrook, D. (2004). *Oxford guide to behavioural experiments in cognitive therapy*. Oxford University Press.

Biglan, A., & Hayes, S. C. (2016). Functional contextualism and contextual behavioral science. In R. D. Zettle, S. C. Hayes, D. Barnes-Holmes, & A. Biglan (Eds.), *The Wiley handbook of contextual behavioral science*. Wiley-Blackwell.

Binswanger, L. (1963). *Being-in-the-World: Selected papers of Ludwig Binswanger*. Harper Torchbooks.

Bishop, S. R., Lau, M., Shapito, S., Carlson, L., Anderson, N. D., Carmody, J., Segal, Z. V., Abbey, S., Speca, M., Velting, D., & Devins, G. (2004). Mindfulness: A proposed operational definition. *Clinical Psychology: Science and Practice, 11*(3), 230–241.

Blenkiron, P. (2010). *Stories and analogies in cognitive behaviour therapy*. Wiley-Blackwell.

Bohart, A. C., & House, R. (2008). Empirically supported/validated treatments as modernist ideology, I: Dodo, manualization, and the paradigm question. In R. House & D. Lowenthal (Eds.), *Against and for CBT: Towards a constructive dialogue?* PCCS Books.

Boss, M. (1963). *Psychoanalysis and daseinsanalysis*. Basic Books.

Brewin, C. R. (2006). Understanding cognitive behaviour therapy: A retrieval competition account. *Behaviour research and Therapy, 44*, 765–784.

Brown, G. P., Roach, A., Irving, L., & Joseph, K. (2008). Personal meaning: A neglected transdiagnostic construct. *International Journal of Cognitive Therapy, 1*(3), 223–236.

Bugental, J. F. T. (1999). *Psychotherapy isn't what you think: Bringing the psychotherapeutic engagement into the living moment*. Zeig, Tucker.

Bunting, K., & Hayes, S. C. (2008). Language and meaning: Acceptance and commitment therapy and the EI model. In K. Schneider (Ed.), *Existential-integrative psychotherapy: Guideposts to the core of practice*. Routledge.

Burston, D. (2000). *The crucible of experience: R. D. Laing and the crisis of psychotherapy*. Harvard University Press.

Burston, D., & Frie, R. (2006). *Psychotherapy as a human science*. Duquesne University Press.

Butcher, P. (1984). Existential-behaviour therapy: A possible paradigm? *British Journal of Medical Psychology*, *57*, 265–274.

Cain, D. J. (2001). Defining characteristics, history, and evolution of humanistic psychotherapies. In D. J. Cain & J. Seeman (Eds.), *Humanistic psychotherapies: Handbook of research and practice*. American Psychological Association.

Cannon, B. (1991). *Sartre and psychoanalysis. An existentialist challenge to clinical metatheory*. University Press of Kansas.

Carleton, R. N. (2012). The intolerance of uncertainty construct in the context of anxiety disorders: Theoretical and practical perspectives. *Expert Review of Neurothearpeutics*, *12*, 937–947.

Castonguay, L. G., & Beutler, L. E. (Eds.) (2006). *Principles of therapeutic change that work*. Oxford.

Cerbone, D. R. (2015). Phenomenological method: Reflection, introspection, and skepticism. In D. Zahavi (Ed.), *The Oxford handbook of contemporary phenomenology*. Oxford University Press.

Chadwick, P., Williams, C., & Mackenzie, J. (2003). Impact of case formulation in cognitive therapy for psychosis. *Behaviour Research and Therapy*, *41*, 671–680.

Chiari, G., & Nuzzo, M. L. (2010). *Constructivist psychotherapy: A narrative Hermeneutic approach*. Routledge.

Cioran, E. M. (2013). *The trouble with being Born* (R. Howard, Trans.). Penguin.

Claessens, M. (2010). Mindfulness based third-wave CBT therapies and existential-phenomenology: Friends or foes? *Existential Analysis*, *21*, 295–308.

Clark, D. A. (1995). Perceived limitations of standard cognitive therapy: A consideration of efforts to revise Beck's theory and therapy. *Journal of Cognitive Psychotherapy: An International Quarterly*, *9*(3), 153–172.

Clark, D. A., & Beck, A. T. (2010). *Cognitive therapy of anxiety disorders: Science and practice*. Guilford Press.

Clark, D. A., Beck, A. T., & Alford, B. A. (1999). *Scientific foundations of cognitive theory and therapy of depression*. Wiley.

Clark, D. M. (1988). A cognitive model of panic attacks. In S. Rachman & J. D. Maser (Eds.), *Panic: Psychological perspectives*. Lawrence Erlbaum.

Clark, D. M., & Wells, A. (1995). A cognitive model of social phobia. In R. G. Heimberg, M. R. Liebowitz, D. A. Hope, & F. R. Schneier (Eds.), *Social phobia: Diagnosis, assessment and treatment*. Guilford Press.

Cohn, H. W. (1995). Authenticity and the aims of psychotherapy. In H. W. Cohn & S. du Plock (Eds.), *Existential challenges to psychotherapeutic theory and practice*. Society for Existential Analysis.

Cohn, H. W. (1997). *Existential thought and therapeutic practice. An introduction to existential psychotherapy*. Sage.

Cohn, H. W. (1999). *With all five senses: Poems* (F. G. Cohn, Trans.). Menard Press.

Cohn, H. W. (2002). *Heidegger and the roots of existential therapy*. Continuum.

Cohn, H. W. (2005). Interpretation: Explanation or understanding. In E. van Deurzen & C. A. Baker (Eds.), *Existential perspectives on human issues*. Palgrave.

Cooper, D. E. (1999). *Existentialism* (2nd ed.). Blackwell.

Cooper, M. (2003). *Existential therapies*. Sage.

Copson, A. (2015). What is humanism? In A. Copson & A. C. Grayling (Eds.), *The Wiley-Blackwell handbook of humanism*. Wiley-Blackwell.

Corrie, S., & Milton, M. (2000). The relationship between existential-phenomenological and cognitive-behaviour therapies. *European Journal of Psychotherapy & Counselling*, *3*(1), 7–24.

Craig, E. (2015). The lost language of being: Ontology's perilous destiny in existential psychotherapy. *Philosophy, Psychiatry, & Psychology*, *22*(2), 79–92.

Crane, R. (2009). *Mindfulness-based cognitive therapy: Distinctive features*. Routledge.

Dahl, J., Stewart, I., Martell, C., & Kaplan, J. S. (2013). *ACT & RFT in relationships*. Context Press.

Dalal, F. (2018). *CBT: The cognitive behavioural tsunami. managerialism, politics, and the corruptions of science*. Routledge.

Datillo, F. M. (2013). *Cognitive behavioral therapy with families and couples*. Guilford Press.

Day, W. F. (1969). Radical behaviorism in reconciliation with phenomenology. *Journal of the Experimental Analysis of Behavior*, *12*, 315–328.

Derrida, J. (2001). *Writing and difference* (A. Bass, Trans.). Routledge.

DeRubeis, R. J., & Feeley, M. (1990). Determinants of change in cognitive therapy for depression. *Cognitive Therapy and Research*, *14*(5), 469–482.

Dobson, D., & Dobson, K. S. (2009). *Evidence-based cognitive behavioral therapy*. Guilford Press.

Dobson, K. S., Poole, J. C., & Beck, J. S. (2018). The fundamental cognitive model. In R. Leahy (Ed.), *Science and practice in cognitive therapy: Foundations, mechanisms, and applications*. Guilford Press.

Doweiko, H. E. (2004). Dreams as unappreciated therapeutic avenue for cognitive-behavioral therapists. In R. I. Rosner, W. J. Lyddon, & A. Freeman (Eds.), *Cognitive therapy and dreams*. Springer.

Dreyfus, H. (1972). *What computers can't do: A critique of artificial reason*. Harper and Row.

Dreyfus, H. (2016). *Skilful coping: Essays on the phenomenology of everyday perception and action*. Oxford University Press.

Dugas, M. J., & Robichaud, M. (2007). *Cognitive-behavioral treatment for generalised anxiety disorder: From science to practice*. Routledge.

Edwards, D., & Arntz, A. (2015). Schema therapy in historical perspective. In M. van Vreeswijk, J. Broersen, & M. Nadort (Eds.), *The Wiley Blackwell handbook of schema therapy: Theory, research, and practice*. Wiley-Blackwell.

Edwards, D. J. A. (1990). Cognitive-behavioral and existential-phenomenological approaches to therapy: Complementary or conflicting paradigms? *Journal of Cognitive Psychotherapy: An International Quarterly*, *4*(2), 105–120.

Efran, J. S., Lukens, M. D., & Lukens, R. J. (1990). *Language, structure, and change: Frameworks of meaning in psychotherapy*. Norton.

Ellis, A. (1992). Constructivism and rational-emotive therapy: A critique of Richard Wessler's critique. *Psychotherapy*, *30*(3), 531–532.

Epstein, N. B., & Baucom, D. H. (2002). *Enhanced cognitive behavioral therapy for couples: A contextual approach*. American Psychological Association.

Fairburn, C. G. (2008). *Cognitive behavior therapy and eating disorders*. Guilford Press.

Fallon, D. (1992). An existential look at B. F. Skinner. *American Psychologist*, *47*(11), 1433–1440.

Felder, A. J., Aten, H. M., Neudeck, J. A., Shiomi-Chen, J., & Robbins, B. D. (2014). Mindfulness at the heart of existential-phenomenology and humanistic psychology: A century of contemplation and elaboration. *The Humanistic Psychologist*, *42*, 6–23.

Fennell, M., & Segal, Z. (2013). Mindfulness-based cognitive therapy: Culture clash or creative fusion? In M. Williams & J. Kabat-Zinn (Eds.), *Mindfulness: Diverse perspectives on its meaning, origins, and applications.* Routledge.

Fewtrell, D., & O'Conner, K. (1995). *Clinical phenomenology and cognitive psychology*. Routledge.

Fischer, W. (1989). An empirical-phenomenological investigation of being anxious: An example of the phenomenological approach to anxiety. In R. S. Valle & S. Halling (Eds.), *Existential-phenomenological perspectives in psychology: Exploring the breadth of human experience*. Plenum press.

Fletcher, L. B., & Hayes, S. C. (2009). Phenomenology and modern behavioral psychology. *Philosophy, Psychiatry, & Psychology, 15*(3), 255–258.

Foucault, M. (1980). In C. Gordon (Ed.), *Power/knowledge: Selected interviews and other writings, 1972–1977*. Pantheon.

Frankl, V. E. (1984). *Man's search for meaning*. (revised and updated edn.). Washington Square Press.

Frankl, V. E. (1988). *The will to meaning. Foundation sand applications of Logotherapy*. Plume.

Freeman, A., & White, B. (2004). Dreams and the dream image: Using dreams in cognitive therapy. In R. I. Rosner, W. J. Lyddon, & A. Freeman (Eds.), *Cognitive therapy and dreams*. Springer.

Freud, S. (1945). *The interpretation of dreams* (A. A. Brill, Trans.). George Allen & Unwin.

Freud, S. (1973). *New introductory lectures on psychoanalysis*. Penguin.

Frie, R. (1997). *Subjectivity and intersubjectivity in modern philosophy and psychoanalysis: A study of Sartre, Binswanger, Lacan, and Habermas.* Rowman & Littlefield Publishers.

Frie, R. (2013). Reconfiguring psychological agency: Postmodernism, recursivity, and the politics of change. In R. Frie & D. Orange (Eds.), *Beyond postmodernism: New dimensions in clinical theory and practice.* Routledge.

Friedman, M. (1991). *The worlds of existentialism*. Humanities Press.

Fuchs, T. (2019). The experience of time and its disorders. In G. Stanghellini, M. R. Broome, A. V. Fernandez, P. Fusar-Poli, A. Raballo, & R. Rosfort (Eds.), *The Oxford handbook of phenomenological psychopathology*. Oxford University Press.

Gadamer, H. G. (2004). *Truth and method*. Continuum.

Garety, P. A., Kuipers, E., Foweler, D., Freeman, D., & Bebbington, P. E. (2001). A cognitive model of the positive symptoms of psychosis. *Psychological Medicine*, *31*, 189–195.

Gendlin, E. T. (2003). *Focusing: How to gain direct access to your body's knowledge*. Ridler.

Gergen, K. J. (1991). *The saturated self*. Basic Books.

Gergen, K. J. (2001). Construction in contention: Towards consequential resolutions. *Theory and Psychology*, *11*(3), 419–432.

Gilbert, P. (2009). *The compassionate mind*. Constable & Robinson.

Gilbert, P. (2010). *Compassion focussed therapy: Distinctive features*. Routledge.

Gilbert, P., & Irons, C. (2004). A pilot exploration of the use of compassionate images in a group of self-critical people. *Memory*, *12*(4), 507–516.

Greenberg, L. S., & Pavio, S. C. (1997). *Working with emotions in psychotherapy*. Guilford Press.

Guidano, V. F. (1991). *The self in process*. Guilford Press.

Guidano, V. F. (1998). Constructivist psychotherapy: A theoretical framework. In R. A. Neimeyer & M. J. Mahoney (Eds.), *Constructivism in psychotherapy*. American Psychological Association.

Guidavo, V. F., & Liotti, G. (1983). *Cognitive process and emotional disorders*. Guilford Press.

Hackmann, A., Bennett-Levy, J., & Holmes, E. A. (2011). *Oxford guide to imagery in cognitive therapy*. Oxford University Press.

Hadot, P. (1995). *Philosophy as a way of life*. Blackwell.

Halling, S., & Nill, J. D. (1995). A brief history of existential-phenomenological psychiatry and psychology. *Journal of Phenomenological Psychology*, *26*(1), 1–45.

Hayes, S. (2004). Acceptance and commitment therapy, relational frame theory, and the third wave of behavior therapy. *Behavior Therapy*, *35*, 639–665.

Hayes, S. C. (2004). Acceptance and commitment therapy and the new behavior therapies. In S. C. Hayes, V. M. Follette, & M. M. Linehan (Eds.), *Mindfulness and acceptance: Expanding the cognitive behavioral tradition*. Guilford.

Hayes, S. C. (2016a). Why contextual behavioral science exists. In R. D. Zettle, S. C. Hayes, D. Barnes-Holmes, & A. Biglan (Eds.), *The Wiley handbook of contextual behavioral science*. Wiley-Blackwell.

Hayes, S. C. (2016b). Analytic goals and the varieties of scientific contextualism. In S. C. Hayes (Ed.), *The ACT in context*. Routledge.

Hayes, S. C., & Hofmann, S. G. (2018). *Process-based CBT. The science and core clinical competencies of cognitive behavioral therapy*. Context Press.

Hayes, S. C., Luoma, J. B., Bond, F., Masuda, A., & Lillis, J. (2006). Acceptance and commitment therapy: Model, processes, and outcomes. *Behavior Research and Therapy*, *44*, 1–25.

Hayes, S. C., Stroshal, K. D., & Wilson, K. G. (1999/2011). *Acceptance and commitment therapy*. Guilford Press.

Heaton, J. (1995). What is existential analysis? In H. W. Cohn & S. du Plock (Eds.), *Existential challenges to psychotherapeutic theory and practice*. Society for Existential Analysis.

Heaton, J. (2014). The other and psychotherapy. In R. Bernasconi & D. Wood (Eds.), *The provocation of Levinas: Rethinking the other*. Routledge.

Heidegger, M. (1962). *Being and time* (J. Macquarrie & E. H. Freund, Trans.). Harper and Row.

Heidegger, M. (2001). *Zollikon seminars: Protocols-conversations-letters* (F. Mayr & R. Askay, Trans.). Northwestern University Press.

Held, B. S. (1995). *Back to Reality: A critique of postmodern theory in psychotherapy*. Norton.

Held, B. S. (2018). Anything goes by the wayside: A reply to Raskin and Debany. *Journal of Constructivist Psychology*, *31*(4), 400–412.

Herbert, J. D., Forman, E. M., & Hitchcock, P. (2016). Contextual approaches to psychotherapy: Defining, distinguishing, and common features. In R. D. Zettle, S. C. Hayes, D. Barnes-Holmes, & A. Biglan (Eds.), *The Wiley handbook of contextual behavioral science*. Wiley-Blackwell.

Herbert, J. D., & Padovani, F. (2015). Contextualism, psychological science, and the question of ontology. *Journal of Contextual Behavioural Science*, *4*, 225–230.

Hersch, E. L. (2015). What existential ontology can offer psychotherapists. *Philosophy, Psychiatry, & Psychology*, *22*(2), 107–119.

Hickes, M., & Mirea, D. (2012). Cognitive behavioural and existential-phenomenological psychotherapy: Rival paradigms or fertile ground for therapeutic synthesis? *Existential Analysis*, *23*(1), 15–31.

Hoffman, L. (1998). *Ritual and spontaneity in the psychoanalytic process: A dialectical-constructivist view*. The Analytic Press.

Hoffman, L. (2009). Knowing and the unknown: An existential epistemology in a postmodern context. *Humana.Mente, 11*, 97–109.

Hoffman, L., & Cleare-Hoffman, H. P. (2011). Existential therapy and emotions: Lessons from cross-cultural exchange. *The Humanistic Psychologist, 39*, 261–267.

Hoffman, L., Jackson, T., Mendelowitz, E., Wang, X., Yang, M., Bradford, K., & Schneider, K. J. (2019). Challenges and new developments in existential-humanistic and existential-integrative therapy. In E. van Deurzen, E. Craig, A. Langle, K. J. Schneider, D. Tatam, & S. du Plock (Eds.), *The Wiley world handbook of existential therapy*. Wiley-Blackwell.

Hollon, S. D., & Beck, A. T. (2013). *Cognitive and cognitive-behavioral therapies. Bergin and Garfield's handbook of psychotherapy and behavior change*. Wiley.

House, R., & Loewenthal, D. (Eds.) (2008). *Against and for CBT. Towards a constructive dialogue?* PCCS Books.

Hughes, S. (2018). The philosophy of science as it applies to clinical psychology. In S. C. Hayes & S. G. Hofman (Eds.), *Process-based CBT. The science and core clinical competencies of cognitive behavioral therapy*. Context Press.

Ihde, D. (1986). *Experimental phenomenology: An introduction*. State University of New York.

Iverach, L. (2018). Death anxiety and psychopathology. In R. E. Menzies, R. G. Menzies, & L. Iverach (Eds.), *Curing the dread of death: Theory, research, and practice*. Australian Academic Press.

Iverach, L., Menzies, R. G., & Menzies, R. E. (2014). Death anxiety and its role in psychopathology: Reviewing the status of a transdiagnostic construct. *Clinical Psychology Review, 34*, 580–593.

James, I. (2001). Schema therapy: The next generation but should it carry a health warning? *Behavioural and Cognitive Psychotherapy, 29*(4), 401–407.

Jaspers, K. (1963). *General Psychopathology* (J. Hoening & M. W. Hamilton, Trans.) (Vol. 1). John Hopkins University Press.

Kabat-Zinn, J. (1982). An outpatient program in behavioral medicine for chronic pain patients based on the practice of mindfulness meditation: Theoretical considerations and preliminary results. *General Hospital Psychiatry, 4*, 33–47.

Kahlon, S., Neal, A., & Patterson, T. G. (2014). Experiences of cognitive behavioural formulation in clients with depression. *The Cognitive Behaviour Therapist, 7*, Article e8.

Kanter, J. W., Busch, A. M., & Rusch, L. C. (2009). *Behavioral activation: Distinctive features*. Routledge.

Kazantzis, N., Dattilio, F. M., & Dobson, K. S. (2017). *The therapeutic relationship in cognitive behavioral therapy: A clinician's guide*. Guilford Press.

Kelly, G. A. (1955). *The psychology of personal constructs*. Yale University Press.

Kelly, G. A. (1973). Fixed-role therapy. In R. R. M. Jurjevich (Ed.), *Direct psychotherapy: 28 American originals*. University of Miami Press.

Kierkegaard, S. (1980). *The concept of anxiety* (A. Hannay, Trans.). Penguin.

Kohlenberg, R. J., & Tsai, M. (1991). *Functional analytic psychotherapy: A guide for creating intense and curative therapeutic relationships*. Plennum.

Kuyken, W., Padesky, C. A., & Dudley, R. (2009). *Collaborative case conceptualization: Working effectively with clients in cognitive-behavioral therapy*. Guilford Press.

Laing, R. D. (1960). *The divided self*. Penguin.

Laing, R. D. (1990). *The politics of experience and the Bird of Paradise*. Penguin.

Langdridge, D. (2013). *Existential counselling and psychotherapy*. Sage.

Leahy, R. L. (2001). *Overcoming resistance in cognitive therapy*. Guilford Press.

Leahy, R. L. (2007). Emotional schemas and resistance to change in anxiety disorders. *Cognitive and Behavioral Practice*, *14*, 36–45.

Leahy, R. L. (2015). *Emotional schema therapy*. Guilford Press.

LeDoux, J. (1996). *The emotional brain*. Simon & Schuster.

Lee, D. (2006). Case conceptualisation in complex PTSD. Integrating theory with practice. In N. Tarrier (Ed.), *Case formulation in cognitive behavioural therapy: The treatment of challenging and complex cases*. Routledge.

Lees, J. (Ed.) (2016). *The future of psychological therapy: From managed care to transformational practice*. Routledge.

Leitner, L. M., & Epting, F. R. (2001). Constructivist approaches to therapy. In K. J. Schneider, J. F. T. Bugental, & J. F. Pierson (Eds.), *The handbook of humanistic psychology*. Sage.

Linehan, M. (1993). *Skills training manual for treating borderline personality disorder*. Guilford Press.

Liu, H., Peng, H., Song, X., Xu, C., & Zhang, M. (2022). Using AI chatbots to provide self-help depression treatment for university students: A randomised trial of effectiveness. *Internet Interventions*, *27*, 1–8.

Lobbestael, J., van Vreeswijk, M., & Arntz, A. (2007). Shedding light on schema modes: A clarification of the mode concept and its current research status. *Netherlands Journal of Psychology, 63*, 76–85.

Loewenthal, D. (2008). Post-existentialism as a reaction to CBT? In R. House & D. Loewenthal (Eds.), *Against and for CBT: Towards a constructive dialogue?* PCCS Books.

Longmore, R. J., & Worrell, M. (2007). Do we need to challenge thoughts in cognitive behaviour therapy? *Clinical Psychology Review, 27*, 173–187.

Lynch, T. R., Trost, W. T., Salsman, N., & Linehan, M. M. (2007). Dialectical behavior therapy for borderline personality disorder. *Annual Review of Clinical Psychology, 3*, 181–205.

Mackessy, J., & Bazzano, M. (2021). Is relatedness a normative ideal? In M. Bazzano (Ed.), *Re-visioning existential therapy: Counter-traditional perspectives*. Routledge.

Macquarrie, J. (1973). *Existentialism: An introduction, guide and assessment.* Penguin.

Mahoney, M. J. (1991). *Human change processes.* Basic Books.

Mahoney, M. J. (1999). Continuing evolution of the cognitive sciences and psychotherapies. In R. A. Neimeyer & M. J. Mahoney (Eds.), *Constructivism in Psychotherapy*. American Psychological Association.

Mahoney, M. J. (2003). *Constructive psychotherapy: A practical guide.* Guilford Press.

Maitland, D. W. M., Kanter, J. W., Manbeck, K. E., & Kuczynski, A. M. (2017). Relationship science informed clinically relevant behaviors in functional analytic psychotherapy: The awareness, courage, and love model. *Journal of Contextual Behavioral Science, 6*, 347–359.

Mansell, W. (2008). What is CBT really, and how can we enhance the impact of effective psychotherapies such as CBT? In R. House & D. Loewenthal (Eds.), *Against and for CBT: Towards a constructive dialogue?* PCCS Books.

Martell, C. R., Addis, M. E., & Jacobson, N. S. (2001). *Depression in context.* W. W. Norton.

Mathews, A. (2006). Towards an experimental cognitive science of CBT. *Behavior Therapy, 37*, 314–318.

Maturana, H. R., & Varela, F. J. (1987). *The tree of knowledge: The biological roots of human understanding*. New Science Library/Shambhala Publications.

Maxfield, M., John, S., & Pyszczynski, T. (2014). A Terror management perspective on the role of death-related anxiety in psychological dysfunction. *The Humanistic Psychologist, 42*(1), 35–53.

May, R. (1981). *Freedom and destiny*. Dell Books.

May, R. (1983). *The discovery of being*. W. W. Norton.

May, R., Angel, E., & Ellenberger, H. F. (1958). *Existence: A new dimension in psychiatry and psychology*. Basic Books.

McEvoy, P. P., & Erceg-Hurn, D. M. (2016). The search for universal transdiagnostic and trans-therapy change process: Evidence for intolerance of uncertainty. *Journal of Anxiety Disorders, 41*, 96–107.

McGregor, H., Lieberman, J. D., Solomon, J., Arndt, J., Simon, L., & Pyszczynski, T. (1998). Terror management and aggression: evidence that mortality salience motivates aggression against worldview threatening others. *Journal of Personality and Social psychology, 74*, 590–605.

McLeod, J. (2004). Social construction, narrative and psychotherapy. In L. E. Angus & J. McLeod (Eds.), *The handbook of narrative and psychotherapy: Practice, theory, and research*. Sage.

McManus, F., Peerbhoy, D., & Clark, D. M. (2010). Learning to change a way of being: An interpretative phenomenological perspective on cognitive therapy for social phobia. *Journal of Anxiety Disorders, 24*, 581–589.

Menzies, R. E., & Dar-Nimrod, I. (2017). Death anxiety and its relationship with obsessive compulsive disorder. *Journal of Abnormal Psychology, 126*, 367–377.

Menzies, R. E., Menzies, R. G., & Iverach, L. (Eds.) (2018). *Curing the dread of death: theory, research, and practice*. Australian Academic Press.

Merleau-Ponty, M. (1962). *The phenomenology of perception* (C. W. Cobb, Trans.). Northwestern University Press.

Messari, S., & Hallam, R. (2003). CBT for psychosis: A qualitative analysis of clients' experiences. *British Journal of Clinical psychology, 42*, 171–188.

Montangero, J. (2009). Using dreams in cognitive behavioral psychotherapy: Theory, method, and examples. *Dreaming, 19*(4), 239–254.

Mooney, K. A., & Padesky, C. A. (2000). Applying client creativity to recurrent problems: Constructing possibilities and tolerating doubt. *Journal of Cognitive Psychotherapy, 14*, 149–160.

Moorey, S., & Lavender, A. (2018). *The therapeutic relationship in cognitive behavioural therapy*. Sage.

Moran, D. (2000). *Introduction to phenomenology*. Routledge.

Moreno, J. L. (1946/2019). *Psychodrama: Volume 1* (4th ed.). American Society of Psychodrama.
Moss, D. P. (1992). Cognitive therapy, phenomenology, and the struggle for meaning. *Journal of Phenomenological Psychology*, *23*(1), 87–102.
Nanda, J. (2010). Embodied integration: Reflections on mindfulness based cognitive therapy (MBCT) and a case for mindfulness based existential therapy (MBET). A single case illustration. *Existential Analysis*, *21*, 331–350.
Neimeyer, R. A. (1999). Constructivist psychotherapies: Features, foundations, and future directions. In R. A. Neimeyer & M. J. Mahoney (Eds.), *Constructivism in psychotherapy*. American Psychological Association.
Nelson, K. M., Yang, J. P., Maliken, A. C., Tsai, M., & Kohlenberg, R. J. (2016). Introduction to using structured evocative activities in functional analytic psychotherapy. *Cognitive and Behavioral Practice*, *23*, 459–463.
Nilsson, T., Svensson, M., Sandell, R., & Clinton, D. (2007). Patients' experiences of change in cognitive-behavioral therapy and psychodynamic therapy: A qualitative comparative study. *Psychotherapy Research*, *17*(5), 553–566.
O'Conner, K. P. (2015). *A constructionist clinical psychology for cognitive behaviour therapy*. Routledge.
O'Donohue, W. (2013). *Clinical psychology and the philosophy of science*. Springer.
O'Donohue, W. T., & Ferguson, K. E. (2016). Historical and philosophical dimensions of contemporary cognitive-behavioral therapy. In C. M. Nezu & A. M. Nezu (Eds.), *The Oxford handbook of cognitive and behavioral therapies*. Oxford.
Onslow, L., Woodward, D., Hoefkens, T., & Waddington, L. (2015). Experiences of enhanced cognitive behaviour therapy for bulimia nervosa. *Behavioural and Cognitive Psychotherapy*, *44*, 168–178.
Ottens, A. J., & Hanna, F. J. (1998). Cognitive and existential therapies: Towards an integration. *Psychotherapy*, *35*(3), 312–324.
Owen, I. R. (2013). Using mindfulness as a teaching aid for phenomenology. *Indo-Pacific Journal of Phenomenology*, *13*(2), 1–16.
Padesky, C. A. (1993). Socratic questioning: changing minds or guiding discovery? *Keynote address at the European Congress of Behavioural and Cognitive Psychotherapies*, London, September 24, 1993.

Pain, C. M., Chadwick, P., & Abba, N. (2008). Clients' experience of case formulation in cognitive behaviour therapy for psychosis. *British Journal of Clinical Psychology*, *47*, 127–138.

Perls, F., Hefferline, R. F., & Goodman, P. (1951). *Gestalt therapy: Excitement and growth in the human personality*. Julian Press.

Polkinghorne, D. E. (2004). Narrative therapy and postmodernism. In L. E. Angus & J. McLeod (Eds.), *The handbook of narrative and psychotherapy: Practice, theory, and research*. Sage.

Pyszczynski, T., Greenberg, J., & Koole, S. L. (2004). Experimental existential psychology: Exploring the human confrontation with reality. In J. Greenberg, S. L. Koole, & T. Pyszczynski (Eds.), *Handbook of experimental existential psychology*. Guilford.

Pyszczynski, T., Solomon, S., & Greenberg, J. (2015). Thirty years of terror management theory: From genesis to revelation. *Advances in Experimental Social Psychology*, *52*, 1–70.

Rafaeli, E., Bernstein, D. P., & Young, J. (2011). *Schema therapy: Distinctive features*. Routledge.

Raskin, J. D., & Debany, A. E. (2018). The inescapability of ethics and the impossibility of "anything goes": A constructivist model of ethical meaning making. *Journal of Constructivist Psychology*, *31*(4), 343–360.

Redhead, S., Johnstone, L., & Nightingale, J. (2015). Clients' experiences of formulation in cognitive behaviour therapy. *Psychology and Psychotherapy: Theory, Research, and Practice*, *88*, 453–467.

Rhodes, J. (2014). *Narrative CBT: Distinctive features*. Routledge.

Riso, L. P., & McBride, C. (2007). Introduction: A return to a focus on cognitive schemas. In L. P. Riso, P. L. du Toit, A. J. Stein, & J. E. Young (Eds.), *Cognitive schemas and core beliefs in psychological problems: A scientist-practitioner guide*. American Psychological Association.

Rogers, C. (1961). *On becoming a person: A therapist's view of therapy*. Constable.

Rosen, H. (1993). Developing themes in the field of cognitive therapy. In K. T. Kuehlwein & H. Rosen (Eds.), *Cognitive therapies in action: Evolving innovative practice*. Jossey-Bass.

Rosner, R. I. (2018). Three myths and truths about Beck's early years. In R. L. Leahy (Ed.), *Science and practice in cognitive therapy: Foundations, mechanisms, and applications*. Guilford Press.

Rosner, R. I., Lyddon, W. J., & Freeman A. (Eds.) (2004). *Cognitive therapy and dreams*. Springer.

Rush, A. J., Beck, A. T., Kovacs, M., & Hollon, S. D. (1977). Comparative efficacy of cognitive therapy and pharmacotherapy in the treatment of depressed outpatients. *Cognitive Therapy and Research, 1*, 17–37.

Safran, J. D. (1990). Towards a refinement of cognitive therapy in light of interpersonal theory I: Theory. *Clinical Psychology Review, 10*, 87–105.

Safran, J. D. (Ed.) (1998). *Widening the scope of cognitive therapy*. Jason Aronson.

Safran, J. D., & Greenberg, L. S. (1998). Hot cognition and psychotherapy process: An information processing/ecological approach. In J. D. Safran (Ed.), *Widening the scope of cognitive therapy*. Jason Aronson.

Safran, J. D., & Messer, S. (1998). Psychotherapy integration: A postmodern critique. In J. D. Safran (Ed.), *Widening the scope of cognitive therapy*. Jason Aronson.

Safran, J. D., & Muran, J. C. (1990). *Negotiating the therapeutic alliance: A relational treatment guide*. Guilford Press.

Safran, J. D., & Segal, Z. D. (1996). *Interpersonal process in cognitive therapy*. Aronson.

Salkovskis, P. M. (2002). Empirically grounded clinical interventions: Cognitive-behavioural therapy progresses through a multi-dimensional approach to clinical science. *Behavioural and Cognitive Psychotherapy, 30*(1), 3–11.

Sartre, J. P. (1991). *Being and nothingness: An essay on phenomenological ontology* (H. Barnes, Trans.). Routledge.

Schachter, J. (2021). Measure for measure: unconscious communication in dreams. In K. Robinson & J. Schachter (Eds.), *The contemporary Freudian tradition: Past and present*. Routledge.

Schneider, K. J. (2008). *Existential-integrative psychotherapy: Guideposts to the core of practice*. Routledge.

Segal, Z. V., Williams, M., & Teasdale, J. D. (2002). *Mindfulness-based cognitive therapy for depression*. Guilford Press.

Seymour, R. (2019). *The twittering machine*. Indigo.

Shearing, V., Lee, D., & Clohessy, S. (2011). How do clients experience reliving as part of trauma-focused cognitive behavioural therapy for posttraumatic stress disorder? *Psychology and Psychotherapy: Theory, Research and Practice, 84*, 458–472.

Shutz, A. (1972). *The phenomenology of the social world*. Heinemann.

Skinner, B. F. (1987). What happened to psychology as the science of behavior. *American Psychologist, 42*(8), 780–786.

Smith, J. A., Flowers, P., & Larkin, M. (2009). *Interpretative phenomenological analysis: Theory, method, and research*. Sage.
Smucker, M. R., & Dancu, C. V. (2005). *Cognitive-behavioral treatment for adults survivors of childhood trauma: Imagery rescripting and reprocessing*. Jason Aronson.
Sotskova, A., Carey, T., & Mak, B. (2016). Applying Goldfried's concept of assimilative psychotherapy integration: The process of synthesizing Existential and Cognitive Behavioral Therapy models. *Journal of Psychotherapy Integration, 26*(1), 36–48.
Spinelli, E. (1994). *Demystifying therapy*. Constable.
Spinelli, E. (2001). *The mirror and the hammer: Challenges to therapeutic orthodoxy*. Continuum.
Spinelli, E. (2005). *The interpreted world: An introduction to phenomenological psychology* (2nd ed.). Sage.
Spinelli, E. (2014). An existential challenge to some dominant perspectives in the practice of contemporary counselling psychology. *Counselling Psychology Review, 29*(2), 7–14.
Spinelli, E. (2015). *Practicing existential therapy: The relational world* (2nd ed.). Sage.
Spinelli, E. (2016). Relatedness: Contextualising being and doing in existential therapy. *Existential Analysis, 27*, 303–329.
Spinelli, E. (2019). What's so existential about existential therapy? *Existential Analysis, 30*(1), 59–79.
Stanghellini, G., Broome, M. R., Fernandez, A. V., Fusar-Poli, P., Raballo, A., & Rosfort, R. (2019). *The Oxford handbook of phenomenological psychopathology*. Oxford University Press.
Stolorow, R. D., & Atwood, G. (2019). *The power of phenomenology: Psychoanalytic and philosophical perspectives*. Routledge.
Stram, H. J. (2001). Introduction: Social constructionism and its critics. *Theory and Psychology, 11*, 291–296.
Sullivan, H. S. (1953). *The interpersonal theory of psychiatry*. Norton.
Teasdale, J. D. (1997). The transformation of meaning: The interacting cognitive subsystems approach. In M. Power & C. R. Brewin (Eds.), *The transformation of meaning in psychological therapies*. Wiley.
ten Napel-Schutz, M. C., Abma, T. A., Bamelis, L., & Arntz, A. (2011). Personality disorder patients' perspectives on the introduction of imagery within schema therapy: A qualitative study of patients' experiences. *Cognitive and Behavioral Practice, 18*, 482–490.

Tillich, P. (1980). *The courage to be* (2nd ed.). Yale University Press.

Tsai, M., Yoo, D., Hardebeck, E. J., Loudon, M. P., & Kohlenberg, R. J. (2019). Creating safe, evocative, attuned, and mutually vulnerable therapeutic beginnings: strategies from functional analytic psychotherapy. *Psychotherapy*, *56*(1), 55–61.

Valle, R. S., & Halling, S. (Eds.) (1989). *Existential-phenomenological perspectives in psychology: Exploring the breadth of human experience.* Plenum Press.

van Deurzen, E. (1998). *Paradox and passion in psychotherapy: An existential approach to therapy and counselling.* Wiley.

van Deurzen, E., & Adams, M. (2011). *Skills in existential counselling and psychotherapy.* Sage.

van Deurzen, E., Craig, E., Langle, A., Schneider, K. J., Tantam, D., & du Plock, S. (Eds.) (2019). *The Wiley World Handbook of existential therapy.* Wiley-Blackwell.

van Deurzen-Smith, E. (1988). *Existential counselling in practice.* Sage.

van Deurzen-Smith, E. (1995). Ontological insecurity revisited. In H. W. Cohn & S. du Plock (Eds.), *Existential challenges to psychotherapeutic theory and practice.* Society for Existential Analysis.

van Deurzen-Smith, E. (1997). *Everyday mysteries. Existential dimensions of psychotherapy.* Routledge.

Vos, J., Craig, M., & Cooper, M. (2014). Existential therapies: A meta-analysis of their effects on psychological outcomes. *Journal of Consulting and Clinical Psychology*, *83*(1), 115–128.

Waddington, L. (2002). The therapy relationship in cognitive therapy: A review. *Behavioural and Cognitive Psychotherapy*, *30*(2), 179–191.

Walser, R. D. (2019). *The heart of ACT.* Context Press.

Wells, A. (2000). *Emotional disorders and metacognition: Innovative cognitive therapy.* Wiley.

Wells, A. (2005). The metacognitive model of GAD: Assessment of meta-worry and relationship with DSM-IV generalised anxiety disorder. *Cognitive Therapy and Research*, *29*, 107–121.

Wessler, R. L. (1992). Constructivism and rational-emotive therapy: A critique. *Psychotherapy*, *29*(4), 620–625.

Westbrook, D., Kennerley, H., & Kirk, J. (2017). *An introduction to cognitive behaviour therapy.* Sage.

Wheatley, J., Brewin, C., Patel, T., Hackmann, A., Wells, A., Fischer, P., & Myers, S. (2007). I'll believe it when I see it: Imagery rescripting of intrusive sensory memories in depression. *Journal of Behavior Therapy and Experimental Psychiatry, 38*(4), 371–385.

Williams, M. J. G., & Kabat-Zinn, J. (2013). *Mindfulness: Diverse perspectives on its meaning, origins, and applications*. Routledge.

Williams, R. N. (1987). Can cognitive psychology offer a meaningful account of meaningful human action? *The Journal of Mind and Behavior, 8*(2), 209–222.

Wills, F., & Sanders, D. J. (1997). *Cognitive therapy: Transforming the image*. Sage.

Winter, D. A. (2008). Cognitive behaviour therapy: From rationalism to constructivism? *European Journal of Psychotherapy and Counselling, 10*(3), 221–229.

Wolfe, B. E. (2008). Existential issues in anxiety disorders and their treatment. In K. J. Schneider (Ed.), *Existential-integrative psychotherapy: Guideposts to the core of practice*. Routledge.

Woolfolk, R. L., & Richardson, F. C. (1984). Behavior therapy and the ideology of modernity. *American Psychologist, 39*(7), 777–786.

Woolfolk, R. L., & Richardson, F. C. (2018). Behavior therapy and the ideology of modernity (revised). In D. Loewenthal & G. Proctor (Eds.), *Why not CBT?: Against and for CBT revisited*. PCCS Books.

Yalom, I. D. (1980). *Existential psychotherapy*. Basic Books.

Young, J. E. (1990). *Cognitive therapy for personality disorders*. Professional Resources Press.

Young, J. E., Klosko, J. S., & Weishaar, M. E. (2003). *Schema Therapy: A practitioners guide*. Guilford press.

Zahavi, D. (2015). Self, consciousness, and shame. In D. Zahavi (Ed.), *The Oxford handbook of contemporary phenomenology*. Oxford University Press.

Zyl, F. N., van (2018). A social constructionist model of therapeutic factors. *Journal of Constructivist Psychology, 31*(4), 440–459.

Index

Note: Page numbers in *italic* refer to figures and tables.

d

m

n

o

p